Praise for Boy Racer

"*Boy Racer* is Mark Cavendish's brash, brutal and honest story of his life on the bike, full of the sound and fury of hand-to-hand combat at the finish line. Cavendish holds nothing back."

—SAL RUIBAL, *USA TODAY*

"*Boy Racer* . . . catch[es] the inner conflict between the impetuousness that makes Cavendish such a daunting competitor and the introspection that makes him such an interesting person."

—*THE GUARDIAN*

"Refreshingly frank and entertaining."

—*SCOTLAND ON SUNDAY*

"*Boy Racer* is essentially a master class in the art of winning, relayed through the eyes of a young, hungry, and sometimes impatient embryo superstar with a penchant for entertaining industrial language. It is also highly personal and revelatory and gives you a unique insight into one of Britain's most successful and respected sportsmen worldwide."

—*DAILY TELEGRAPH*

"Few have brought the terrifying and visceral art of sprinting to life. *Boy Racer* redresses the balance."

—*THE TIMES*

"This book surprises and inspires with outspoken views, insider insights, and a life story to date full of fantastic highs and devastating lows. With the 2008 Tour de France as a backdrop, Cavendish takes us on a whirlwind tour of his life so far—a meteoric rise from young Isle of Man 'scally' to double World Champion track star. Along the way we learn of his apprenticeship with the GB track development team, getting taken on by the infamous T-Mobile squad (now Columbia-Highroad), and winning the Milan–San Remo classic. Inspiring reading."

—WWW.SPOKE.IE

"Offers a unique account of the world's fastest sprinter."

—WWW.ROADCYCLINGUK.COM

"I have read a large number of sporting autobiographies in my time; some very good, many distinctly mediocre. This might just be the best one I have ever read.

"The book reads in much the same way the man conducts himself in interviews: He shoots from the hip with his heart on his sleeve, occasionally inserting foot in mouth. But anyone who has ever seen Cav speak would expect no less; in a PC, PR-conscious world, here is a sportsman who is as brutally honest as he is fast. At times, it is painfully obvious who he does and does not respect in the cycling world, and yet he is surprisingly self-critical, self-effacing, and not afraid to admit when he has been proven wrong about someone. The book is full of little insights into the mindset of a master practitioner and behind-the-scenes revelations of what it is like to be a professional road cyclist, which make this a cut above the average sporting autobiography. Add this to the fleshing out of a personality far more complex, meticulous, and magnanimous (to his team) than the one-dimensional cocky narcissist sometimes portrayed in the media, and what you have here is a compelling tale that had me tearing through the pages much like the man himself does when he has the sniff of the finish line in his nostrils.

"*Boy Racer* was unputdownable. I'll be first in line to buy the next chapter of the story of this incredible young man."

—SPORTINGREFLECTIONS.BLOGSPOT.COM

"Love the man or hate him, you won't find much in *Boy Racer* to change your mind. It's pure Cav—honest, outspoken, occasionally aggressive, imbued throughout with that trademark self-confidence you already find either charming or annoying. Even if you're not a fan, this kind of peek into the peloton makes the book well worth reading. But if (like me) you do harbor a certain fondness for the Manx Express, chances are you'll tear through this book with sheer delight and find yourself quoting bits of it for weeks to come."

—WWW.PODIUMCAFE.COM

"Can a youngster obsessed with barging his way through several other bicycle missiles in a 70-kph scrabble string more than a couple of words together? Happily, the answer to that one is a resounding yes. This is an exceptionally well-written book; well-constructed, never tedious, well-paced, and above all else, highly interesting.

"There won't be any difficulty getting to [the final page]; probably more of a problem putting it down in between. Quite a surprisingly good book."

—WWW.THEWASHINGMACHINEPOST.NET

BOY RACER

BOY RACER

MARK CAVENDISH

My Journey to Tour de France
Record-Breaker

BOULDER, COLORADO

Published in 2009 by Ebury Press, an imprint of Ebury Publishing
A Random House Group company

U.S. edition with additional material published in 2010 by VeloPress

Printed in the United States of America

1830 55th Street
Boulder, Colorado 80301-2700 USA
(303) 440-0601 • Fax (303) 444-6788
E-mail velopress@competitorgroup.com

Distributed in the United States and Canada by Ingram Publisher Services

Library of Congress Cataloging-in-Publication Data
Cavendish, Mark.
Boy Racer: my journey to Tour de France record-breaker / Mark Cavendish.
p. cm.
ISBN 978-1-934030-64-6 (pbk.: alk. paper)
1. Tour de France (Bicycle race). I. Title.
GV1049.2.T68C38 2010
796.6'20944—dc22
2010015130

For information on purchasing VeloPress books,
please call (800) 811-4210, ext. 169, or visit www.velopress.com.

Cover design by Katie Jennings
Interior design by Anita Koury
Cover photograph by Graham Watson
Text set in Whitman

10 11 12 / 10 9 8 7 6 5 4 3 2 1

CONTENTS

PROLOGUE

"Brian, I need you to do me a favor. I need you to call Unibet."

Brian was Brian Holm, my Columbia Sportswear team's Danish directeur sportif, and Unibet was an online betting company. Brian knew what I meant. I could tell from the way he was smirking; but sitting next to him, my other directeur, Rolf Aldag, thought he'd either misheard or that I'd gone insane. He leaned over Brian in the passenger seat to get a clearer view and asked me to repeat what I'd just said.

"I need you to call Unibet and put a grand on Mark Cavendish to win today's stage. Got it?"

Now Rolf was laughing. . . .

A hundred kilometers to go. A hundred kilometers and not much more than two hours until the most important ten seconds of my life. Hopefully. I spotted the huge bundle of varicose veins that belongs to my teammate George Hincapie, and I kicked through a little window of daylight between the bodies and on to his shoulder. "Hey, George, I just went back to the car and told them I needed them to call Unibet for me. . . ." By the time I'd finished the story, he was laughing so much he nearly fell off his bike.

Ninety kilometers, 80, 70, 60 to go. It was hot—the first really warm day of the Tour, and the sun happened to have showed up on a day when there was precious little shelter, just endless wheat fields acting like giant solar panels. *Drink, Cav, gotta keep drinking.* Four riders were still off the front, but now wasn't the time to start fretting. Not yet. At the

50-kilometers-to-go mark, I'd start picking my way through the maze and into the top twenty or thirty positions, close to my teammates and as far as possible from danger. My teammates might not see me, but they'd see my long white socks—the socks I wore deliberately so they could pick me out in the melee—I'd drift on to a wheel, maybe George's, maybe Bernie's, maybe Kosta's, then the thinking, the planning, the wondering would all stop and the focusing would start. Nothing would count except the next turn of the pedals, the next shift of the gear lever, the next tweak of the handlebars, the next inch of tarmac.

As far as I was concerned, you could psychoanalyze a bike race as much as you liked, but it basically boiled down to just you, the bike, and the road. The British Cycling team's full-time psychiatrist, Steve Peters, had earned a lot of praise for his work with track stars like Chris Hoy and Victoria Pendleton, and rightly so, because I could see how much Steve had helped them.

I could see that Steve had helped them think logically, override emotion and doubt—but I didn't need any of that. I'd been to see Steve once, before becoming world Madison champion in Los Angeles in 2005, but nothing he'd said had really helped me to conquer my nerves. What I needed was the approach favored by another of the staff at the British Cycling Federation, Shane Sutton: Basically, I needed sunshine blown up my arse.

A lot of professional athletes have performance anxiety or whatever psychology wants to call it, but winners, born winners like me, just want sunshine blown up their arses. Or if you prefer a slightly less vulgar translation, I don't want the truth—I just want to be told I'm the best. Logic states that a sprinter can't win the Tour de France overall. That's because it's written in the laws of nature that the same muscles that allow me to touch speeds of 70 kilometers an hour on the flat make me a liability in the mountains, which is invariably where the Tour is won and lost. But that's only logic; if you could wire Shane Sutton to blow sunshine up my arse twenty-four hours a day, seven days a week, then forget a thousand pounds on me winning a sprint stage—you could do worse than putting a few grand on me winning the whole bloody Tour.

I've told Steve Peters my views on sports psychology, and he's not offended. We get on fine. I just don't think I'm like most other athletes, not even the Olympic medal winners in the British team, and Steve accepts that. The other thing to consider is that a lot of people whom Steve has helped are doing timed events on the track, where the variables can be controlled and performances quantified in terms of minutes, seconds, and milliseconds. What I was doing here was different, and that's why I loved it. It was pointless telling me, "You've done your best, everything you can do"; it was pointless showing me a line on a graph that told me how much I was improving. The only line I looked for was the finish line.

Fifty kilometers. An hour, hour and ten minutes, at this speed. We weren't going to make the same mistake as two days ago and let the break stay away. I wasn't going through that again: the anger at having let down my teammates, the self-loathing, the regrets, the silence on the team bus, the dumb questions from journalists. . . . Fortunately, the gap was now down to two minutes and falling fast. Our jerseys had flooded the front of the bunch—seven of us in blue, then Kim Kirchen in the green that denotes the leader of the points competition and Thomas Lövkvist in the white worn by the best rider under the age of 25 on the general classification. Marcus Burghardt and Adam Hansen were on the front; over the next two and a half weeks, those two would rarely be anywhere but on the front, riding themselves to a pulp to keep me, my team, and everyone else in the race exactly where we wanted them.

Stay there, Cav, stay there. And on the intercom radio with Brian and Rolf: "Cav, how are you feeling?"

"Fucking amazing . . ."

I was cruising right in the sweet spot—that magical place, like a magic carpet, right at the base of the arrowhead, maybe twenty positions behind the point of the triangle, where your energy expenditure—and risk—is minimized. Fifteen kilometers to go.

Come on, Cav, nothing silly now.

At the Giro, I'd locked my radio to "on" with 10 kilometers to go so that my teammates and directeurs could hear me but couldn't relay back any information or instructions. Here in France, I'd asked if we could do the same and been outvoted. I'm not sure which approach is better, but I do know that when I heard a crackle in my ear and the words "George has punctured, George has punctured," I was absolutely sure I'd seen George Hincapie for the last time on Stage 5 of the Tour de France.

I'd ridden enough Tour stages now to know that if I've dropped out of the top thirty positions anywhere in the final 30 kilometers, when the pace never drops below 50 kph, I've also dropped out of contention to win the stage. Lose touch with the peloton, be it because of a crash or a puncture, and you can forget about it altogether . . . except, apparently, if your name's George Hincapie. No sooner had I written him off than, with 7 kilometers to go, suddenly there was that varicose spaghetti again, and George was back in the game. To get there, he'd had to stop, wait for the team car, change wheels, almost rip the cranks off his bike to get back to the bunch, accelerate again, up the gutter, overtaking about 150 of the best cyclists in the world riding at full bore, giving his life insurers a nasty fright in the process, then compose himself to slot back into my sprint train and start the real hard work. And people ask me what I mean when I say I've got the best teammates in the world.

There's a clip on YouTube that shows us 5 kilometers out—Adam Hansen on the front, Marcus Burghardt on his wheel, then Tommy Lövkvist talking on his radio with me in his shadow—all set to the Safri Duo track "Rise." It still gives me goose pimples. I could sense the other sprinters' teams—Liquigas, Quick-Step, and Crédit Agricole—trying to move up and muscle in, but today it was our turn to dictate. All day we'd been dictating.

Four kilometers. Three. Ideally, you'd want at least four men at this point. However, Adam had just popped, and so had Tommy. That left two—Bernie Eisel and Gerald Ciolek. In our eagerness, in the excitement, we'd committed too early.

Come on, Cav, stay calm. Just hold the wheels. Remember the tight right-hander with 2 kilometers to go—then the last kilometer's straight and wide. Don't think about Hushovd or McEwen or Steegmans. You're the quickest today. Focus. Watch the wheels. And remember that right-hander. . . .

The right-hander, Cav, the right-hander! Too wide. Blown it. Now you're going backward. Boxed in. Five back, ten back . . . Where's Gerald? There. Legend. He's taking me round the outside. "I'm with you, Gerald." There's the red flag: a kilometer to go. A kilo—? Gerald's already in the wind, and he can't hold a kilometer. No way. Just do what you can, Gerald. I'm here. Stay calm, Cav.

Everyone who's never been there wants to know what's going through your mind in the last kilometer of a sprint. The answer may be a disappointment: It's nothing, except what's needed to process precisely what's flashing in front of your eyes at any given moment. There's no reflection, no calculation, no speculation—just endless, split-second decisions and gambles. It's "Left or right?" "This wheel or that wheel?" "Wait or go?" It takes hundreds of these decisions to win a sprint, but it might take only one to lose it.

If it's not instinct, it's the closest thing to it.

How long is a Tour de France sprint? Two hundred fifty meters? Three hundred? Are we talking the whole drumroll or just the climax? The 50-kilometer, hour-long, 600-watt test of collective power, endurance, and concentration or the ten-second, 1,200-watt, 70-kph drag race that everyone sees and remembers?

A great sprinter doesn't need to be a great strategist. When you're on that finishing straight, timing trumps tactics every time. At the Tour, the black distance markers at the side of the road act as your countdown: one every 100 meters in the penultimate 500 meters, one every 50 in the last 500—300 might be too soon to go, 200 too late. Sometimes it's someone else who takes the initiative, and you simply don't have any option but to step on the gas.

Seven hundred. Six hundred. What's that jersey up the road? Fuck me! We haven't even caught the break yet! One of them's still up the road. How did that happen? How the fuck did he . . . No, forget it, Cav. Focus. You'll catch him. Focus on the sprint.

We're on the outside of the swarm, and suddenly there's a surge. I don't see it, but I feel it. I can always just feel it. It's too early and Gerald's already had to do too much, but I need one last effort. I scream, "Gerald, you've got to go!" So he goes, like an Exocet, right into the wind, and he goes and goes and goes. Last 500, last 450, he's still going, last 400, 375, and is he still . . . *no, he's not, he's seizing up, starting to swing. He's gonna blow any second* . . . and I can feel someone coming on my right. It's a green jersey, it's Crédit Agricole, it's Mark Renshaw, with Thor Hushovd on his wheel, and I wait for Hushovd to appear on my right shoulder, then I swing across Gerald and suddenly level with Hushovd's back wheel.

The most important ten seconds of my life. The next ten . . .

INTRODUCTION

H i everyone . . ."

Well, at least I nailed the first two words . . .

If only they taught you this at school. You're twenty-two years old, less than six months into a first season that began with your team's coach saying you were fat and useless, in a sport where the hierarchies are steeper and harder to climb than any mountain—a sport where nothing comes at a price that isn't blood, sweat, and often tears—and here you are writing to ask for a place in the 2007 Tour de France.

My two wins in the spring Tour of Catalunya were fresh in my mind and those of my T-Mobile team managers. I'd barely gotten back to my teammate Roger Hammond's place in Belgium, barely had time to put down my suitcase before I'd gone into the living room, turned on the computer, and started typing. I'd spoken to my coach from the British Federation, Rod Ellingworth, to untangle my thoughts and smooth out my arguments. I was ready to make my case . . . yet I was hesitating. I never hesitated.

Finally, the words started flowing.

Hi everyone,

I am sorry to drop this on you all, considering you all have other things to think of, but I'd appreciate it if you took this request seriously.

Simply—I would like to start the Tour de France.

I know I am only in my neo-season, so I am still naive to how hard the Tour actually is, and this is why I have left it until now to ask. After Dunkirk, I started to wonder whether to ask you all, but I wanted to see how I could handle the ProTour first, which is why I waited until after Catalunya. I wanted to be confident in myself before I asked you all, and not just jump in with my head in the clouds.

I have really thought long and hard about this, and discussed it in depth with various people, with mixed reactions ranging from "completely push for it" to "definitely way too early, leave it a few years," but I have come to the decision that I would like to try one week to ten days.

If even the first week is way too deep for me, I still think this is a positive thing, as I will know exactly what my current level is so I can work towards the race in the next years. I know I have good form at the moment, but I also know I have more to come in the next month, and I truly don't think there are many riders at all faster than me in world cycling at the moment.

Thank you all for considering this, and please let me know your thoughts on it.

Regards, Mark

Twelve months separated the start of the 2007 and 2008 Tours de France, but it could have been light-years as far as I was concerned. The Grand Départ in London in 2007 should have told the world that a British sprinter was about to embark upon a brilliant Tour de France career. Instead, it started and ended in tears.

The reaction to my letter surpassed even my expectations. Within minutes of me clicking "send," replies were pinging back to my inbox and my phone. "Bloody hell, you've got balls," said one e-mail, the first of several with the same message. The next day the phone rang and I heard the familiar Australian drawl of Allan Peiper, one of the directeurs, on the end of the line. "You're in like Flynn, mate!" he said. "Keep it on the low, but yeah, it's pretty unanimous."

I was buzzing. I called Rod. Called my dad. Called Melissa. "Keep this to yourself . . . but I think, I think I'm doing the Tour de France."

It wouldn't be long before I was wishing it'd all remained a secret until the moment I rolled off the start ramp opposite Downing Street forty days later on 7 July 2007. Or at least until the posh do to introduce our nine-strong Tour team at Fifteen, Jamie Oliver's restaurant in Shoreditch, the day before. Hardly ever before and never since has pressure or expectation or scrutiny affected me, but there came a point, or rather one interview, when I couldn't bear it anymore and the emotional wheels came off completely.

It was all the more infuriating because I'd trained so hard. Three weeks before the Tour, I was flying . . . then it started. The phone calls, the interviews. The endless bloody interviews. Cycling's rare—if not unique—among modern, mainstream sports, as journalists will regularly call top riders for a quote or a quick chat, and it generally works because there's a mutual understanding—among the riders, the team's press officers, and journalists—of what's reasonable and what's not. These unwritten rules only break down when the company that sponsors the team gets involved, which is what happened with T-Mobile. I would get home from seven-hour training sessions, then find that T-Mobile had scheduled two hours of interviews, one every fifteen minutes, almost all of which would end up running overtime. Some days, I'd end up doing four hours of interviews, most of them with journalists whose lack of even the most basic knowledge about cycling should have made me laugh, but which at the time I just found maddening. Finally, one day, I dissolved into tears; I then turned off my mobile and vowed not to speak to another journalist or PR person until I arrived in London.

I arrived in London, and the pressure hit me like a tidal wave. Where was the little upstart who'd had the audacity to write to his team managers explaining exactly why they should pick him for the Tour team rather than one of the dozen or so other squad members with more experience and, you'd think, far better prospects? Lost—that was where. As they are at every race, my teammates were my sanctuary—their banter, their advice, their confidence in me—but stepping outside was like going from comfort zone to war zone. "The easiest mistake Mark could make would be thinking too much about the sprint finish on Sunday," my roommate, Kim Kirchen, said in the press on the Saturday morning. He might as well have been pissing in the wind.

The prologue time trial in London was never likely to be my cup of tea. I finished 69th. The next day—the first stage from Tower Bridge to Canterbury, the last before the race went back to France, and surely the first sprint finish of the Tour—was going to be the Big One.

We've since found out that more than one rider in that Tour was doped up on one thing or another, whether it was testosterone, EPO, or their own transfused blood. If you saw me riding that day, you'd have said that if anyone was high, it had to be me, not because I was so fast but because of the way I was bouncing off bodies as soon as the Tour director's flag went down to indicate the start of the stage. My thoughts were racing faster than I was, from all the people who'd been telling me for days that they had money on me for the first stage to exactly how I was going to get them their money. I don't remember the sights so much as the sounds: the constant white noise, the screams—"Cavendish! Cavendish!"—and then a voice over my shoulder belonging to the Spanish rider from the Rabobank team, Juan Antonio Flecha. He was imploring me to calm down. But I couldn't. I punctured at a time when the peloton was just pootling along, slow enough to make changing wheels and regaining touch no more an inconvenience than retying your shoelaces, yet I was screaming into my intercom radio as if not just the stage but also my life depended on it. I was manic, drowning in the deep end.

The race was the only thing that wasn't moving too fast. Then it happened: the Rush. The Tour was the one major race that my teammate Roger Hammond hadn't ridden in a career spanning over a decade, but he'd tried to put my mind at rest. After all, he said, it was the same riders I'd already been racing against and often beaten since the start of the season, often when I wasn't nearly as fit as now. Right? Sorry, Roger, wrong: It was faster, a lot faster, 5 kilometers an hour faster—and it didn't matter whether it was uphill, downhill, round corners, on narrow roads or wide ones. Yes, they were the same riders, the 189 best in the world, and yeah, I'd already beaten most if not all of them at some point or another, but not all in the same race. In no other race had every bloke in the peloton trained to peak for precisely the second they rolled off that start-ramp in the prologue. In no other race could a good ride, any day out of twenty-one, change a fella's life. The stakes, the noise, the hype, the adrenaline—it was all just *more*. Five kilometers an hour *more*.

Fifty kilometers to go. They said make sure you're in the top twenty or thirty positions with 50 kilometers to go. I did what I was told. Twenty-five kilometers later, I was in the perfect spot, near the front but on the side of the peloton, which is exactly where you should be; stay in the center and you can soon get vortexed—as teams and riders rotate at the front, you start spiraling backward. So, I'm right there, fine, comfortable, calming down, feeling good . . . and then *boom*, I've hit something. I'm on the ground. I look around and see my bike mangled, my glasses on the tarmac, and I'm screaming, "Who the fuck was that?" But really I just want my bike. My directeurs are telling me to keep my cool and get back to the peloton, but now I'm screaming at them, "I can't! My bike's fucked." I see the whole peloton flash past me, then finally the team car with my replacement bike. I hop on and start pounding on the pedals, weaving through the race convoy, my speedometer showing 50 kph, heart hammering in my rib cage; then one of the race officials, the commissaires, rides alongside me, wagging his finger; he's telling me that if I keep riding in the team cars' slipstream, I'll be demoted and fined. Usually, if the rider loses his place in the bunch because of a crash or mechanical problem, the commissaires will let you get shelter behind the bumpers until you bridge the gap. Not this time. Now it was my Italian directeur sportif, Valerio Piva's, turn to raise his voice—not that it made any difference to the commissaire. I looked in vain for a colored jersey in the distance, a body, a hope. Nothing. Just tears. So many tears that I lost sight of where I was going and crashed into the back of the Barloworld team car.

I rode alone, crying, all the way to the finish line. I got there two minutes after the main pack, as replays of Robbie McEwen's winning sprint flickered on the giant video screen. I bustled through the journalists and the photographers to my team bus, which was parked on a playing field next to those of all the other teams. I leaned my bike against the side of the bus, climbed aboard, and sat at the back sobbing for another half hour.

It had started in tears and ended in tears.

Wednesday, 2 July 2008. What a difference a year makes.

I looked around at Brest, its grey skies, buildings, and streets, and thought . . . well, to put it politely, I thought it wasn't London. Grand Départ, they were still calling it, but, from where I was standing, there was nothing grand about it. London had been spectacular, memorable, monumental in every sense; this was the Tour going back to its earthy, homegrown roots. The people here didn't need billboards or hype or a photogenic backdrop; even now, three days before the action was due to start, the man in the street took one look at my Columbia race jersey and doffed his beret or waved or shouted a few words of encouragement. Contrast this with the previous year, when one team went out training in the lanes of Essex and got hounded back to their hotel by White Van Man.

I felt relaxed, confident; nothing like the previous year. Okay, after winning two stages in the Giro d'Italia in May, the first Briton ever to do so, I would have liked to savor that achievement, gather my forces, and focus squarely on the Tour; instead, two weeks before leaving for the Tour, I was still in Manchester, at the request of the British Federation, trying to divide my time, my concentration, and a daily quota of about 200 kilometers between practicing on the track for the Olympics and training for the Tour on the road. At least this time I'd put my foot down about the media commitments—it was an hour a day, fifteen minutes per journalist, and when those fifteen minutes were up, so was the interview. I spent the last week before the Tour in our new house on the Isle of Man, relaxing and training just like I always had, the way that suited me: no structures, no worrying about heart rates or power outputs; just simple, hard rides of three, four, or sometimes five hours with a couple of long sprints thrown in at the end. Proper old-school.

My flight was on the Tuesday morning before the Tour. Melissa took me to the airport, just like for any other race. I flew to Birmingham, then took a connecting flight to Brest the next morning and, from there, made my way to the team hotel, which just happened to be directly opposite the start line. None of my teammates was arriving until the evening, so I unpacked my stuff, put on my kit, and headed out for a spin.

After a couple of hours, I rode back via the high street. I had some shopping to do: My roommate for the Tour was going to be the Australian Adam Hansen, and, before he arrived, I wanted to buy him a token to say thanks for all of the incredible, lung-exploding, ego-burying work he'd done for me at the Giro. I located Brest's best jeweler, brought my bike inside, and started scouring the display cabinets for something to suit Adam—something classy but also techy and with a bit of an edge. I saw a Breitling Chronomat with a red strap. Perfect. I had it gift-wrapped, handed over my credit card, then went straight back to the hotel, straight back to the room, and placed it on Adam's pillow.

I was in a massage in another room when Adam arrived. I went back to the room and noticed right away that he hadn't seen the box on his pillow. I played dumb. He had one look at me, one look at the box, then walked over and started unwrapping. He opened the box and beamed at me.

People might think that it's just false appreciation or some kind of formality when I thank my teammates after a race win. It's not. There are two aspects to it: One is genuine recognition. My guys aren't just any old teammates, they're special athletes, special individuals with whom I have a special bond and without whom I'd never win a race. The other reason is that I know what warmth and satisfaction I get when someone thanks me for the work I've done, like Adam did that day. Without wanting to sound too soppy, it's not about politeness or protocol—it's about sharing a moment. When I win a race and struggle through the crowd to get to my teammates, it's not because I want to be congratulated or even say thanks; it's because I want to be with the people who have made that win possible, who have worked for it with me. It's because I want to see the joy on their faces.

That first night was great. The whole team had arrived, the piss-taking was rampant, and everyone was excited. Most of all we were confident: In 2007, the spring had been dominated by doping scandals; this year, we'd dominated, full stop. The mood was one of a band of mates about to set off on one great big adventure.

The next two days flew by. Partly thanks to our brilliant results in the spring, our manager, Bob Stapleton, had finally found a sponsor to replace T-Mobile, the German telecommunications giant that had pulled out at the end of the previous year when the team's leader, Jan Ullrich, had been involved in a major doping scandal and more details had started trickling out of ugly medical practices that involved not only T-Mobile riders but several other big names. The new name on the jersey—the new name of our team—was Columbia Sportswear, the California-based outdoor clothing and footwear company. Our new jerseys were electric blue.

In those last forty-eight hours, there were meetings with people from Columbia, the usual glut of interviews and photo shoots, a couple of fairly gentle training rides . . . and a first brush with the opposition. The size of the Tour and every team's entourage is such that the Tour organizers can never squeeze more than a couple of teams into any one hotel, and for the few days before the Tour we'd been paired with the Italian squad

Liquigas. This made no odds to me, but it did mean I'd be under the same roof as probably my least favorite rider in the peloton: Filippo Pozzato, the self-styled playboy of Italian cycling.

My beef with Pozzato dated back to the Tour of Catalunya the previous year. In Stage 1, the whole peloton had been slipping and sliding down a wet, dangerous descent and Pozzato had singled out me, the first-year pro, as an easy target. *"Amatore!"*—amateur—I kept hearing, and I didn't need to turn around and see his overmoisturized smug mug to work out that it came from him. We finished the descent, the road kicked up steeply toward the finish, and I ended up winning. This was despite the fact that the run-in really shouldn't have suited me; it was my first ProTour race, and, on top of all that, I'd lost a couple of seconds when I'd bumped into the Australian Aaron Kemps and my foot had unclipped from my pedal with 200 meters to go. I crossed the line, spent but elated, then almost immediately felt a hand on my back. It was Pozzato again: *"Amatore, amatore . . ."*

He'd set me up perfectly. "Not bad for an amateur, am I? Now fuck off!" I hissed. And with that I rode away.

Since that incident over a year ago he'd had several digs at me through the media, so when, on one of those last nights before the Tour's start in Brest, I walked with my teammates Gerald Ciolek and Bernhard Eisel into the lift and saw Pozzato, I took one look at him and walked back out of the lift. It was petty, I know, but I was being deliberately melodramatic to make my point. One day maybe I'll tell Pozzato what his problem is: I think he fancies me!

The following evening, we all sat behind a huge stage in a packed main square in Brest and waited to be unveiled to the public in the official team presentation. The cue came from the Tour's official speaker, Daniel Mangeas, and out we marched. *"Messieurs, nous vous présentons, les neuf coureurs de l'équipe Columbia . . ."*

And here we were. . . .

Adam Hansen. Age 27. Hailing from Queensland, Australia. A former mountain biker who'd come to road racing late but, in the season and a half that he'd been on our team, had built a reputation for his incredible horsepower on every terrain. Top man, top rider, and my roommate. We were yin and yang, he the quiet, studious type, I all heart and mouth. Adam wasn't even supposed to be here, but his performances in the Giro in May had made it a no-brainer. He'd been twitchy in the peloton the previous year, but now, in his second season, he was the archetype of the perfect domestique—a French word literally meaning "servant" but in cycling terminology indicating a tireless, strong, unstintingly loyal teammate. Adam put more into me winning a sprint than I put in myself.

Kanstantin Sivtsov, or "Kosta," as we call him. A 25-year-old Belorussian. Didn't speak a word of English when he joined the team at the start of 2008, didn't smile . . . then, one day at the Giro d'Italia in May, someone teased a little grin out of him, and now he's a changed man. In fact, he's become a sarcastic bastard, but he cracks us up. And he loves being on the team, loves being part of something successful. Kosta will be on the front working for you on the flat, he'll work for you on the mountains, where he's absolutely brilliant, and it's all because he loves that euphoria of the team winning. His English has even improved. Not everyone understands it, but then, many don't understand me, either.

Kim Kirchen. Kosta's roommate. "Little Kim" to us, "Grim Kim" to the press, since the phrase "hangdog expression" could have been invented for him. The Jack Dee of cycling because he's actually hilarious. Biscuit-dry but hilarious. Born in Luxembourg and speaks seven languages, all more or less fluently. One of the best riders in the world, certainly one of the men of the 2008 season before the Tour, and our man for stage wins in time trials and mountains and for the general classification. An überpro who could fill an encyclopedia with all the wisdom he's picked up from working with some of the most famous and successful directeurs in cycling. Thirty years old as of two days before the Tour, team leader, top bloke, and top rider.

Thomas Lövkvist. Swedish. Self-confessed eccentric Scandinavian with boy-band looks. Tommy's the guy whose elbow you'll feel in your ribs when some egghead from an equipment supplier comes in to do a seminar at our preseason training camp; then you'll see his arm go up, and, innocent as you like, he'll ask the most intricate, complex, unanswerable question you could possibly imagine, just for his own and the other riders' amusement. Face of an angel, devil's sense of humor. On his bike, he's proper hardcore. At training camps in the winter, he's always on the front, always going hard, always doing more than everyone else, then he goes back to Sweden, puts spikes on his tires, and goes out training in the snow for four hours a day. He's 24, but he's been a pro for years. A super, super talent, and another one who just loves being on our team.

Gerald Ciolek. German. 22 years old. Tommy's roommate. A freak: freakishly good on a bike, freakishly selfless. We are the same age, are both sprinters, yet I was the one who was winning more and bigger races and had been picked for the Tour the previous year at his expense. Now he was the one being told to literally act as my water carrier, then launch me in the closing straight before peeling off to let me take the glory. He could have resented my success. But I'd realized very early on that Gerald was special. We'd ridden against each other as amateurs in Germany, then in 2007 joined T-Mobile at the same time. He was the German wunderkind, the youngest-ever national champion; we should have been at each other like a pair of pecking hens, but we bonded straightaway, partly because neither of us hit it off with the team's coach. Now, a year and a half later, we were the Starsky and Hutch of sprinting—I, Starsky, the curly-topped tearaway, and he the floppy, flaxen-haired straight man, Hutch. We had such a good partnership that we'd even discussed marketing and selling ourselves as a two-man package, then spending our entire career working for each other in different races. We also had a feeling that this was going to be our Tour.

Marcus Burghardt. German. East German, in case you hadn't guessed from the ear stud or the blond highlights in his straggly, shoulder-length hair. As tall and strong as an oak. Twenty-five years old. I didn't like the guy . . . or rather, I hadn't the previous year. One issue was the language: I'd picked up enough German in my season with the amateur team Sparkasse in 2006 to understand most of the banter between the German lads and directeurs on our team, but, because of his accent, when Marcus spoke I didn't understand a word. Then there was the 2007 Tour, when he was supposed to be one of the guys working for me in the sprints. I'd gotten the impression he didn't fancy wasting precious energy for the sake of a rookie who wasn't yet looking the part, especially when Marcus had already won Ghent-Wevelgem, one of the biggest one-day races on the calendar, earlier that spring. It became so tense between us that I think we both realized we had no choice but to make an effort to get on. The outcome was that we gradually started to respect each other; then, at the team training camp in January 2008, suddenly we were like best mates. Partly because of that, partly because I knew I'd earned his respect as a rider, and partly because he was fresh after a nasty knee injury that spring, in this Tour, Marcus was exactly the kind of guy I needed on my side.

Bernhard Eisel, 27 years old. Big Austrian beefcake . . . or so he'd like to think. Bernhard and I have a running joke about who's the best-looking guy in the team. If we ever let you into our bathroom when we're sharing at a race and you saw the array of aftershaves, creams, and hair products, you'd say we were just a pair of tarts. Bernie's like the laughing gas in the team; I've almost never seen the guy with anything but a big grin on his face. And yet he's also the ultimate pro, the ultimate team man—the bloke who, when I won my first pro race at the Grote Scheldeprijs in Belgium in April 2007, had been under orders to bury himself for the team's other sprinter, Andre Greipel, which Bernie did . . . but then he saw me in trouble and buried himself *again* to pilot me back through the peloton with a kilometer to go. If you can imagine a 400-meter runner doing one race, then stopping a few seconds and doing it all over again, all out of pure selflessness, you get the idea. Bernie was like Ciolek: They'd both been signed as big-name sprinters, yet here they were, selected for the Tour team on the understanding that they'd spend most of the race sacrificing their own chances for mine. And not only did they never complain, they gave more for me than I'd give for myself. Their devotion left me speechless and, if ever I lost, frankly embarrassed.

George Hincapie. New Yorker of Colombian origin. At 35 years of age the grand old man of the team and the only one allowed his own room. Thirteen Tours and counting. He's perhaps best known as Lance Armstrong's friend and teammate at the Motorola, U.S. Postal, and Discovery Channel teams. I'd grown up watching U.S. Postal in the Armstrong years—this relentless blue train, rattling along at the front of the Tour peloton every day, their eyes shielded by Oakley sunglasses, their emotions hidden behind a rigid game face—and I'd assumed that every one was probably a real bastard. I was wrong. George Hincapie is the nicest man in the world. I'd never spoken to him in my life until, in one stage of the 2007 Tour, when he was still riding for Discovery, we were trundling along in the pack, and I heard a voice, and I looked round, and there was George. "Hi," he said. "Good to meet you. You're fucking fast. . . ." I think I was too starstruck to carry on the conversation, but it didn't matter—I'd met George Hincapie, veteran of seven victorious Tour de France campaigns, peloton legend, and the nicest man in the world. Actually, correction—the second-nicest man in the world, because I've since met his brother and business partner, Rich, who's even nicer. George had joined the team at the start of the 2008 season and had been rejuvenated. At the Tour of California in February he was practically skipping to the start line; he'd spent years grinding away on the front for Armstrong under intense pressure, intense scrutiny, then he came to us and we were like a bunch of kids let out of school for the afternoon. He was loving every second. It actually pained me to think that the second-nicest man in the world and one of the best riders in the sport had never had this much fun in his whole career.

And finally we came to me: Mark Cavendish. A 23-year-old from the Isle of Man. Joker, firebrand, self-acknowledged sometime bastard, immature, emotional, generous, recovering scally (a Liverpool term for "casuals," meaning an urban teenaged ne'er-do-well), a team leader, and the fastest man in the world. Maybe.

As the man said, we had three weeks, twenty-one stages, and 3,559 kilometers to find out.

STAGE 1

Saturday, 5 July 2008
BREST-PLUMELEC
197.5 KM

I have a mate, Dools, my best friend from the Isle of Man, who often asks me what it's like to ride a stage of the Tour de France. Dools, like most amateur cyclists, is curious to know how long he'd last in one of the Tour's first half-dozen, routinely quite flat stages as the race makes its way toward the mountains. He wants to find out whether he'd be able to last the pace for 10, 50, or maybe even 100 kilometers.

"Dools," I tell him, "you wouldn't even make it through the neutralized zone. I can only think of about three people on the Isle of Man who would."

The Tour de France starts in the neutralized zone on the first stage, but I swear that for most even competent amateurs, that's also where it would end. The neutralized zone is the stretch between 1 and 10 kilometers used by the race organizers to take the peloton safely and slowly out of the main street or town square where the stages inevitably begin and at the same time give the public at the side of the road a decent view of the race. In theory, it's the Tour's no-fly zone, "neutralized" inasmuch as all racing and attacks are off until its end point—or "kilometer zero" of the race proper. In practice, it's like sharing a tightrope with a herd of buffalos.

Danger is a topic you're often asked about as a sprinter. The common perception is that the final 200 meters of a Tour stage are the most dangerous and the most frightening. That might be half right, but while it may hold true that the final few seconds of a bike race are fastest and apparently chaotic, at 70 kph and 200 heartbeats per minute, there's simply no time for anxiety. Adrenaline, yes. Instinct, sure. But fear, no. The day I begin to be afraid of taking risks, afraid of crashing, afraid of my own fearlessness, will be the day I also start worrying about my future as a top sprinter.

We were scoobying along at no more than 30 kph, yet I meant what I told Dools—he wouldn't even have made it to the start line, not because he wasn't fast or fit enough but because of the feats of bike handling required just to stay upright. At any one time, you could have laid a hand on about six different riders, so closely were the bikes and bodies huddled together. I was climbing up curbs and bunny-hopping over grass verges. It was chaos, absolute, utter chaos—the kind that leaves you mentally drained after five minutes . . . and we still had 197.5 kilometers to ride just to earn the right to do it all again the next day.

We passed the kilometer zero mark. Tour director Christian Prud-homme's flag came down to indicate the start of the race, and it was as though someone standing at the side of the road had turned on a giant hair dryer. On a bridge immediately after the start line, wind whipped in from the estuary and slanted across the road at 90 degrees, almost taking the entire peloton with it. "Everyone sitting uncomfortably?" it seemed to say. "Okay, then, *bienvenu au Tour. . . .*"

Not many people knew it, but I wasn't even supposed to be here. I had been selected the previous year at Gerald Ciolek's expense, and the plan at the beginning of the 2008 season had been that I'd skip the Tour to concentrate on preparing for my shot at gold in the Madison at the Olympics. In my absence, Gerald would be the team's sprinter at the Tour. But then came the Giro d'Italia, or Tour of Italy, in May, when my two stage wins forced a rapid reassessment of how Gerald and I would now be spending the month of July. Gerald and his sprinting would have been the fulcrum of almost any other team's objectives for the Tour; now he accepted the role of my understudy with a grace and professionalism that both humbled and amazed me.

On today's stage, at least, Gerald would have his chance. The finish line was at the top of a nasty 1-kilometer climb, the Côte de Cadoual, that would scatter the pure sprinters like me or Robbie McEwen but might suit a rider like Gerald, whose finishing kick relied more on power than leg speed. Most mornings, in our prestage briefing, Brian Holm's instructions could be condensed into some variation on "Have fun!"—and today he didn't need to tell us that a break would go early in the stage. A break always went early in the stage. There'd be attacks, counterattacks, full-blooded accelerations, halfhearted ones; then five or six riders would open up a gap of 100 meters, 200, 300, before, finally, the main peloton would hand them the rope with which to hang themselves before scooping up the suicide victims somewhere in the final 10 kilometers. It was one of those accepted clichés of cycle racing, especially stages in the first week of the race.

Even by Tour standards, this was a tense, fast, nervous opening stage. Sure enough, the break was reeled in before the final climb up the Côte de Cadoual, but the pace proved too hot and the slope too steep for me and for Gerald, who was spat out three-quarters of the way up the hill. At around the same time, at the front of the bunch and the race, Little Kim kicked hard around the penultimate bend, leaving a chasm behind him. Unfortunately, the Spaniard Alejandro Valverde had timed his move perfectly and swept past Kim in the final few hundred meters. Kim lived up to his other nickname by hanging on grimly for 4th.

The landscapes in Brittany reminded me of the Isle of Man. The roads, too, were similar to those on which I'd grown up—narrow, gnarly, and constantly undulating, with coarse grey tarmac that gripped your tires like a fifth brake pad and wind that seemed to gust in every direction except at your back.

If the Tour really was to be the journey of a lifetime, my lifetime, then this certainly seemed like a fitting place to start.

The home of Manx cats, the Bee Gees, the TT motorbike race, and Mark Cavendish is a green, windy island in the middle of the Irish Sea, two and three-quarter hours' ferry ride from Belfast to the west, a bit less from Liverpool to the southeast, about 32 miles long, and 15 miles across at its widest point. It is also, you often hear, a "strange place."

The Island is what's called a crown dependency, which means it's not strictly part of the United Kingdom, although it has the same head of state—the queen. The contradictions begin rather than end there: Our passports say, "British Citizen," but we have our own parliament, Tynwald, which is supposedly the oldest parliament in continuous existence in the world, dating back to the first Norse invasions just over a thousand years ago. We have the same dialing code as the UK but our own mobile phone networks and, bizarrely, international tariffs for calls to the UK. While to many people our accent sounds Scouse—a legacy of the fact that, historically, most people came to the Island on the ferry from Liverpool, where Scouse is spoken—islanders can easily make the distinction; we use the same currency units as the mainland but different notes and coins; English and Manx Gaelic are our official languages, though the last native speaker of the latter died in 1974 and only 2 percent of people on the Island claim to know any Manx Gaelic; we have the same awful trends and fashions, except that they arrive on the Island later and take even longer to shift; and finally, there's the local delicacy—chips, cheese, and gravy, which, as far as I know, hasn't yet made it over the water.

Perhaps because of these idiosyncrasies, for some people on the Isle of Man, going over to England is a bit like traveling to another planet. The Island has its own quirks and folklore, which are a pretty minor part of Manx life but do give people who live there a strong sense of identity.

Dutch, Belgian, and even British journalists who come to see me at home in Laxey lap up local color like the legend of the Fairy Bridge—a road bridge on the way from the airport to Douglas where it's unlucky not to say hello to the fairies as you cross, preferably in Manx Gaelic. Even people who aren't particularly superstitious won't dream of breaking that rule. Then there's the law that says a Manxman is allowed to shoot a Scot, as long as he's on the beach and wearing tartan—though don't ask me if anyone's ever taken advantage of that particular loophole.

I'd love to tell you that the Cavendish family is just as much of an institution as the Island myths and folklore that people find so fascinating, but I somehow doubt it. My grandmother on my dad's side does claim to have a family tree that goes back to the 1600s, although I don't have a clue about the details. That's the Manx side of the family. My mum, Adele, hails from Harrogate in Yorkshire. She met David, my dad, when she came over to the Island on holiday with her mum's cousin, whom we always knew as Auntie Ruth. My parents fell in love and, pretty soon, were married with two kids. I was first, and fifteen months later, along came my brother, Andy.

I was born in Douglas on 21 May 1985. With a population of just over 25,000, which equates to just under one-third of the Manx population, Douglas is the largest town on the Island and its capital. With a 2-mile promenade that loops around a beautiful, windswept bay, the seafront has been compared to the famous palm-flanked Promenade des Anglais in Nice, historically the setting for the final stage of the Paris-Nice stage race. Others disagree; they reckon it's a bit like Blackpool.

I inherited my physique from my mum's side of the family. The short, muscular legs, the ample backside—sorry, Mum, but you know what I mean. My dad's the total opposite—small and skinny. My parents both have passionate natures, though that passion expresses itself in very different ways. My mum is either blessed or cursed with the same heart-on-the-sleeve attitude to life that many see in me. She's spontaneous, fiery, transparent—an emotional volcano. My dad is every bit as wholehearted but in a completely opposite, very studious, and occasionally slightly obsessive way. Their personalities both clashed and complemented each other; as a legacy to my fledgling career as a sportsman, you could say that Mum supplied the fire and Dad the ice.

My mum will tell you that I always was a headstrong little so-and-so. Whenever she tried to breast-feed me, I'd push her away, and it was always the same later when she tried to choose what I was going to wear. I always wanted be ahead with everything, whether it was potty-training or maths lessons at school. My first-ever memory is of lining all the other kids up and racing them across the room at the nursery, Knotfield, where Mum used to take Andy and me when she was at work in the bridal-wear shop that's been in the family for decades.

I hated Knotfield. I obviously had a pretty sharp sense of injustice even then because I couldn't fathom why the women who ran that place acted as though they were doing us a favor, even though Mum and Dad were paying a fortune for us to go there. One day Andy and I decided to take matters into our own hands. I was about 10 at the time, at primary school, but we'd still get taken to Knotfield after school to wait for Mum to finish work. One afternoon, we decided to attempt our first breakaway, waiting until the monitors went into the kitchen to prepare dinner at ten to five, then bombing up the stairs and out the front door, leaving our bags behind to add to the panic and confusion. The next day, we went into the nursery to discuss what had happened, but instead of showing concern and trying to find out why we were so unhappy there, the lady in charge, Val, blew her top. "What would have happened if there'd been a fire?" she shrieked. If Mum hadn't already made up her mind about us never going back, she did when she witnessed Val's reaction.

It's another cliché, but Mum and Dad made sure we never went short of anything. We weren't wealthy, but between the bridal shop, which later diversified to sell dancewear, and Dad's job in the IT department of an accountancy firm, we had a comfortable life in a comfortable 1930s, four-bedroom, semidetached house on the outskirts of Douglas. Mum and Dad gave us every opportunity to pursue our interests, whether it was playing the cornet or the euphonium, or football, or ballroom dancing. We'd go on family holidays to Tenerife or Florida or to see Mum's family in Yorkshire. In almost every photo from those years, we're smiling, and so, usually, are Mum and Dad.

My first bike was a Christmas present when I was 3—a little red thing with a white saddle, which, now I think about it, may have been a girl's bike. I have a clear image of Dad running up and down the garden, holding my saddle, until finally, one day, I made it to the other end without falling off. They then bought me a black BMX for my birthday, which I absolutely adored. We had the same yellow-and-red Early Learning Centre slide that every other kid on the Island seemed to have, only Andy and I reinvented ours as a BMX ramp sloping down from the garden onto a paved terrace. We spent hour after hour, day after day, zooming down that thing. That slide brought me endless fun and my first major crash—an unrehearsed, unintentional Superman dive that ended in a face-plant on the patio and a chipped tooth.

My parents weren't especially sporty, but that was offset by one considerable advantage: They never put any pressure on us. Some of the pushy parents I used to see at our soccer matches or, later, bike races made me wince. As for me watching sport, I was, like every kid, mad about soccer, especially as Leeds United, my mum's team, was in the middle of a renaissance. It was the era of Eric Cantona, Gary Speed, the Premiership title. The halcyon days.

As a player, I was strong, fast, and two-footed, best deployed as a left wingback. That was when I was deployed at all, before the headmaster at my infant school decreed that soccer might interfere with my academic performance, and therefore I shouldn't be picked. My reputation as a budding Einstein was later enhanced when I took the entrance exam for King William's, a private school with optional boarding near the only airport on the Island in Ballasalla. There was a choice of three questions: Write a poem, tell us about a musical instrument you play, or write a short story. I did all three, a feat that earned me the only scholarship up for grabs. Given my level of application and interest in schoolwork—and also my appetite for mischief—King William's should probably count itself lucky that I opted to follow my friends and go to the Ballerkemeen comprehensive school in Douglas.

Have you ever noticed how, in interviews, athletes will often refer to a single day or incident in their childhood as the "moment that shaped their future" or the "turning point in their lives"? As if, say, a professional golfer would now be working in a butcher's shop or a call center if his dad hadn't bought him those plastic clubs when he was 4 years old. They see their lives and careers a lot like *Sliding Doors*, the 1990s chick flick starring Gwyneth Paltrow, whose character's life takes two completely different paths according to whether or not she squeezes inside the closing doors on a London Tube train.

If I had to choose my *Sliding Doors* moment, one day in 1995 stands out quite clearly: the afternoon when Andy came home from school and announced that he wanted to go along to the cycling league for kids that took place every Tuesday night at the National Sports Centre (NSC) on the road out of Douglas. When I piped up that I'd like to give it a go as well, my mum said, "Why not?" After school the next Tuesday, she rounded us up, and off we trooped to the NSC.

One thing I can say quite emphatically about that evening is that I could hardly have looked less like someone poised to embark on a journey toward a career in professional sport, least of all in cycling. My chosen battle gear that and every other Tuesday for the next few months was more Lee Chapman than Lance Armstrong, what with my Leeds United home shirt and oversized red helmet. Not that I'd have been fazed as I took my place on the start line, glancing left and right, sizing up the opposition. There were maybe twenty kids, and I was the smallest of the lot. I gripped the handlebars of my BMX tightly and listened for the signal to send all that adrenaline rushing to those pudgy little legs. One second, two seconds, ready, steady, *go!* and two minutes later, I'd finished the course—a single lap of the NSC car park—in last place. Dead last. In my first race.

I was gutted but also, somehow, sufficiently exhilarated to want to come back for more. And I would keep coming back, keep finishing last or, on a good day, second from last, and keep drawing both motivation and humiliation from the experience. One Tuesday night that summer, I was in my customary position, somewhere at the back, when I caught sight of Mum at the edge of the track, smirking. At the end of the race, I rode over and asked her what she'd been smiling about. Her answer was mortifying: "You look like you're out for a Sunday stroll." I blurted out that maybe if I had a bike with gears like all the other kids, I might have a chance one day, a notion she found even funnier.

My next birthday, Mum and Dad finally caved in and allowed themselves to be dragged to the bike shop, Castletown Cycles. I picked out a purple mountain bike, bigger than its red predecessor, and with gears. Crushingly, the next Tuesday's race was canceled due to rain, but all that meant was a delay to the start of what was soon to become a rampant winning spree. After the first win came a second and a third, and, pretty soon, thanks partly to the gears and partly to my mum's unwittingly goading remarks, I'd become nigh on invincible. It seemed that defeat and ridicule were the best bait for whatever lurking talent needed coaxing out. Thus, the same year, when I competed in a mountain bike league off Douglas Head, I ended race one sobbing in a gorse bush and vowing never to go back, only to go on later to dominate there as well. At around the same time, I entered a British Cycling Federation Challenge consisting of a short time trial and an obstacle course, with the winner going on to a national final in Manchester. I thought I'd done pretty well in both and said so to Mum and Dad as we stood waiting for the results. I was rabbiting away, "I'd absolutely love it if it was me."

Mum sniggered. "Ha. Don't be silly, it's not going to be you."

The next voice was the one we all heard over the loudspeaker—"And the winner is . . . Mark Cavendish." I was on my way to Manchester for the national final.

If I was pleased with myself then, I'd be even more delighted and amazed when, a few weeks later, on a course that consisted of a road race and a time trial, both effectively laps of the Manchester velodrome car park, I won the Challenge overall. My prize was a Raleigh mountain bike. It had been tipping it down with rain that whole day, but as I sat on the ferry that night, sopping wet, you could have toasted bread on my cheeks.

Winning an event organized by British Cycling meant that I was now on the national federation's radar, and so started a period of several years where you'd have seen me down the Ferry Port in Douglas of a Saturday morning, bike slung over my shoulder, off to some race or event. It was also around that time that my life took a completely unexpected and unwelcome twist: My parents announced that they were splitting up. I automatically connect the two things simply because the day that Mum, without warning or preamble, told us the news, I was due to go over to the mainland for a race, this time with the Island athletics team.

An hour or so later, I was on the ferry with all the other kids, but I was the only one sitting on his own crying his eyes out. That whole weekend I was crestfallen. There'd been none of the warning signs you expect—the constant blazing rows, the silences, the simmering tension. Okay, our parents had the odd argument, but nothing out of the ordinary. Maybe we had just been too preoccupied with whizzing around on our bikes, or maybe I'd shut it out. I never really dwelled on it in the years following, but now when I think about it, the rawness of the emotion takes me by surprise.

For a while, at first, Dad carried on living with us, but there was never any question that they weren't going to get a divorce. Thinking back, it was surreal; the first time it really dawned on us that Dad was gone for good was when Andy and I were riding around Douglas on our BMXes one day, weeks or maybe months after Mum broke the news, and we saw his car parked in a drive that wasn't our own. There were no tears, just a stark realization: "Oh, okay, so that's where Dad's living now." After that, we pretty much got on with things. If we misbehaved, which wasn't that often, or if we were hyperactive, which was pretty much all the time, Mum would blame it on the divorce, but that was just her fretting and perhaps feeling guilty. When it wasn't the divorce, she was blaming Coco-Pops or apple juice and banning them from the kitchen cupboard.

I don't know if Andy would agree, but in general, I think Mum and Dad breaking up made us grow up quite quickly and recognize that, even as a pair of kids, we had to take some responsibility. The hardest part was Christmases, as I suppose it is for a lot of kids with divorced parents. At school, I'd be aware of the other kids looking forward to Christmas, while I'd be quietly dreading it. We were lucky in that Dad still wanted to be a part of our lives, but the flip side of this was that we'd spend Christmas Day getting ferried from one family to another. It's only in the years when I was with Melissa that I started to like Christmas and even love it.

I don't think the divorce changed me particularly; it just happened to come at a time when I was changing a fair bit anyway. I'd been gobby at infant school, and now I started puberty before everyone else and became even more confident. Headmasters' comments spanned the gamut from "bone idle" to "too smart for his own good."

There are many common misconceptions about the Isle of Man, one of them being that an island measuring 50 kilometers in length couldn't possibly offer the variety of roads and terrain that arc the spice of a cyclist's life and training. The misconception is, in fact, almost as vast as the 400-kilometer road network that zigzags the Island, and which, by the age of 13, I knew by name, number, gradient, and texture of tarmac.

I'll always maintain that the roads are one of the main reasons why the Island has produced so many decent riders. One of the best known before me was probably Steve Joughin, who won national titles and stages of the Milk Race in the 1980s. Mike Doyle was another one who turned pro in that era. Going back further, Peter Buckley won the Commonwealth Games gold medal in 1966 but was tragically killed when he was out training three years later. Over the past few years, it's amazing how many riders from the Island have represented Great Britain at some level or ridden for pro teams either in the UK or abroad: Mark Kelly, Christian Varley, Andrew Roche, Jonny Bellis, Peter Kennaugh, Timmy Kennaugh, Mark Christian, and I.

It's hard to explain if you're not a cyclist and you haven't been to the Island, but take it from me, there are two prerequisites for riding a bike there: You have to be tough, and you have to be passionate. Without those two key requirements, there's just too much wind, too much cold, too many hills, and too many excuses to do something else—something that doesn't feel suspiciously like self-harm.

By the time I was 13, cycling was still a game, but one that I was taking increasingly seriously, and with increasing success. The Manchester Youth Tour gave me my first experience of racing against the best in my age group from all around Europe, and a couple of sprint wins proved that I was far from out of my depth. At home, I was a member of one of the two main clubs on the Island, the Manx Viking Wheelers, and at the club dinner that winter, I can remember asking the guest of honor for the evening, Shane Sutton, for a few training tips.

Shane would later become one of my best and most influential coaches at the British Cycling Federation—a good road racer in the '80s and '90s; a brilliant manager; and your original, straight-shooting, straight-talking Aussie. His advice to me that night was typical Shane—simple and brilliant. He said, "It doesn't matter what you do, just do sixteen hours a week."

My bullshit radar had always been a finely tuned instrument, and I recognized straightaway that this advice was coming from someone with the right credentials to give it, so I went straight home and started drawing up a training plan with my mate, training partner, and sometime nemesis, Christian Varley. Sixteen hours a week, every week, all winter, come rain or shine. And we stuck to it. Religiously. It was the first time I'd trained properly rather than just riding my bike with fitness as a collateral benefit—and the results were incredible. Once upon a time in cycling circles, training was considered no less an outrageous and unethical shortcut to better performance than anabolic steroids or EPO are today, and now I could see why: I attacked 200 meters into the first race of the next season in Saltayre, lapped the field twice, and could have stopped for a light picnic and still won. That was also the year of the Youth Olympics. We turned up at the trial in Cleveland, and I asked if I could ride in the Under 16s rather than in the Under 14s, where the competition would no doubt be less challenging and the gears were restricted—the theory being that younger and less-developed riders could damage joints and muscles by pushing too hard on the pedals.

The organizer pointed me in the direction of the Under 16s, and I swear to this day that I would have won and not come in 2nd had Christian not told me to launch my sprint too late. The races kept coming, and so did the improvements—and the wins. Every Wednesday night back on the Island meant a 10-mile time trial, and pretty much every week I'd take a big chunk of time off my personal best. I'd started off doing twenty-nine minutes, then it was twenty-eight, then twenty-seven, until one week one of the lads from Bikestyle, the shop in Douglas, lent me his lo-pro—a bike whose frame slopes down from the saddle toward the handlebars for a lower and more aerodynamic position. That night I went under what time trialists refer to as the "magical" twenty-four minutes for the first time. I was 13 years old.

I had become "The Manx Express." Pretty soon, I'd also be a double British champion. The road race was in Hillingdon, near London, and I attacked incessantly before settling into the main pack and comfortably winning in a sprint. The race was an omnium, the track-cycling equivalent of the decathlon: a series of different events of varying number and type, with points added up in an overall league table based on your finishing position in each event. I'd never really ridden on a track before, so Mike Kelly, the coach from the Manx Road Club, and Andrea Ingham, a friend of Mike's, had given me a bit of a crash course a week before the championships. Mike had also lent me a rear disc wheel and an aerodynamic helmet. They had the desired effect: I stopped the clock in 12.3 for the flying 200—200 meters with a rolling start—which was about two seconds faster than anyone else, then in under two minutes for the 1,500-meter individual pursuit—sixteen seconds better than 2nd place.

I left the velodrome that day with my second British title and a new certainty, more meaningful than any trophy or medal, or any amount of bluster or bravado: I was bloody good at this.

STAGE 1: BREST-PLUMELEC, 197.5 KM

1. Alejandro Valverde Belmonte (Spa), Caisse d'Epargne, 4:36:07 (42.91 kph)

120. Mark Cavendish (GBr), Team Columbia, 2:00

STAGE 2

Sunday, 6 July 2008
AURAY–SAINT BRIEUC
164.5 KM

I'm sure someone must have said it before, but for three weeks, the life of a Tour de France rider bears a strong resemblance to the recurring, twenty-four-hour nightmare faced by Bill Murray's character in the film *Groundhog Day*.

It's not as though the daily grind on the Tour is necessarily very different from that of any other race. The average pro bike rider races seventy to a hundred days a year. That's potentially a hundred days of chain hotels, chain-hotel breakfasts, chain-hotel dinners, and chain-hotel beds. It's a hundred alarms and a hundred times the same kaleidoscope of excitement, tiredness, and sometimes dread that accompanies the same waking thought: "Here we go again." All that changes at the Tour is that everything gets magnified as though for every extra spectator, every extra ounce of prestige and pressure, every extra day in the hottest, harshest cauldron in professional cycling, or perhaps any other endurance sport, the emotional hangover gets heavier—heavier than at any other race, and heavier than it was the day before.

Some riders will tell you they know what kind of day it'll be as soon as they open their eyes and feel the dull aches and pains in their legs, which will multiply as the race goes on. Not me: *Que sera, sera* is my philosophy. Now, on the second morning of the race, I rubbed away the sleep, rolled gingerly off the bed, no differently than billions of adults on every working day all over the world, pulled on a pair of tracksuit bottoms and a T-shirt, and shambled down to the nondescript dining room du jour.

The breakfast table's one of the best places to observe the other rituals, superstitions, and dietary eccentricities that are as much a part of cycling lore as the Tour itself. Some are grounded in science, some in personal experience, some in nothing more than myth and legend. One of my more irrational superstitions is my refusal to take a shower on the morning of a race; I also steer clear of cow's milk, having once read something in a magazine about dairy products encouraging the buildup of lactic acid in the muscles, and I'll never eat meat because proteins are hard to digest. You'd think everyone would abide by the same principles, but, on the morning of some of her most important races, I've seen the British Olympic and world champion Nicole Cooke drinking a pint of milk to wash down a dirty big fry-up. It goes without saying that my team coaches and nutritionists will take some convincing before they frog-march us to the nearest greasy spoon.

An interesting study in the nutritional habits of a leading cyclist it may be, but breakfast is also one of the least interesting parts of the day on the Tour. Very early in the race, sleep and rest become an obsession, and any time not spent on the bike or not dedicated to either of those two activities can seem wasted. Today, the banter was typically subdued. Depending on how bleary-eyed and brain-dead everyone is, and how many column inches are dedicated to the team in the morning papers splayed across the breakfast tables, the highlight of the whole twenty minutes to half an hour is choosing from the array of cereals laid out by our soigneurs—the assistants-cum-masseurs-cum-chefs who are an integral part of every team. After three bowls of Chocomix or Special K, a splash of soya milk, a croissant or bread roll, two espressos, and my laundry bag of freshly washed kit from the soigneurs, usually, like today, I'm ready to roll.

My race number at the Tour was 43. That's another of my superstitions, this one passed on by Axel Merckx, son of the greatest cyclist of all time, Eddy: Never pin your number on your jersey until the morning of the race. That left about twenty minutes after breakfast to inflict four stab wounds on a square sheet of paper marked "43," change into my kit, fasten the number, pack up my suitcase, and report to the bus five minutes before the departure time advised by the directeurs sportifs the previous evening. Why five minutes early? Simple—the closer to the advertised stage start time you arrive, the more problems and stress you create for your teammates, your mechanics, your soigneurs, and your directeurs—and the more likely you are to get an almighty bollocking, even from our relatively mild-mannered directeurs sportifs.

Stage 2, or the second of twenty-one Groundhog Days? For the next two hours, it'd sometimes be hard to tell. . . .

Two hours to start:

Sometimes your hotel's an hour away from the start village, sometimes half an hour, as was the case this morning from the Ibis in Vannes to the start in Auray. Either way, the timetable for the entire morning—when you get up, when you eat, when you leave—is geared toward arriving an hour and ten minutes before the start. Today, like most mornings on Tour, the mood is sleepy and subdued, the conversation muted; everyone jumps on, on time, and the wheels roll.

One hour fifty-seven minutes to start:

Give or take a couple of seconds, this is when, in most cases, the iPods go in and the eyes slam shut; sometimes, seen from afar, you'd think the Tour was a sleeping competition, the team bus a mobile dormitory, not a mode of transport. Occasionally, you'll see someone with their head in a book—a novel, a real book—but, really, the only required reading at the Tour is the race manual, or "road book," containing the maps and course profiles of every stage. Last night, like every night, I spent fifteen or twenty minutes poring over the detailed map of the last 4 kilometers of today's stage, and, this morning, I repeat the review session as soon as the bus pulls out of the hotel car park.

One hour fifteen minutes to start:
The bus groans through streets now lined with fans, banners, and tricolor flags and into the area allocated for "Parking Équipes," or team parking. All eyes are now wide open and darting between the riders, journalists, officials, and spectators choking the road and sidewalks on either side. Unseen and un-heard behind our bus's tinted windows, this is also where the banter can start. "Check her out. . . ." "There's that prat. . . ." "Cav, in fifteen years, when you've retired and you're a fat bastard, you'll look just like that bloke over there. . . ." It's all in good heart. Honest.

One hour ten minutes to start:
The engine stops, the bus rocks to a standstill, and the directeurs sportifs ar-rive for our ten-minute briefing. No fists on tables; just a few pointers about the route, a brief outline of tactics, perhaps a couple of questions, then everyone's mind on the job. Today, it's "We work to bring back the breakaways, for a sprint finish. Couple of bumps in the last kilometer, but we try to set up Cav. Okay?" Okay. Over and out.

One hour to start:
One of the guys disappears into the bathroom. Four minutes later, a foul stench, a deluge of expletives, and, finally, laughter fill the air.

Forty minutes to start:
Slap on chamois cream. Pick out selection of energy bars and gels from stash replenished every morning by team soigneurs. Tell Bernie Eisel I'm definitely better-looking than him.

Half an hour to start:
Ride the 100 meters or so to the sign-on podium. You always know where to go, because, from about 100 miles, never mind 100 meters, you can hear Daniel Mangeas, Tour speaker and institution, reciting some irrelevant statistic about

how an obscure Spanish rider once finished 12th in Stage 4 of the Vuelta a España. I arrive, sign the sheet indicating that I'm present, correct, and ready to ride, wave to the crowd, retrieve my bike, then muscle through more fans, journalists, VIPs, and gendarmes back to the team bus while Mangeas rasps his way through a list of my most significant achievements.

Twenty minutes to start:
Perhaps pop outside for two or three very short interviews, at request of team press officer. Every day, for fifteen minutes or even half an hour, some riders will camp out in the "Village Départ" or start village, a sprawling hospitality area where you can read the papers, drink coffee, and even get a haircut . . . but where you're also besieged by reporters, sponsors, guests, or former Tour stars now recycled as chauffeurs or PR men. In 2007, this had all been a novel, prestage diversion; now, in 2008, it is much less stressful and much more sensible to count down the last few minutes before a stage start in the calm and comfort of the bus.

Five minutes to start:
Down the stairs, out of bus, helmet on, take bike, check radio, right foot in, left foot in, and away we go. See you in 164.5 kilometers, in Saint Brieuc, in about three and three-quarter hours' time, on the top step on the podium, with any luck.

Three hours, forty-five minutes, and thirteen seconds, to be precise. That's how long it took Thor Hushovd—but, sadly, not me. Those "bumps" we talked about in the briefing turned out to be somewhat harder than expected, so much so that, on the penultimate rise, a kilometer and a half from the line, my legs suddenly seized up and my chances evaporated. As I dropped backward, one rider's tumble led to a mass pileup, which forced me to slam on the brakes and skid to a halt. When I finally started moving again, I was in fiftieth position, and it was all I could do to reach for the microphone on my intercom radio, press the *on* button, and bleat the order to forget about me and ride for Gerald Ciolek.

From twenty-seven places back—which was exactly where I would finish—I could just about make out Hushovd's raised arms and both Kim and Gerald lunging in vain at his heels.

Kirchen 2nd. Ciolek 3rd. Cavendish 27th.

Or, if you like, another day, another defeat.

"Fat wanker." That's what the *Guardian* called me. Or rather, that's what I called myself, according to an article by William Fotheringham the day before my Tour de France debut in London in July 2007. William was one of the scores of journalists that my team, T-Mobile, had fixed up with phone interviews in the run-up to the Tour's Grand Départ, nearly driving me to despair, and I'd been telling him about how my coach at the British Cycling Academy, Rod Ellingworth, had transformed me from a slightly chubby 16-year-old into the rider everyone now said was going to be the revelation of the 2007 Tour. The line wasn't the best, but I thought he'd heard okay. There were even faint gurgles of laughter down the phone. Well, you would, wouldn't you? It was one hell of a quote—"Rod turned me from a fat wanker to a world champion in fifteen months."

I know I'm not the most lily-tongued 24-year-old on the planet, and I'm not proud of it, but would I really call myself a "fat wanker"? To the *Guardian*? I suppose at that point, not many people knew I'd spent a couple of years in my teens working in Barclays Bank in Douglas, trying desperately to raise a few quid for what I expected to be an expensive couple of years when I'd have to travel abroad to race and get myself noticed. From "fat banker" to world champion; I'll grant you that it's a strange enough concept for one or two people to get their wires crossed.

I'd known I was going to leave school at 16 right from when I'd had to choose my GCSE (General Certificate of Secondary Education) options two years earlier. You know how it goes: Kid tells parents and headmaster that he's going to be a professional athlete, parents and headmaster roll their eyes and mutter some cliché about "having qualifications to fall back on," kid shakes his head and sulks, and parents and headmaster usually win. In my case, the bone of contention was whether I was going to do just French or German; I was passably good at both and could well understand how French could be useful for my cycling career, at least, but simply didn't see the point of taking German instead of physical education, which was what they were advocating. They ended up convincing me, and for reasons that'll later become clear, it's no bad thing that they did.

They were an eventful couple of years, 2001 and 2002. There was one event in particular that changed my life forever, and that was meeting Melissa, who would become my fiancée. People still laugh when I talk about my past life as a teenaged ballroom-dancing prodigy, but I always tell them not to knock it because, without it, I would never have met the girl who, eight years on, was the person who'd done more for me than anyone else in the world—the girl whom I called the best thing that ever happened to me.

The date was sometime early in 2002—the year of my GCSEs—the occasion a Saturday night when I had just returned from my first race of the season, the Eddie Soens in Aintree. I was never much of a drinker or a party animal as a teenager, mainly because those vices aren't compatible with the lifestyle of a budding professional cyclist, but all of my mates were going to a "Battle of the DJs" at the Villa Marina, on the front in Douglas, so I decided to tag along. Straightaway I recognized Melissa. We'd been introduced by my ballroom-dance partner, Laura, at a party a couple of months earlier, and I'd been downright snotty with her. We'd spoken for a minute, then I'd pretended to be bored and sloped off to talk to someone else. Now, though, I saw her across the dance floor and turned to my mate. "That girl has to be mine," I whispered. To cut a long and fabulous story very, very short—at least for now—eight fabulous, sometimes tempestuous years later, we were still together and due to get married in October 2009.

Most kids at that age launch themselves into relationships without a moment's thought for where it's all leading, what kind of emotions or practical choices are going to be involved in a few months' time. It shows just how sure I was about Melissa that after a few weeks I'd turned to her with both a warning and the option of quitting while we were ahead: I was going to be a professional cyclist, and chasing that dream would mean trips to the mainland every weekend and to Europe every so often, and pretty soon it might mean spending weeks or months at a time away. She nodded, unperturbed, but I'm sure she hadn't grasped the full implications of what I was saying, probably because it did sound a little bit presumptuous coming from a 15-year-old. There'd be plenty of tears shed by both parties over the next few years as we realized that, if anything, I'd underestimated the extent of the sacrifices we would both make and the heartache they'd cause.

Melissa's arrival on the scene coincided with the buildup to my GCSEs, for which I showed a total lack of enthusiasm. Melissa was in the school year above me, which meant she was studying for AS Levels at the same time that I was doing my GCSEs, but she was intent on devoting more time to helping me than to her own revision. Even without doing homework or much revision, I scraped by in the classroom as well. My GCSE results came through that August: five As, six Bs, and two Cs.

Staying on at school and A-Levels was never really an option. Cycling was the axis on which my world now turned, and everything else, as far as I was concerned, was a waste of time—especially the ten and a half months per year that weren't summer holiday. "Holiday" perhaps isn't how other people would describe a strict regimen of six hours on a bike every day, but to me, those six hours weren't obligation or drudgery or even training—they were pure, unvarnished fun. Every day, I'd either head out with the group that met in the mornings at the Quarter-Bridge or ride on my own for about three hours, then go out for another three with the crowd who trained after work. I loved the company, the piss-taking, the exhilaration, and, of course, like every kid, the gratification that comes with praise and success.

It was around this time, as my obsession grew, that my brother's interest in cycling began to wane. I've said in numerous interviews that Andy was perhaps a more naturally blessed rider than I, and my view on that hasn't changed. One year, for instance, Andy put his bike away in September, dusted it off again the following March, trained for a week, then went straight to Liverpool and won the Merseyside Divisional Championships in his age group. I, meanwhile, had ridden all winter but could only finish 2nd to my soon-to-be best mate, the Scouser Matt Brammeier.

Andy lacked nothing as a cyclist except perhaps a little bit of perseverance and passion. Those, fortunately, were the two commodities I possessed in abundance.

I officially became a Barclays employee in September 2001. I had the next phase of my life all mapped out: A lot of riders in the junior, or Under 18, category are effectively full-time cyclists who live, eat, train, and race pretty much like the pros who ride the Tour de France, but to me, that seemed senseless. I always knew that the key years, the ones that would determine whether or not a big pro team would be willing to take a punt on me, were the three that came later, when I'd be classed as an amateur, or Espoir, or Under 23 rider. They were years when I'd need discipline, contacts, the right diet, the right results, and also a few grand in my pocket to make time off the bike as comfortable, uncomplicated, and conducive to good performances as possible. Mike Kelly, my coach, mentor, training partner, and mate from the Manx Road Club, recommended Barclays in Douglas; his son, who'd been a really good rider as a junior, had worked there and said they'd been great, always happy to give him the odd day to go and race as well as moral support and even a bit of sponsorship. I was so keen that I felt compelled to tell a white lie in the Record of Achievement that I had to submit as part of my application: I said I aspired to a career in professional cycling *or* banking. It obviously worked because I got the job.

Like most people and their banks, over the next two and a half years, Barclays and I developed a love-hate relationship. The job itself was great. I was a cashier, which may not be the most interesting role in itself, but I made it as stimulating as I could by treating it a lot like I treated my cycling: in other words, by working hard and fast. There was an unofficial record at the bank for the number of transactions a cashier completed in a single day, and I soon set about beating it. There was no such record for flirting with the old ladies, but I had a pretty good stab at that as well. It was the only way of making it bearable—learning the customers' names, humoring them, bantering with them. I still go to the bank sometimes to say hello to one of the women who used to work with me, and she still maintains that I was the best cashier they ever had. It still makes me smile.

As modest as the wages were, it was a relief to be earning properly for the first time. Up to that point, my only job had been a newspaper route, the proceeds of which would inevitably be spent on cycling gear, as would all my Christmas and birthday money. I think my parents, and my dad in particular, had exactly the right attitude when it came to buying me equipment for my bike; if, for example, I bought some carbon Campagnolo brake levers, crashed, and wrecked one of them, I'd be able to go to my dad to ask for money for a replacement, but he'd always ask me why I needed the carbon ones, which were only five grams lighter than the slightly less fancy, less expensive alloy versions, and he'd buy me those instead. At the time, I'd be slightly miffed, but now I realize that I grew up appreciating good equipment, just as I still appreciate it now, as well as everything else that my team's backup staff does for me. I can be fairly sure that the pro riders who I see now taking their bikes and their masseurs and mechanics for granted picked up that attitude when they were kids, when they only had to whistle for a new piece of carbon fiber to fall from the sky.

You could say that the clue's in the name, but the "fat banker years" were never intended to be my most productive from a cycling point of view. There were the cream cakes, sure, plus the half-dozen or so kilos of extra blubber they left me carrying, but the real issue was the limited time I had to dedicate to riding my bike. Fortunately, when I did train and race, I was proving to myself and others that I could compete and win, not just on a domestic level but also against my contemporaries from all over Europe. That had been one of the conclusions I'd taken home from the Assen Youth Tour in Holland, which I'd ridden for the British Schools team in my last year at Ballerkemeen. That race was as memorable for my encouraging performances as for a couple of incidents involving my pal and partner-in-scallydom Matt Brammeier. I'd ordered a LOOK adjustable stem a few days before the race and had it sent to Brammeier's in Liverpool, where I was due to stay before we went over to Holland. Of course, when I got off the ferry and arrived at his place, the stem—all £150 worth of it—was already on Brammeier's bike, and he was adamant that it wasn't coming off, arguing that it was "payment" for my board and lodgings. We then pitched up in Assen, at a lodge in the woods where all the other riders and officials were staying, and ran amok. In the race, I won the prologue and finished 2nd on the next stage, a time trial, despite having to suffer the indignity of watching Brammeier riding to 5th place with the LOOK stem I'd ordered specifically with that stage in mind. I won my second stage the following day, then, in the penultimate, attacked on a cobbled section and escaped with a group of eight. I was convinced I had the general classification sewn up until I glanced back and saw the yellow jersey zigzagging through the team cars, sheltered from the crosswinds. I knew then that it was over. My consolation was another win in the final stage, the points jersey, and, most importantly, confirmation that I could hold my own against even the best kids in Europe.

Later that summer, Dad started taking me to track races on the mainland. I loved those trips—just me, my dad, and my bike in the back of our Citroën AX, buzzing up and down the motorways. After my first winter at Barclays, I trained for no more than a fortnight before the British junior track championships, yet still won the Scratch race and was the fastest qualifier in the flying 200 meters (in 11.1 seconds) and the kilometer time trial ahead of Matt Crampton, who sometimes gives Chris Hoy a run for his money in the sprint events these days.

On the track, I could get away with a bit of calorific overindulgence. There were no hills in the velodrome, no gravity to defy, and my finishing speed was intact. On the road, alas, it was a different story. In 2002, my first full year at Barclays, I'd very much hoped to ride and, if possible, win the junior world championship road race on what was said to be an unusually flat and sprinter-friendly route in Zolder, Belgium, but had been badly penalized by a series of hilly routes in the Peter Buckley Trophy. The "Buckleys" were the most coveted, hard-fought junior races on the domestic calendar, not to mention the British Cycling Federation's main measuring post when it came to selecting teams for the Worlds. In 2002, the climbers had flourished while I had flattered to deceive, the result being that Great Britain went to Zolder with a team full of climbers who were desperately ill-equipped for such a flat course. A Frenchman won; the Brits ended medal-less while I sat at home ruing what might have been.

My last year at the bank, 2003, was also going to be my last as an Under 18, or junior. Mike Kelly had set me up with Dataphonics, a junior team based in Cambridge, and Barclays allowed me to have much of that summer off on a short sabbatical. Having missed out the previous year in Zolder, I set my sights on the 2003 Worlds in Hamilton, Canada, but was left fuming again as the selectors snubbed me for the second straight year. The day after the team was announced minus my name, I luckily had the opportunity to make amends in what was to be the final Buckley of the season. My rivals that day had the Federation to thank for a performance that was as angry as it was dominant and, most importantly, triumphant.

STAGE 2: AURAY–SAINT BRIEUC,164.5 KM

1. Thor Hushovd (Nor), Crédit Agricole, 3:45:13 (43.84 kph)

27. Mark Cavendish (GBr), Team Columbia, 3:45:13

GENERAL CLASSIFICATION

1. Alejandro Valverde Belmonte (Spa), Caisse d'Epargne, 8:21:20

100. Mark Cavendish (GBr), Team Columbia, 2:00

STAGE 3

Monday, 7 July 2008
SAINT-MALO–NANTES
208 KM

There are many things you'd like to do when you've just blown your chance in a stage of a Tour de France, but trust me when I say that giving a television interview is a fair way down your list of priorities.

We were now three stages and three missed opportunities into the Tour. Admittedly, with its hilltop finish, Stage 1 had almost been written off in advance. Stage 2 was hardly the kind of pure test of sprinting speed I'd expected, either. Today, though, ought to have been the Day.

Instead, I crossed the line in 10th place, two minutes behind the four-man breakaway group we'd mystifyingly failed to catch. I had lots of questions of my own but no answers.

Unfortunately, answers were exactly what the man with the microphone wanted, and he didn't care that my mood was as dark or wet as the weather.

"Mark, Mark, can we have a word?"

He must have seen from the look on my face that the prospect didn't exactly fill me with glee, but the guy had a job to do. Anyway, as soon as the camera starts rolling, you're trapped; tell him to stick his microphone where there's never any sun on the forecast, or even put it more politely, and you've just starred in your own version of *How to Lose Friends and Alienate People*.

I shrugged and mumbled, "Okay."

First question: "What happened there?"

I glared at him. Did he want a comprehensive analysis from the start of the stage until the end, all six hours of it, while I was standing here in the pissing rain, having just risked my life? Did he want me to run through how I'd effectively sacrificed three teammates—Marcus Burghardt, Bernhard Eisel, and Adam Hansen—ridden them into the floor, all for nothing, because, for some reason that escaped my understanding, no other team wanted to chase? Did he want me to spell out to everyone at home that the six or seven stages on the route that weren't time trials, or didn't feature major climbs, equated to my six or seven shots at a stage win *at best*—and that I'd not so much missed the target as fired a blank?

I looked at him through narrowed eyes. "What do you mean?"

"Well, you didn't catch the break, did you?"

"Well, no—"

"So when did you decide to chase the break?"

"Er, as soon as it went . . ."

Translation: You always know you're going to chase a break as soon as it goes. No, forget that: On a day like today, when the route was predominantly flat, the stars seemed aligned, and everything was set up for me to take my first Tour stage win, we'd known even *before* the stage that we would chase any break. Of course that doesn't mean that when four blokes attacked right from the gun that morning—two Frenchmen, Romain Feillu and the eventual stage winner, Samuel Dumoulin; the Italian Paolo Longo Borghini; and the American William Frischkorn—we were going to mobilize straightaway; it was only when the gap immediately went out to ten minutes after 15 kilometers that we sent Adam, Burghi, and Bernie to the front, just to keep things ticking over, to keep a handle on the situation.

Next question . . . actually, no, the same one as before.

"So when did you decide to start chasing the break?"

"When the break went . . ."

"Who made the decision to start chasing the break?"

"The directeurs, as always . . ."

Translation: With 100 kilometers to go, the gap was still ten or eleven minutes, but we assumed, and the directeurs assumed, that (a) the guys in the break would start tiring and their advantage start plummeting, as per usual, and (b) we'd get some help from a couple of other sprinters' teams and maybe the team of the current yellow jersey, Alejandro Valverde. We were wrong: Everyone could see how motivated I was, purely from how active my team was at the front of the bunch, and they decided we could do all the work on our own. In normal circumstances, we'd still have caught the breakaway quite comfortably, but today, the farther we rode, the more we felt like we were the victims of some cruel practical joke. With 30 kilometers to go, Adam Hansen was drilling on the front and I was in the sweet spot and absolutely flying, yet somehow the gap was refusing to budge. It was still five minutes. Then we turned left into crosswinds with 20 km to go, the peloton split, and we knew it was *bonsoir*.

"So what have you learnt from today?"

"Nothing."

Translation: Mate, I respect that you have to do your job, but not now—not after that stage. I know that everyone watching will think I'm a petulant little sod, and they'll be rushing to say so on message boards and blogs about two minutes from now, but that's my problem, not yours. With me, I'm afraid that what you see is what you're going to get. On a day like this, don't expect a charm offensive.

To give the guy credit, it took him a while, but he finally took the hint. I then rode off in the direction of my team bus, even angrier than I'd been when I crossed the line.

Usually for twenty minutes after everyone's cleaned up and washed down and before we've all flaked out on the seats, the chat in the bus revolves around the race. Not today, no doubt fortunately for all concerned. Only as I told my teammates about the interview did I come up with what would have been a good answer to that final question, albeit one that would have had repercussions way beyond the Internet forums that would be humming with talk of my "antics" the following day.

Interviewer: "So what have you learnt from today?"

Me: "That journalists sometimes ask some stupid fucking questions."

"I want to win stages of the Tour de France . . . oh, and be Olympic champion."

That was my answer to a better question: "What do you want to achieve as a cyclist?"

A yard or two away, on the other side of the table, sat John Herety, Simon Lillistone, and Rod Ellingworth, all former professionals and members of what was rapidly becoming the most highly regarded coaching team in the UK, perhaps even in world cycling. Herety: small and bald, in his mid-40s. Lillistone: younger, medium build, mousey hair. Rod: in his mid-30s, taller, stockier, with spiky ginger hair and a cherubic, friendly face that, you sensed, hid a ruthless streak. They nodded skeptically at my reply.

This wasn't your usual interview. But then I suppose it wasn't your usual job. I'd always intended to leave Barclays at the end of 2003 to dedicate myself full-time to cycling, hoping that a pro contract would be waiting for me at the end of two or three seasons in the Under 23, or amateur, category. Belgium, Holland, Italy, France—they all had a sprawling network of amateur clubs, many with six-figure budgets, top-notch bikes and backup, international race programs, and often feeder agreements with the best pro teams in the world. Soon enough, I'd decided, one of these teams would also have me on their books.

All that had changed when, late in 2003, the British Cycling Federation announced it was launching a two-year residential "Academy" for six Under 23 riders, to be selected in interviews at the end of November. The program was to be lottery-funded and aimed to produce future Olympic champions—which meant a clear emphasis on the track, where (at that time, anyway) there were far more medals available. Although I was far more interested in the romance, the history, and the prestige of the road, I nonetheless knew a good opportunity when I saw one.

There was only one potential glitch: I wasn't sure how highly some of the coaches at the British Federation rated me. I got the impression that one, Marshall Thomas, thought I was downright useless. That year, I'd been entering Nations Cup events with the British junior track team and regularly winning Madisons with Tom White, another of the lads who was applying for the Academy, yet when we'd gone to the European track championships in Düsseldorf that summer, Marshall Thomas had wanted to leave me out of the team pursuit. It was lucky for me that another British coach, the German Heiko Salzwedel, had been one of my biggest admirers ever since he'd first seen me ride at 16 years of age and immediately compared me to Robbie McEwen, who at the time was just about the best road sprinter in the world. In Düsseldorf, Heiko laid down the law; he told Marshall that I had to be in the team pursuit, no questions asked.

Now I scanned their expressions: Herety's, Lillistone's, then Rod's. I got the impression—later confirmed to me—that Lillistone wasn't a fan. Rod was hard to read, but he at least knew that I respected him as a coach. Earlier that year, I'd been invited for a weekend of "coach-led" racing at the Manchester velodrome—a two-day, multidiscipline crash course with Rod providing technical advice and feedback at the end of every session. At the end of the weekend, on my way out of the car park, I'd seen Rod and wandered over to tell him, quietly and sincerely, that it had been the best two days I'd ever spent on my bike. Now Rod and Herety both seemed impressed with my answers, especially the ones about racing. "You're in a group of twelve, 10 kilometers from the finish, and people are starting to attack. What do you do?" Herety asked.

I said I'd start by sussing out who were the strongest riders and marking them because I knew they could use up a lot of energy, finish tired, but still win in a sprint.

He nodded. "Good answer."

There were more unusual questions. Like "How did you get here today?"

Apparently they weren't just looking for athletic or even tactical ability but also for quick wits, street smarts. I knew the road names and exactly how long it had taken, probably because I'd been used to finding my own way off the Isle of Man and to all kinds of race venues for years. Apparently some of the other lads were clueless; they'd just sat in the backseat, with their parents driving, and could barely work out which country they'd come from, let alone the name of the motorway. Rod later said they'd drawn up a matrix plotting our scores in every different department—from motivation to passion to the number of watts we could produce on the bike—and that overall, Ed Clancy and I had been comfortably the best.

For all my bravado, though, and despite the fact that only eight of us were up for six places, I left that interview room without the merest inkling of whether I could expect good news.

A week went by, then two, then three. I carried on training, waiting, hoping. Finally, in December, the phone call arrived. It was Lillistone. I held my breath. I'd been quite open in the interview about how little riding I'd done over the previous two years that I'd been at Barclays, and I'd also told them I was about to have my wisdom teeth out, which would set me back another couple of weeks. I now wondered whether honesty had been the best policy.

Lillistone paused. "Mark," he said, "er . . . congratulations. You've made it. We want you in Manchester for your induction on the eighth of January."

My heart leapt. I was buzzing. I got off the phone to Lillistone and immediately called Christian Varley, the other lad from the Island who'd applied for a place. He hadn't heard anything; I feigned sympathy while privately congratulating myself.

But Varley was soon the least of my worries. The next person who needed to know was Melissa. When I told her, she threw open her arms

and whispered words of congratulations. It was only five minute
when I found her sobbing silently in her sister's bedroom, that the imp
of what was about to happen struck us. We'd known this day was coming,
but that didn't make it any easier.

"Oh . . . my . . . God."

They say a picture's worth a thousand words, but, if that's true, there
are certain facial expressions that are worth a million.

Rod Ellingworth's face was that picture. He worked in Manchester;
he'd seen a scally before; I just don't think he expected to see a pair of
them piling out of a bright gold, souped-up Vauxhaull Corsa in the car
park of the Manchester velodrome. Not today, anyway. Not when he was
here to meet the six teenagers who were meant to form the next genera-
tion of Olympic-medal-winning cyclists. Not in Lacoste tracksuits in that
chav-mobile, with that stereo pumping, and that "007 Man" number
plate, and the "Goldfinger (no. 007)" sticker on the front windscreen.

Matt Brammeier and I had made quite an entrance. I'd stuffed the
Corsa full of my gear, cranked up the sound system, rolled off the ferry
in Liverpool, and gone straight to Brammy's place to pick him up. We'd
then bombed down the M62 into Manchester, across the city, and into
the velodrome car park with a skid, a wheelspin, and more sparks and
sound effects than your average fireworks display.

Having taken several seconds to catch his breath, Rod told us to go
fetch our pedals to put on the new Trek road bikes that were the first
big perk of being in the Academy. Christian Varley turned to his parents.
"Mum," he said, "can you go and get my pedals out of the car for me?"

The coaches looked at each other. Rod later told me that the precise
words flashing through his head at this point were "What the fuck have
we got here?"

The joy of six. Somehow, I don't think whoever coined that phrase
was thinking of us at the time. The least you could say about us was

ıde interesting raw material for a sociological ex-
ny—the scallies and wannabe alpha males; Bruce
—big, dopey Bruce, a domestic disaster area but
e; Varley—my old training partner from the Isle
a place after all; Tom White—decent rider but a
rtue of the fact that he'd grown up in a plush area
of south London, whereas most of us were from the North; and redhead
Ed Clancy, who sometimes seemed to have come from another planet
and had the extraterrestrial strength to match but had actually grown up
in Holmfirth in Yorkshire. It was the kind of lineup that the producers
of *Big Brother* would probably have rejected on the grounds that the mix
was too volatile.

For us, there was no secret location, no diary room, just two fairly
ordinary houses—one in Fallowfield, a nice end-terrace but in a rough
area, and one a semidetached near the university campus, close to a
lot of the popular student bars and restaurants. I wanted to live with
Brammy, but the coaches weren't stupid; the British Cycling Federation
performance director, Dave Brailsford, said he was going to allocate the
houses, and we could draw lots for the rooms. One scally per household
was apparently the limit: I ended up in Fallowfield with Bruce Edgar and
Ed Clancy, and Brammeier was kept at a safe distance, a couple of miles
away, with Varley and Tom White.

In that first year of the Academy, we would learn a hell of a lot about
bike racing but more about ourselves, and even more about life in general. We'd all been living at home until then, and for all my supposed
tidiness, I'm the first one to admit that I'd happily leave my plate on the
table for my mum to clean up. When we joined the Academy, though, I
knew straightaway that no one would clean up after us, and I couldn't
figure out why some of the others didn't get it. The concept of basic
hygiene seemed totally alien to Ed and Bruce.

One of the questions you're often asked as a professional athlete is
whether you feel you've "missed out" on being a student. Boozing, drug-

My fondness for junk food isn't new, as you can see from this picture taken outside my auntie Ruth's house. © MARK CAVENDISH

Maybe it's pictures like this that my critics are referring to when they say I've always been a "big-headed little so-and-so." Clearly, for Mum, I was already a handful.

© MARK CAVENDISH

One of my first wins, at the Ballacloan Infant's School sports day. Aptly, as it would be the site of my first triumphs as a cyclist, the Isle of Man National Sports Center in Douglas provides the backdrop. © MARK CAVENDISH

My younger brother, Andy, and I standing outside our old house in *Douglas*. Our first real cycling jerseys were the same as those worn by Lance Armstrong at the start of his professional career.
© MARK CAVENDISH

Starstruck, posing with Dave Millar during Cycling Week in 1999. © MARK CAVENDISH

Winning my first British national road race title in the Under 14 division at Hillingdon in 1999. Second across the line, in the blue shorts, is Matt Brammeier, my friend and future partner in crime at the Academy. © MARK CAVENDISH

Sporting my new National Champion's jersey on the podium at Hillingdon in 1999. On my left, Matt doesn't appear too upset at finishing 2nd. © MARK CAVENDISH

The mean machine: By 2005, the motley crew of scallies that had assembled when the British Cycling Academy was launched in 2004 had developed into a formidable unit. In training mode from left to right, here we see me, Geraint Thomas, Ed Clancy, Matt Brammeier, and, hidden from view, Tom White.

© BRITISHCYCLING.ORG.UK

The Beach Boys . . . but not as you know them. This picture was taken on Bondi Beach in Australia during a training camp with Rod Ellingworth in the winter of 2004. From left to right: Matt Brammeier, Tom White, me, Geraint Thomas, Matt Crampton, and Ed Clancy.

© ROD ELLINGWORTH

Ever since I joined the British Cycling Academy in January 2004, when Rod Ellingworth talked, I listened. Here is Rod setting the agenda for a training session with the Academy in 2005. © BRITISHCYCLING.ORG.UK

Here I am attacking in vain, en route to 14th place in the points race at the 2004 British National Track Championships. Two days later, despite my oft-stated dislike for the team pursuit, I would be one of the gold-medal-winning quartet in that event. © BRITISHCYCLING.ORG.UK

Max Sciandri and I got off on the wrong foot in 2006, when Max was not too impressed with my approach to racing and training. These days we're good mates, not to mention neighbors when I stay and train in Quarrata, Italy. © BRITISHCYCLING.ORG.UK

British Cycling performance director Dave Brailsford (left) and head coach Simon Jones pictured at the Athens Olympics in 2004. The track team's exploits in those Games would win Jonesy the "British Sports Coach of the Year" accolade. I neither rated nor liked him. © BRITISHCYCLING.ORG.UK

A rare photo of me in the colors of the Isle of Man, taken before the road race at the 2006 Commonwealth Games in Melbourne. A winner of the scratch race at the track a week earlier, I should have won a medal in the road race, but I only managed to finish 7th.
© BRITISHCYCLING.ORG.UK

A magic moment: my first pro win at the Grote Scheldeprijs in Belgium in April 2007, nicked on the line from sprint legend Robbie McEwen, at far right. © GRAHAM WATSON

Brad Wiggins and I were inseparable and perfectly in sync at the Track Cycling World Championships in Manchester in March 2008. © GRAHAM WATSON

Clearly over the moon, I am on the podium with Brad after winning the world Madison title in Manchester in 2008. Germany and Denmark completed the top three. © BRITISHCYCLING.ORG.UK

A skilled lip reader could have told you that there was something amiss very early in the Madison in Beijing. Watching from the stands, Prime Minister Tony Blair could hear most of what I was saying . . . and probably wished he couldn't. © GRAHAM WATSON

taking, living in a crappy single room in a tower block they like to call a "hall of residence"—I don't exactly know what it is that you're supposed to have missed out on, but that's what everyone seems to think.

If university life was about booze and drugs and skipping lectures, then, yeah, I missed out. If it was about having a laugh and living with two mates who cooked bad food and turned the place into a shithole on a daily basis, then I think life with Bruce and Ed was a fairly decent substitute.

Five years on, someone might look back on those first few weeks we spent at the Academy and see them as a landmark in the all-conquering recent history of the British Cycling Federation, but to us, they were just the equivalent of your average 18-year-old's first term at university, right down to the shopping trips to IKEA to buy cheap furniture. In the past, any British youngster who aspired to turn pro relied on contacts and his own initiative; he had to overcome homesickness, loneliness, and often a language barrier, not to mention the bias foreign teams usually show toward their own riders. A few really resilient souls even made it, but they'd done so in spite of, rather than because of, the system. Or perhaps not—because according to one school of thought, the likes of Sean Yates, Robert Millar, and Graham Jones had arrived and then thrived on the continent *because* the very lack of any formal support was the best possible quality control—"naturally selecting" only those with the requisite physical and mental toughness.

Rod might tell you that I would have made it even without the Academy. That's certainly my view, but then I'm also the first to admit that, if the Academy was a kind of *Top Gun* for the best young cyclists in Britain, then the memorable quote directed at Tom Cruise's character, "Maverick"—"Your ego's writing checks your body can't cash"—was equally applicable to a certain Mark Cavendish.

One day from those first few weeks in Manchester will forever be lodged in my memory and Rod's. It must have been the end of February or beginning of March—a typical damp, cold, late-winter day. We set off toward the Peak District—the six of us, with Rod following in the car—and soon, the first climb had claimed its first casualty. Whoever named that narrow, gnarly stairway to my private hell at least had a sense of humor, because they'd called it Gun Hill, and I was shot straight out of the back.

To someone who's never raced bikes, it's hard to convey the agony of blowing up on a climb, compounded by the horror of seeing your opponents or—even worse—your mates disappearing up the road. Just take my word for it when I say that there aren't many more humbling experiences. The climb can't have been more than a mile or so long—maybe three minutes of riding in normal circumstances—but I later realized that Rod had told the others to stop waiting and press on at the top because he was worried they'd catch cold. I finally lurched up the last ramp, zigzagging from one side of the road to the other to take some of the sting out of the gradient, maroon-faced, wheezing like a dodgy exhaust. I noticed Rod's car parked on the side of the road, made one final lunge to grab the back bumper, and in doing so toppled sideways into the grass verge. The car door swung open. Rod walked round the side of the car and found me sprawled on the tarmac, pity in his eyes and tears in mine.

"I'm so sorry, Rod," I blubbed. "I'm trying my best, but I'm not getting any better. I don't know what I can do. I'm so sorry. I won't let you down. I promise I won't let you down. I'm so sorry. . . ."

Most coaches, even experienced ones, wouldn't have known how to respond, but Rod's a master psychologist, cycling's answer to Brian Clough. Now, as I sat weeping, he knew exactly what to say and how to say it. "What are you doing to improve? Riding your bike, and sticking to a good routine? Okay, you're already doing that, so there's no need to apologize," he urged. "Just stick at it, and eventually it'll come. Now, get back on your bike and let's carry on working. . . ."

Revived by the pep talk, I somehow finished the ride that day, and sure enough, within a couple of weeks, without my even noticing, my body had started to undergo a slow, subtle transformation. The first big race of the season was over Easter weekend—the Girvan, a three-day stage race up in southwest Scotland with bags of history and all of the top UK-based pros competing. In theory, all the Academy lads were eligible to ride for the main Great Britain national team, but in practice, only Varley was picked. Brammy, Bruce, and I were farmed out to what was effectively the Great Britain "B" team, sponsored by Persil.

Five kilometers into the first stage, I went for an intermediate sprint prize—basically a race within a race, with the first three over the line getting a few quid in prize money and points toward the sprint or points jersey. I crossed the line first and after a few seconds instinctively looked around and saw a group starting to form behind me, and behind it a widening gap to the main field. That was the last we'd see of them all day.

I was dropped on every climb and clawed my way back on every descent, the last of which came down within a few kilometers of the finish. My chain in my biggest gear, my legs and lungs screaming, I wove my way through the following team cars and on to the back of the breakaway group with about 5 kilometers to go. I was just catching my breath when one of the riders on the main GB team, Tony Gibb, rode alongside me; he said he wanted me to lead him out in the sprint.

It was my first big race since joining the Academy, so I didn't protest. Instead, I moved up the side of the group with about 2 kilometers to go and starting cranking up the pace, ready to launch Gibby about 250 meters from the line. I kept pushing, accelerating, and waiting for someone or something to appear out of the corner of my eye . . . except no one ever did. I raised my arms as I crossed the line, half in jubilation, half in confusion. It took a few seconds to register: I'd only gone and bloody won.

I couldn't keep the leader's jersey over the next two days, but that didn't matter. Those dark days in February and March, the doubts and the question marks, had been banished in one afternoon. Well, almost. Our next big race was also our first on the continent—the deceptively leisurely-sounding Triptyque des Monts et Châteaux in southern Belgium. I was like the proverbial kid in the candy shop; I hadn't been a big one for heroes and idols growing up, but one guy who had inspired me was the Belgian Johan Museeuw, who'd forged his reputation on the kind of bone-jangling, teeth-chattering cobbled roads that we rode in training in the couple of days leading up to the race. It was my first time on the legendary *pavé*, or cobbles, and even on a gentle training ride, the fearsome, fang-like stones were also my cue to unleash hell. Behind, in the team car, a different coach or team manager might have wondered why I was wasting energy in a training session; instead, Rod told me later, he just turned to the mechanic in the car and said with a chuckle, "I bloody knew Cavendish would attack there. . . ."

There was precious little to laugh about over the next few days, at least not at the time. "Baptism of fire" hardly did it justice. On the first stage, half of the peloton came down on wet tram tracks; I avoided those but promptly wiped out into a trailer on the left-hand side of the road a few kilometers later. Typically, Bruce, when he noticed me lying half dead in the gutter as he shot past at 50 kilometers an hour, looked half appalled, half excited to see me. "How are you, Cav?" were, I think, his exact words.

I eventually staggered to my feet, climbed back on my bike, and started grinding on the pedals. My arm was in such pain that I couldn't hold the handlebars, couldn't brake, yet I was still catching people. One of the stragglers looked like Bruce—well, if you could imagine what Bruce would look like after he'd been eaten by a shark. There was blood and Lycra everywhere. We later found out that a lorry had pulled out onto the course; Bruce had swerved into a ditch to avoid it and ended up scraping his whole body and bike along a barbed-wire fence. When the other Academy lads and I tell that story now, we piss ourselves laughing. At the time, it was anything but comic.

I was the one who'd actually end up worst off. Rod took me to the hospital for X-rays that night, and it turned out I had a badly bruised collarbone. I looked dolefully at Rod; the next day was the cobblestones. I couldn't lift my arm, but I told him I wanted to ride. He was probably half delighted that I was determined and half resigned to the fact that it was pointless arguing. He said I could ride.

We were like the Andrex puppies—bouncing left and right, falling down, getting up, and going back for more. The next day it was Ed. I'd started the stage with my shoulder strapped and just trying to stay out of trouble, which was what I was doing, tucked in behind Ed's wheel, until suddenly I saw Ed stub his foot on someone else's pedal crank, his bike go flying, his head plunge toward the road, his glasses smash, and, finally, the side of his face sandpaper along the tarmac. It was horrific. If the previous day Bruce had looked as though he'd spent the afternoon on the set of *Jaws*, the way Ed was walking down the road now, dragging his bike behind him, staring into space, half of his cheek hanging off, he was like Mel Gibson in *The Man Without a Face* or the Phantom of the Opera minus the mask. "What am I doing? Why am I here?" he kept saying.

We were shockingly out of our depth. The Dutch equivalent of our Academy, the Rabobank Under 23 team, was cleaning up, and there we were in the last stage, reduced to me and Matt Brammeier. That day, both of us were dropped and were riding in the last group, the so-called gruppetto, yet Rod still wanted us pulling on the front. The foreigners couldn't fathom it; usually, in cycle racing, there has to be a sound tactical reason for using up valuable energy and leading a chase, but Rod wanted to see us competing and fighting purely for the experience. When the Belgians began ranting at us, Matt and I shrugged and gestured in the general direction of Rod in our team car. Rod later told us that one or two of the Belgies rode alongside the driver's door and started tapping on the window, mouthing insults in English. Cool as you like, Rod wound down the window: "Oh, you understand English, then? In that case, you'll understand this: Fuck off!"

I loved that about Rod: He was always the first to defend us if someone was trying to intimidate us. And he was equally quick to let us know when we weren't keeping our part of the bargain. There was a good example one day on that trip, after the Triptyque des Monts et Châteaux, when Rod told us we could have an "easy" training day and "only" do three hours with a café stop near the end of the ride. He trusted us, so he was going to stay at the hotel and get on with some work. Our mistake, or rather Brammeier's, was bringing his digital camera to the dinner table that night and showing the lads some of our snaps from earlier in the day. Rod happened to catch a glimpse of one of the photos. Straightaway, I could see his expression changing.

"Er, lads, did I say three hours with a café at the end of the ride?" he asked. "I did, okay? And did you tell me when you got back today that's what you'd done? Right, so why, in this photo, are you sitting drinking coffee in the center of a town I recognize, and which is nowhere bloody near here?"

The only other bit of that conversation I remember is "Right, go upstairs and get your fucking kit on because you're doing four more hours."

The next day we were due to ride a hard, one-day circuit race, what the Belgians call a kermesse, but Rod didn't care; how could he trust us to carry out instructions in races if we were telling him lies about where we'd stopped for cappuccino? We almost compounded the damage by fiddling with the settings on our cyclocomputers—changing the wheel circumference so we'd get back and Rod would think we'd clocked up more kilometers than was the case. We were still giggling to ourselves when, just as we were leaving, we heard the sound of a growling motor and turned around to see Rod, revving up and ready to follow us in his car.

He was wasting his own free time that night, barking orders at us from behind a steering wheel when he could have had his feet up in the hotel, yet he did it because it was in our best interests. Rod had once been a lot like I was now—19 years old, passionate, and ambitious. He'd ridden as a pro for the UK-based Ambrosia team in the mid-1990s but quickly realized that, partly due to a lack of opportunity, partly due to a lack of the kind of outstanding talent that would get him noticed by a top European team, and perhaps partly due to a lack of luck, his dreams of riding the Tour de France were destined to remain just that—dreams. Now, a decade on, his passion was still alive, and he also possessed the theoretical know-how to go with his own firsthand experience, the same firsthand experience that left him mortified by the idea of lads, who perhaps had more natural ability and certainly more opportunities than he'd had, not fulfilling their potential.

It was that same frustration—more for us than with us—that spilled over at a national Under 23 series event in Penzance later that spring. In theory, as the national Academy team, we were the best riders in the field that day, and Rod would tell you that we had the swagger to match. Rod never minded if we weren't physically strong enough to follow a break-away, but he'd be fuming if we let one slip because we were distracted or lazy, and that day there was simply no excuse for the entire team missing out when a group escaped in the first fifteen minutes of the race. We spent the whole day chasing, and Brammy ended up catching the last survivor from the breakaway 5 meters . . . after the line. We'd blown it. While all of the other teams were packing away, swigging their energy drinks, and comparing stories, Rod told us all to stop what we were doing and line up next to our minibus.

Poker-faced, he moved up the line, asking every one of us the same questions: "Did you see the break go?" "Were you tired at that point or were you not?" He didn't give a shit if someone started sniggering; all that mattered was that we knew he wasn't joking. He told us to pack up our stuff and not to say a single word from when we got in the car to when we got back to Manchester that night. Sure enough, the next time anyone opened his mouth was when we pulled up at half eleven, and that was Rod telling us to be at the velodrome at half past eight the next morning ready for a long bike ride. The following day was as advertised, the training session from hell: five hours of "through and off"; in other words, a revolving line where everyone takes it in turns to do short, sav-age bursts on the front, like in a team pursuit. Every now and again, we'd glance back and notice that Rod was no longer following in his car, at which point we'd think it was safe to ease off. We'd then hear a familiar voice, a familiar command to go "Faster!"—then see Rod's bristly red hair peeping over the top of a bush at the roadside.

The Academy was a test of survival, and some couldn't hack it. Chris-tian Varley had been homesick and off the pace in most of the races, and he went back to the Isle of Man for good after three or four months. The daily routine back in Manchester was no less punishing than the racing, sometimes more so. A typical day started with an alarm at half six, breakfast at seven, then a slalom through the morning traffic to get to the velodrome by half seven. Anyone who was late got sent home. In that first 2004 season, we'd often be out on our road bikes from eight o'clock, whereas in the second year we'd usually kick off with a twenty-minute warm-up on the rollers—the cycling equivalent of a treadmill—followed by an hour of team pursuit training, with everyone alternating fifteen-second sprints with forty-five seconds of spinning, just like you would on the track. At nine o'clock we'd get off the rollers and into track for another three hours—again, more often than not, team pursuit work.

Lunch was at midday, followed by a two-hour French lesson. Those classes could be a pain in the derrière, not because French wasn't going to be useful for a career in cycling—it was—but because a couple of the other lads didn't take it seriously. Brammy was good, and Ed picked it up pretty quickly, but Bruce was no Zinedine Zidane, and Tom White used to Google his homework and think he was smart. I'd been studying French since I was 6 years old and had gotten a B in it in my GCSE at age 14. Now I was being made to start all over again with *"bonjour," "je m'appelle,"* and *"je suis."*

I used to be glad to get back on the track for the afternoon session at three o'clock, this time usually for Madison practice or "go till you blow" sessions, when we'd ride behind Rod's moped, and he'd keep going faster and faster until there was no one left. That would take us to six o'clock and home time, unless it was a Tuesday, when we'd have dinner at the track, then ride in the track league against the weekend warriors—blokes who worked in offices during the week but lived for battering themselves on a bike on Saturdays, Sundays, and Tuesday nights. Usually, we'd annihilate them; occasionally, we'd just be too tired, and you'd hear them muttering, "These GB lads aren't that good, are they?" Of course, you'd hear different comments from the guys who knew that we'd been on the track since eight in the morning. Or from anyone who happened to see us when we were riding back to the house at eleven at night, including one occasion in the middle of a blizzard.

On our bikes there was no doubt that we improved fast in that first year. The last race we did in Belgium in 2004, a circuit race in Diest, was both the perfect bookend and counterpoint to that first trip of the season to the Triptyque des Monts et Châteaux, with me winning after a textbook lead-out from the other lads. It was in a couple of other areas—such as discipline and, in Ed's and Bruce's case, hygiene and cleanliness—that we still needed work. Unlike my roommates, I understood that it was important to come back to a tidy, comfortable house every night, especially because what we were doing during the day was so hard, and I understood that Rod kept harping on about us "structuring our lives" for exactly that reason.

The discipline issue was harder for me to take on board simply because mischief and piss-taking came as naturally as scooting around a velodrome. Rod didn't mind as long as it didn't spill over into our lives at the Academy, but sometimes, inevitably, the inner scally reared its curly mop—or, in my case, at that time, its shaven head. That was quite literally what happened at the European track championships in Valencia that first summer.

The first thing to point out is that I'd been ill before the trip and was hopelessly out of form; consequently, in my events, I went like the proverbial bag of spanners. The other point to make is that Rod wasn't expecting much and might have been sympathetic . . . had he not heard a racket coming from the fire exit in our hotel one day that week and wandered out to see what was going on. He showed up just in time to see my shiny slap-head bobbing up the last flight of stairs, steam rising off its surface, Brammeier crouched over a stopwatch, and pretty much the entire GB squad—juniors, Under 23s, girls and boys—gathered on the landing, bawling either encouragement or abuse. I noticed how it had suddenly gone quiet when I hauled myself up the last few steps, leg muscles howling, the sweat dripping off me, and then saw Rod standing in the corner. He was shaking his head. "What the fuck do you think you're doing? You didn't even try this hard in the bike race. Not good enough. Not fucking good enough."

That trip confirmed to me that Rod didn't miss a trick. On the last night, he'd told us to go to bed early; the whole week had been a disaster, and we needed to be on the case as soon as we arrived back in Manchester. So what did we do? Had a party in one of the rooms, of course. It was about one in the morning, and we'd all spilled out onto the balcony, when I happened to peer over into the car park and saw what looked like someone sitting on the curb, on his own, in the pitch black, maybe a couple of hundred feet below. I squinted through the darkness; it was Rod, watching us, making mental notes. Again, he was sacrificing his own free time because he cared about us mucking about and wasting our opportunities.

There were all sorts of other little lapses, but with Rod, the punishments were always consistent and fair. Telling us off didn't give him any pleasure. He used to set us little thousand-word essays on cycling-related topics—one might be on "Life in the Academy," another on "The Career of the Cyclist Stuart O'Grady"—and on one occasion, I thought I'd outsmart him by writing my latest magnum opus in longhand rather than sending it in on the computer so that Rod couldn't use the word-count tool to check whether I'd done the full thousand. Of course, Rod could see straight through this; he counted the words, and it turned out that I'd done only eight hundred. He said he was sorry, but I would have to do the whole thing again. Rod, though, could put up with my shenanigans because he knew that, in exchange, he was getting a full quota of passion, determination, and willingness to learn when it came to my cycling. That was the difference between Rod and another of the coaches, Simon Lillistone, who sometimes seemed as though he was being strict just to mimic Rod, and to spite us, rather than to enforce rules. He'd do things like taking away our PlayStations, which would achieve nothing because we'd cause trouble through being bored. Take away our game consoles and we'd replace them with something that could do real damage . . . like a paintball gun. That was fun while it lasted—until the gun was confiscated when word got back to the velodrome of us taking potshots at innocent members of the public.

The coaches' problem was that we were too resourceful; short of stripping the house bare and locking us away, there was nothing they could do to stop our high jinks. Evan Oliphant, a Scottish lad who came to stay and race with us for a few weeks, discovered this in that 2004 season when, every night, he'd open the door to his bedroom and think he'd taken a wrong turning to the local Turkish baths. Every night, without fail, about two hours before bedtime, one of us would sneak in, disconnect the pipe at the back of the tumble-dryer that we kept in the corner, press the "on" switch, and pump the air full of hot, sticky steam. Evan knew what we were doing—of course he did—but he also knew that it was a case of our gaff, our rules.

I have so many memories of my two years at the Academy that, one day, I could write a book solely about that period. The physical suffering, the homesickness, the wins, the losses, the laughs, and the tears—there was enough life experience in those two years to fill three autobiographies. Ask me, though, to pick the one episode that encapsulated the highs and lows better than any other, and I don't need to think twice about which one I'd choose. For ease of reference, let's call it "The Tale of the Horse-Drawn Undercarriage."

It all started innocently, with a phone call from Brammeier's little sister. Bless her, she wanted help with her homework, and Brammeier thought one of us might be able to help. "Hey, lads," he said, "I've got my sister here. She wants to know how to draw a horse. . . ."

I have no idea what came over us that day. We rarely, if ever, drank, but for some reason, that day, the prospect of demonstrating my artistic prowess had me practically gurgling with delight. I reached for a black marker and walked over to the window; a minute or two later, a line here, a bit of coloring there, and we had a masterpiece of rare and, er, very graphic detail.

The lads were beside themselves. "That's fucking brilliant, Cav. Absolutely brilliant." So brilliant, in fact, that they didn't want to rub it off. We were heading off for a race the next day, yet somehow it slipped our minds that we were leaving behind a gallery of profanity as liable to cause offense as anything Tracey Emin's ever painted. We'd also forgotten, or rather Brammy had forgotten, that he'd drawn the curtains in his room and left the light on; as a result, for the duration of the weekend, my sketches would be gloriously illuminated in his bedroom window. Another couple of minor details: There was a synagogue a few doors down and a church directly opposite our flat. A church where, what was more, people were rolling up at all hours of the day for art lessons, support groups, and, probably, after they saw my little comic strip, a quiet word with Our Father.

On Monday, when we came back and saw Matt's light on, alarm bells should have started ringing. Instead, later that day, it was our phones that were ringing, and Simon Lillistone on the other end: Apparently the gentleman who lived next door hadn't appreciated our little exhibition and had contacted the landlord. The landlord, in turn, had contacted Lillistone. Rod then showed up at the house. When he saw the window, he stood openmouthed, not sure whether to marvel at our stupidity, our audacity, or the intricate detail of my diagrams. "Lads," he said, "whoever drew it, it *is* funny. I mean, it's a good drawing. It's detailed, it's fantastic . . . *but not on a fucking residential street!* What were you thinking?"

We were soon summoned to the office at the velodrome to see Lillistone and Brailsford, both of whom were seething. The first thing they did was play the recorded message from the landlord. We all bowed our heads and bit our lips, but I would have defied anyone not to laugh. Anyone, that is, except Brailsford and Lillistone, who looked as though they might spontaneously combust. On went the tape: "I was called round by the neighbor, who was horrified by something drawn on the window. I went round to have a look, and I saw some very rude drawings of donkeys. . . ."

Lillistone pressed *stop* and cast his gaze in our direction. "Now, is this all true?"

"No, it's not true," I replied. "It wasn't a donkey. . . . It was a horse."

The next day, we received our punishment, or at least its first installment: three hours riding full gas round the top of the track, with Rod baying, "Faster, faster!" and screaming at us if we strayed too far from the wheel in front. After that physical ordeal came the trial by humiliation: For the next week, Rod said, we'd wash all the staff's cars every day, in full view of everyone arriving at the velodrome.

As if there hadn't already been enough tests of our, ahem, still maturing characters in that first, 2004 season with the Academy, the year was to end with our first taste of the European Six-Day circuit. Almost a sport in its own right, the Six-Day scene is hard to describe to a layman, but if you could imagine a German Oktoberfest meeting the Cirque du Soleil meeting a track cycling event, all held over six consecutive evenings, there are enough images for you to have a rough idea.

And rough is exactly what Six-Day meetings can be, because, contrary to a popular misconception, the racing is hard, hard, hard.

All that saved us initially was that we were racing in the Under 23 category and not with the seniors. That and the fact that we'd spent countless hours on the Manchester boards over the previous few months honing our speed, our bike handling, and also the tactical know-how you needed in these events, the highlight of which were the Madisons. In our first appearance, in Amsterdam, I'd come in 3rd overall with Matt Brammeier and looked forward to faring even better on what was going to be our next outing to Dortmund. Sure enough, despite Brammy's misgivings about his own track skills and a spectacular collision between him and Tom White on the last evening, we ended up holding on for a win that was merely the latest evidence of how far we'd come since our first day at the Academy the previous January, when the only thing we'd looked likely to win was an ASBO (Antisocial Behavior Order).

We headed home from Dortmund, tired but none too quietly thrilled. We then relaxed—or at least I did—barely riding my bike for a month. This would have been fine if my next races had been on the road and three months away, in January or February, but we were due back on the track for the Six Days of Ghent at the end of November. To compound matters, by this time there was a new intake of Academy lads, and one of them, Geraint Thomas ("Gee"), was absolutely flying. If Geraint and his partner, Tom White, made the British Federation, Rod, and the Academy look very good indeed that week, the way Brammy and I rode made Gee and Tom look even better. In short, we were utterly, embarrassingly, excruciatingly woeful.

Rod was fuming. More importantly, though, I was fuming at myself. The unexpected success of Dortmund had been so exhilarating, so rewarding; yet within the space of a month, I'd contrived to fritter it all away like a lottery winner with his winnings. I said it was embarrassing, but really, that doesn't convey quite how it had felt, all six nights in that packed, smoky, raucous Ghent velodrome; what it had been was downright degrading.

It was also—I would make sure—the very last time that I was ever going to allow myself to take such a horrendous beating.

Thus, over the next few weeks, I trained more than ever before and indulged less, a win-win combination, the effects of which have to be seen in photos from that winter to be believed. On a typical day, I'd go out at seven o'clock in the morning, do a two-hour loop, then, at nine fifteen, swing by the Quarter-Bridge roundabout, outside the NSC, where there's a group that gathers every single day of the year, even Christmas. I'd then do two hours with them, followed by two more hours on my own, after which I'd arrive home and call Geraint Thomas. Gee would barely have picked up the receiver before the one-upmanship would start: "So how many hours today, Gee? Ah, only five? I did six. . . ."

At the end of a year when the lessons had come thick and fast, apparently, the best and most valuable—a true turning point in my career—had waited until last.

STAGE 3: SAINT-MALO–NANTES, 208 KM

1. Samuel Dumoulin (Fra), Cofidis–Le Crédit par Téléphone, 5:05:27 (40.91 kph)

10. Mark Cavendish (GBr), Team Columbia, 2:03

GENERAL CLASSIFICATION

1. Romain Feillu (Fra), Agritubel, 13:27:05

85. Mark Cavendish (GBr), Team Columbia, 3:45

STAGE 4

Tuesday, 8 July 2008
CHOLET-CHOLET
(INDIVIDUAL TIME TRIAL) 29.5 KM

O n the night of 8 July, the 2008 Tour de France was four days old, my overall Tour career was now into its second fortnight, and I still wasn't a stage winner. To understand the significance of this, you need to understand that a Tour stage win is a rite of passage in professional cycling. The Giro d'Italia, or Tour of Italy, and its Spanish counterpart, the Vuelta a España, or Tour of Spain, may be on the same theoretical footing as cycling's big major tour, but whereas victory in those races brings recognition within the sport's niche community, a stage win in the Tour de France—*the* Tour—guarantees exposure outside the goldfish bowl and respect within cycling's deeply hierarchical confines.

For sprinters in particular, the Tour is more than just the most important race on the calendar. A Tour stage win on your curriculum vitae is the cycling equivalent of "PhD" after your name—a status symbol that earns not only plaudits but also privileges. To put it another way, not only can you expect more nods and backslaps, more *"ciaos"* and *"bonjours"* from fellow pros in the Tour's start village, you'll also notice that, when the racing begins, where once you would have had to scrap and jostle for certain positions, now potential obstructions will move respectfully to one side like a bellboy at a posh hotel.

There is another side of the same coin, of course: As a sprinter, as long as you haven't won at the Tour, any claims you may have to a standing among the elite in your field of expertise simply can't and won't be validated by your peers, the media, or the fans. As someone who, for several months now, had been assuring everybody who cared to listen that he wasn't just one of the fastest but *the* fastest bunch sprinter in the world, obviously this left me with something of a problem.

I'm blessed in that I'm not one of these athletes who's ever been plagued by self-doubt. I've already mentioned the British Cycling psychologist Steve Peters and the brilliant work he's done in helping our track riders, but I can honestly say that I've only ever had momentary, very, very occasional dips in self-confidence—never full-blown crises, and certainly nothing a good win or ego massage from one of my coaches or teammates couldn't fix. Fortunately, what doubts I haven't created for myself, other people have been more than happy to supply for me. I say "fortunately" because there's only one tactic that trumps what I like to call the sunshine-up-the-arse motivational method (bombarding me with adulation and flattery), and that method is equally uncomplicated: Just tell me, "Cav, old pal, you can try but I don't think you're gonna make it. . . ."

Some people might say I have a persecution complex. That most kids, at the age of 9 or 10, would have just laughed or ignored their mum when she said that instead of racing around the NSC car park, they looked like they were going for a Sunday stroll. Or that they'd have shrugged it off when, a few years later, more than one coach told them they were overweight and would never amount to anything. Lance Armstrong once said about the teams, riders, and journalists who'd crossed him, "I just keep a list, a mental list. And if I ever get the opportunity, I'm gonna pull out that list." Now, not only do I keep exactly the same kind of list, but in the same way that Armstrong's longtime team manager, Johan Bruyneel, claimed at the end of 2008 that Lance had "always drawn his strength from anger and resentment," it may just be that all those who have doubted and discounted me have been among the most influential figures in my career to date.

Tour stage winner, or journeyman pro scraping by on the International Cycling Union's minimum wage of €30,000 a year? Take your pick . . . because plenty of people who knew exactly what it took seemed pretty sure that professional cycling was no place for a pudgy kid from the Isle of Man with fast legs but an even faster mouth.

I'm not naive or pigheaded enough to suggest that if, at times, I have sensed a disproportionate skepticism about my ability as a cyclist, it's been due to any personal malice or prejudice. On the contrary, with a few exceptions, the individuals who have questioned me over the years haven't so much misunderstood my capacities as, to my mind, they've misunderstood cycle racing.

My problem is maybe that I just don't look like a cyclist. Pro bike riders come in a range of well-chiseled sizes, but my short, stubby legs and long body are at least unusual and maybe unique in the pro peloton. More to the point, I don't look like a bike rider in front of what some coaches regard as the one mirror that never lies—the one that is kept in the gym or the physiology lab, with two pedals, a saddle, wheels that move without traveling, and a digital display programmed, it seems to me—to communicate to the world exactly how Mother Nature was having an off day when she made me.

All cyclists hate stationary bikes, or "rigs," mainly because they're synonymous with leg-butchering, lung-perforating fitness tests, but no one hates them more than I do. At the Academy I'd almost literally kick and scream even before I was put through one of these ordeals, to the point where eventually the coaches decided it was too much melodrama to bear and agreed to let me opt out. All the feedback I've gotten from these tests could be condensed into a single message—and the same one you often hear directed at opposing fans at football matches: "You're shit, and you know you are. . . ." Hearing this once might fire me up; hearing it time and time again was guaranteed to kill any motivation I'd ever had.

As for the real mirror, well, I didn't need one, nor did my coaches, to confirm that my muscles didn't ripple quite as close to my skin as some of my colleagues'. While the average pro's body is generally between 4 and 10 percent fat, mine had occasionally been close to 20, particularly before my "epiphany" at the Ghent Six at the end of 2004. In the past, my weight had also fluctuated dramatically; in a manner probably most familiar to female readers, I'd go through purges during which I'd aim to eat no more than 1,000 calories a day, alternating with times when all self-control was lost completely. Like many people, unfortunately, I use food, and especially junk food, as an antidepressant. Rig tests depressed me because they told me I was useless, and feeling depressed made me hungry. The obvious and convenient conclusion to draw was that if I wanted to stay away from food, I should also steer clear of anything resembling a rig.

In a sport growing ever more obsessed with science, a kid whose performances on the road simply didn't seem to translate into watts in the lab was likely to be confusing and sometimes infuriating. Generally, leading teams were (and still are) managed by old pros who knew from their own experience that cycling is much too complex to reduce to a mathematical equation, but in recent years, ironically, cycling has seen sports scientists as the revolutionary soldiers to lead cycling out of its doping crisis. The argument goes that anyone who competed as a pro in the 1970s, '80s, or '90s either doped or raced with and against doped athletes and therefore had by definition been "contaminated." The theory falls down not only because such generalizations are unfair and inaccurate but also because a lot of sports scientists live up to only about half of their job description: They know plenty about science and sod all about sport.

Given my views on the matter, Simon Jones and I were never likely to hit it off. He'd been taken on by British Cycling in 1998 and had since graduated to the position of head coach, with a particular focus on the endurance disciplines on the track and especially the team pursuit. When Great Britain won one gold, a silver, and a bronze in endurance events at the Athens Olympics in 2004—and a lot was made in the press of the team's studious, scientific approach—Jonesy was voted British sports coach of the year.

My contact with him was limited until my first senior track World Championship in Los Angeles in 2005. Even there it was minimal simply because, in the team pursuit, Jonesy seemed to have found the perfect focus for his theoretical know-how and attention to detail. My event— and by extension I—were neglected at best, ignored at worst. My preparation for what turned out to be a World Championship–winning ride with Rob Hayles consisted of circling the track behind the team pursuiters, I on my upright track bike, they on their aerospace-engineered speed machines.

One thing Jonesy did seem fascinated by straightaway was my diet. That week in LA, I spent a lot of time with the sprinters, who happened to do a lot of eating, albeit in a highly structured, scrupulous way . . . most of the time. However, one day, Chris Hoy and Jamie Staff announced that they were heading out in Chris's courtesy BMW X5 on a mission to locate some Krispy Kreme doughnuts. They raised no objections when Ed Clancy and I bundled into the back.

It turned into quite an adventure: A couple of wrong turns soon took us into the ganglands of Inglewood, where there was not a Krispy Kreme in sight and Chris was too frightened to ask for directions. When, later, we finally stumbled upon the deep-fried gold at a drive-through and decided it was safe to wind down the windows, I chirped from the backseat that Jamie and Chris should tell the waitress they were with Mark Cavendish and they'd probably get a free order. She had another idea: She said we could have free doughnuts if Jamie danced. So that was what he did.

We got back and Jonesy went apeshit; little did he know that we'd guzzled only twelve of a possible twenty-four on the way home . . . or that Jamie's tango had saved us about five dollars.

Jonesy's nagging continued all through that week. I was only 19, and his lack of interest in my event probably saved me more grief. Still, though, at dinner, I could sense his eyes following me around the buffet table. "Cav, isn't that sauce a bit creamy for you?" "Cav, no sauce on your pasta, please. . . ." It was depressing. And we all knew what I did when I was depressed.

I was depressed again the following winter . . . only this time, for a brief period, maybe clinically so. In that spring of 2005, our second with the Academy, in the post and out of the blue, two German racing licenses had arrived bearing the names "Ed Clancy" and "Mark Cavendish." We'd called Rod, who'd matter-of-factly announced that he was sending us to race with the German Sparkasse team. A few weeks later, equally matter-of-factly, we'd stuffed our worldly possessions into a pair of suitcases, pitched up in Germany, performed impressively all summer, and then, in autumn, headed straight for the Six-Day circuit.

The high-four-figure appearance fees I was banking on as a world Madison champion did nothing to ease the cumulative fatigue that came with these events, with their five-hour racing sessions and three-in-the-morning bedtimes. Unfortunately, those fees had become a means to an end, as British Cycling had just told me and Ed that, since we were now riding in Germany with Sparkasse, it would no longer provide or pay for our accommodation. In theory, as a world Madison champion, I ought to have been on the top grade of lottery funding, i.e. £24,000 a year, but the Federation decided that was too much for a rider under the age of 21 and changed its own rules. It ended up giving me £12,000—three times what I'd been earning at the Academy, but now I also had to pay for my own place to live.

Ed and I moved in with the Scottish sprinter Craig MacLean in the Cheadle area of Manchester. Craig was great, the flat was great . . . but unfortunately Ed's new girlfriend, an American who also happened to be

Matt Brammeier's cousin, drove me insane. She was bossy—really bossy. As the weeks went by, the exhaustion of continual trips to Europe for the Six-Days were grinding down my patience, and every time I came back to the flat, Ed's girlfriend had her feet a little bit further under the table. In the end, in desperation, I turned to . . . Walker's crisps.

I'm not sure if the Federation knew about my dietary habits that winter. Or that my training regimen consisted almost entirely of "intervals"—repeat journeys to Cheadle to buy large bags of Walker's Sensations. I was addicted. So addicted that I ate nothing else. For a few weeks, my days all looked the same; to be precise, they looked like the view from Craig's sofa with the curtains drawn, my mind a fog, and a bag of Sensations tantalizingly open somewhere between me and the TV screen.

It sounds funny now, but it wasn't at the time. My fitness or mental health had barely improved that Christmas when I went home to the Isle of Man. One thing that was usually guaranteed to boost my mood, besides junk food, was a ride with the usual gang on the Island—the Kennaugh brothers, Peter and Timmy, Jonny Bellis, and anyone else who wanted to tag along. One day between Christmas and New Year, we all headed out for what would probably be the last session of 2005.

Little did I know that all of the problems of the previous couple of months—or indeed any problem, in any month—were about to fade into the cruelest perspective.

It was a normal day, a normal ride out to the café in St. Johns, and my normal reaction to sprint into the slipstream of a caravan that overtook us on the route home. Peter Kennaugh darted after me. The first sign that something was amiss came a kilometer or so up the road, when we saw what looked like a giant lorry wheel rolling down the hill and needed all the reflexes we'd learned on the track to miss it.

Instinctively, we turned around to warn the others. It was too late. All we could do was watch the loose wheel plowing right into the middle and taking out our smallest rider, a 13-year-old called James Berry.

We panicked. At 20 years old, I was the oldest in the group, so it was natural for everyone to look to me to take charge, but I was in shock. James's bike was in pieces on the road, so was his helmet, and his eyes were flickering. "James, James, wake up!" I cried, but there was no response. "James. *James . . .*" but still nothing. Within a minute or two, someone had produced a mobile phone and we'd called James's dad and an ambulance. After a few more minutes, the ambulance had arrived and James's motionless body had been lifted inside on a stretcher. By this time, I'd rung Melissa to pick me up; I couldn't bring myself to get back on my bike.

We heard nothing until the following day. We knew James had been knocked unconscious but nothing more about the precise nature of the injuries. I woke up early that morning and drove to Douglas to see the Isle of Man racing director, Gary Hinds, at the bike shop, Bikestyle. I was hoping he had heard something, or at least knew which ward James was in at the hospital. I'd parked the car and was on my way in as another of the lads who'd been there the previous day was on his way out. Before I even had the chance to ask, he said, "Have you heard the news? James has died."

I called Jonny and Peter and Timmy. We were all incredulous and distraught. Really, though, at times like these, words were and still are redundant. All I will say is that, in spite of grief that dwarfed anything we might have been feeling, James's dad was fantastic. Not only did he say we weren't to blame, he also said James at least died doing what he'd wanted, what he loved—riding his bike. I couldn't know if that was true, but I could promise that I'd win a gold medal for the Isle of Man at the 2006 Commonwealth Games the next spring and dedicate it to James.

The following March, I was as good as my word, winning the Commonwealth Games scratch race on the Melbourne track in homage to James. Sadly, that was all I could do; nothing would bring James back, and nothing could erase his parents' grief, or the horror of realizing that it could all have been avoided if only that wheel had never come loose from that Leyland truck—the same wheel that had been refitted after a repair two days earlier.

The manslaughter trial of the two mechanics accused of gross negligence in refitting the wheel ended in a verdict of not guilty in February 2008.

Everything that had happened before that Christmas of 2005 had suddenly paled into insignificance, but the frustration and fatigue and binge eating had now been replaced by deeper and more unpleasant emotions. In that frame of mind, and in the pitiful physical condition to which I was now reduced, the second-to-last thing I needed was a British Cycling training camp in Majorca. The last thing was a British Cycling training camp with Simon Jones.

The prospect was already enough to make me rip open another bag of Walker's. Then, before the camp, I was told to come to Manchester for a meeting with Dave Brailsford and Simon Jones. Jonesy was the one who did most of the talking; in short, he said the Federation wanted me to turn professional, and it wanted me to do it with Landbouwkrediet, a lowly Belgian team with which the Federation now had a loose "feeder" arrangement. In a sport where there were maybe two dozen good, well-funded teams that had access to the major races, it would be the equivalent of starting a football career with Burnley.

I was aghast. I told them that, no, I had no interest in joining Landbouwkrediet; the world's number-one team, T-Mobile, had already invited me for a three-month trial to begin in August 2006, and I fully intended to sign with them when the trial was over. The meeting ended with me walking out, livid. It took a conciliatory phone call from Dave B. and words to the effect of "We admire your determination, and we still want you to ride for Great Britain," to calm me down.

For a number of reasons, that camp in Majorca merely exemplified my problem with Jonesy. He wasn't a bike rider, and that was reflected in everything he did—right down to the itineraries he'd choose for our training sessions. Training camps are tedious enough as it is, but one of the things that can alleviate the monotony is a nice, varied route in an attractive location, which Majorca definitely is. Jonesy, though, would have told you we weren't there for a pleasure ride; it therefore didn't matter that every day we'd go out in one direction, usually over Puig Major to Soler, then back on exactly the same road.

It was obvious to everyone except Jonesy that I needed base fitness and not the kind of high-end, hyper-regimented team time trial drills that the pursuit lads were doing up and down the seafront. "Cav," he'd say repeatedly, "you're not hitting the numbers. You need to hit the numbers"—meaning watts of power output or some other trivial statistic. And every time, I'd counter with "Simon, I don't need numbers. I just need to ride my bike and lose some weight."

I was like a bug in his computer that ruined all his sums. I had two things he couldn't plot on a graph: passion and an ability to suffer. To me, there was no limit. There was no universal rule of cycling except that the bloke who rode fastest won the race.

Our clash of ideas was always likely to come to a head on that trip. Sure enough, that was exactly what happened at the end of one of the hardest rides of the camp, seven hours over Puig Major and back, with the others stopping at the top of the climbs to wait for me.

All day I'd been yo-yoing off the back, then finally I felt the string snapping on the way home. The pursuiters were all in good form, especially Steve Cummings, and I couldn't hold the wheels. I had lost contact when, above my own puffing and wheezing, I heard the sound of a car engine and tilted my head to see Jonesy leaning out of the car window.

I'll never forget what he said to me next.

"That'll teach you, eating all those chocolate bars at Christmas. . . ."

And then he drove off.

I burst into tears. I'd been trying so hard all day. The lads asked me what was wrong, and I told them, at which point even some of them turned on Jonesy. As for me, well, that was the moment when I stopped simply disliking him and started detesting him.

I pulled myself together just enough to make it back to the hotel. I then called Rod and told him what had happened. I begged him to work with me again: If I needed to, I'd even go back on the Academy program—I just had to get as far away as possible from Jonesy. Rod said he'd call Simon.

An hour or two later, I was in the bathroom, shaving, still enraged, when, in the mirror, I saw the door behind me open. It was Jonesy. I kicked the door in his face, and it slammed shut. It swung open again, and he started talking.

"Cav, it's not easy for me either. I miss my wife and kids as well."

"Well, don't get so perverted with this training, then. I miss my girl-friend as well, but at least no one's being a prick to you."

The insults kept flying, the volume kept rising, but there was nothing new coming out of either of our mouths, no apologies; there certainly wasn't going to be any burying of the hatchet. My relationship with him was finished before it had even started. I couldn't wait until this training camp was finished as well.

The 2006 season was always going to be a crucial one. I'd celebrate my twenty-first birthday in May—alone, in a flat near Dortmund, in Germany, where Ed and I were again spending the summer to gain some experience of racing abroad with Sparkasse—and, although, in theory, I could ride for another year as an Under 23, no one needed to remind me that a third year in that category is cycling's own last-chance saloon.

I was lucky, or at least I'd made my own luck in the sense that then former (he's now returned) team Great Britain coach Heiko Salzwedel had already approached me about a pro deal with the richest team in the world, T-Mobile, which he was then helping with youth development. In 2005, Heiko had seen me win the final stage of the Tour of Berlin in the shadow of the Brandenburg Gate, after which he'd strolled across for a chat about my plans over the following two years. He asked if, at some point, I'd be interested in a stagiaire's contract with T-Mobile, referring to the arrangement whereby top amateurs go on trial for leading pro teams for the final three months of a season. He said that at the end of the three months, if I impressed them enough, I might even be taken on full-time. "Brilliant!" I gasped.

Alas, I was panting for a different reason at the same race in 2006, which this time I rode for Sparkasse. I'd won the second stage with probably one of my most spectacular individual performances to date, spending the whole day in a break, then winning the bunch sprint when we were caught. Unfortunately, I'd also crashed on the first two days, then—not for the first time—wiped out into the back of Ed on the final stage. I said earlier on that after his crash at the Triptyque des Monts et Châteaux in 2004, Ed looked as though he'd been eaten by a shark—well, by the time I left Berlin, I looked as though I'd been in a light sparring match with a grizzly bear.

One of the biggest races of 2006, the Under 23 Tour of Italy, or "Baby Giro," was due to start five days after the Tour of Berlin. Instead of focusing on training, I spent most of that time attending to my cuts, caked in plasters and bandages, drowning in antiseptic rinse—yet it still wasn't enough to get me to Italy in anything resembling my best mental or physical shape. That was one of the few races in 2006 that I was due to ride with the Academy, and I got to Italy and immediately told Rod I didn't feel good; not only was I in pain, I'd also started developing the symptoms of flu. Rod said I should at least try to race, out of fairness to the race organizer, and that I could pull out if things got any worse. I said, "Okay."

The first stage was a strange one: a 10 km prologue time trial up the side of a mountain. I finished second to last. The next morning I steeled myself and promised Rod that, if I felt good, I'd go for the intermediate sprint after 30 km; I hadn't even gotten that far when, having already been dropped for the second or third time, I dragged myself through the race convoy up to Rod in the GB team car, looked sorrowfully across, and said, "Rod, what am I doing here?"

Rod took one look at me, my pallid cheeks, my shredded legs, and nodded. "Get in the car, mate," was his next instruction.

Over the next two days, the race was due to make its way north to Tuscany, and Rod and I had agreed that he would drop me off at the Academy's new base in Quarrata, near Pistoia, where I could spend a few days training and recovering. It was a good idea in principle, but after three days, to say things had started to turn ugly would be a literal as well as a metaphorical observation. Not only had my scabs not healed, they were now oozing a fluorescent orange pus like nothing I'd ever seen outside the Gunk Tank in *Noel's House Party*. The same unidentifiable substance was also streaming from my nose.

I briefed Rod, who in turn contacted Max Sciandri, the British-born, Italian-raised, and Quarrata-based former pro who had recently been recruited by the Academy to act as a liaison, mentor, and coach in Italy. Max arranged for me to see a doctor. The doctor's diagnosis was septicemia, his prescription an intensive course of antibiotics and two weeks of equally intensive rest.

I didn't know Max before that trip. Never the most avid aficionado of the pro scene when I was growing up, I wasn't even particularly familiar with his story, which was that of a gifted one-day rider who, by general consensus, had perhaps also been an underachiever, a bronze medal in the Olympic road race in 1996 in Atlanta notwithstanding. Now nearing his 40s, Max still had the thick golden curls and athletic physique of a much younger man and the lifestyle of someone whose wealth predated his career in cycling. We had a taste in common for expensive cars, clothes, and watches; the only difference was the side of the window on which we could afford to do our shopping.

Ten days or a fortnight after I'd arrived in Quarrata, the other Academy lads had come back and left again for another race, and my symptoms were slowly improving. Max even suggested we go out for a little ride.

I accepted with a clear proviso: "Max," I said, "you've got to remember that I'm still sick. I've got this shit coming from my nose and—"

He interrupted, "Cav, don't worry. It's fine, we'll just go easy, okay?"

So off we rode. Out of Quarrata, on gentle terrain, at a gentle pace, until we hit a climb. Max pressed a little harder, his ego inflating and mine responding; I may have been ill, but my pride wouldn't allow an ex-pro to drop me. He kept accelerating, I kept straining, until finally, I couldn't push anymore; I saw Max disappearing up the hill, made one final lunge, and as I did so called to him to slow down. I never paid any attention to the SRM power meter fixed to my handlebars, but I knew that, on a normal day, on this kind of climb, I'd be scoring in the high 300s, whereas now I was barely edging above 200 watts. In between huge, rasping intakes of air, I tried to explain this to Max. "Max," I wheezed, "I think I'm about to pass out."

I was expecting sympathy. Instead he shook his head.

"Cav, there's something wrong with you, you know. You've got this big engine and you want to turn pro next year, but you don't eat like a pro, you don't act like a pro, you don't train like a pro. What do you want? You want people to help you, but you've got to help yourself. . . ."

I couldn't believe what I was hearing.

"Max, I'm fucking sick. Can you not see that?"

"Nah, Cav, you don't get it. . . ."

I kept protesting, but the more I talked, the more Max thought I was verifying his theory: I simply didn't want to learn. We finished the ride together, still speaking but with conversation now as stilted and uncomfortable as the motion of my empty legs.

There was still friction over the next few days, but it eased slightly over a gorgeous meal at a villa owned by one of Max's friends, a famous architect. That evening, any worries about Max were lost in the luxurious surroundings, plus there was the novelty of David Millar's company to keep me entertained. Dave had confessed to doping in the summer of 2004, and for several months thereafter he'd plunged into a spiral of booze and despair. He had since vowed to come back to the professional scene, and to do it without drugs. His ban was due to expire a few days before the start of the 2006 Tour; this trip to Tuscany would be one of his last training binges before that race.

I'm not the first person and I won't be the last to say that Dave Millar wasn't your typical pro cyclist. The son of a Scottish airline pilot, he was born in Malta, was raised in England and Hong Kong, and had the kind of quirky, bohemian outlook on life you suppose could only come from that upbringing. Bizarrely, I'd met him years earlier, in June 1999, when he'd come to the Isle of Man for International Cycling Week and I'd asked for his autograph. That day, I also asked him how he thought he'd get on in the 60 km time trial held on the same circuit as the Isle of Man TT motorbike race and was shocked and awed when he responded, "Probably shit"—then qualified that by quoting a time around ten minutes better than my personal best at the time. I still have the Cofidis team cap that Dave signed for me that day, while Dave has a photo immortalizing the meeting, which, to his total amazement and bewilderment, I dug out and gave him as a gift a couple of years ago.

A few days after our posh dinner with the architect, Dave, Max, and I were supposed to go out riding, but Max opted out at the last minute, leaving just me and Dave. By now, I was well into the course of antibiotics and generally feeling much better, so much so that I could follow Dave without too much trouble. Admittedly, he was on an easy training day, but still, there was a world of difference between this and the ride with Max a few days earlier. At least that was what I thought until, at one point, Dave turned to me and, in a tone of voice that sounded both ominous and very similar to the one Max had used a few days earlier, announced that we "needed to have a chat."

"Look, Cav," he said, "Max and I have been speaking, and you've got it all wrong. Look at you: You're not lean."

By now my arguments were as well rehearsed as his and Max's were flawed, as far as I was concerned. "Well, I'm the leanest I've ever been, and I've been winning races with Sparkasse all year."

"Yeah, but you want to be a pro, you've got to act like a pro . . ."

"Er, no, Dave, I'm an amateur, so I'm going to train like an amateur. It's not a case of *if* I get a pro contract—it's *when* I get a pro contract, and when I do, I'll change. In winter, I'll train longer and harder. I'll train like I need to train to win pro races."

"Cav, it doesn't work like that."

"It does, Dave. I'll prove to you it does."

Dave sighed and shook his head, again exactly as Max had a few days earlier. He was right—he *had* tried—and, perhaps unbeknownst to him, he'd also reinforced my belief that there were some people who, for whatever reason, may not have wanted me to fail but certainly expected it.

Most importantly, as if I needed any more motivation, Dave had just given me a brilliant incentive to make my doubters eat their words.

In March of the same year, 2006, I'd won the points race at the Commonwealth Games. In April I'd gone to the track Worlds in Bordeaux, quit the scratch race, and finished 4th in the Madison with Rob Hayles because I'd made a pig's ear of the final sprint. In June I'd quit the Baby Giro. In August I started my trial with T-Mobile. In October the season finished. Throughout the whole time, I had zero contact with Simon Jones.

The Federation now knew my feelings about Jonesy and also about the team pursuit. It was also adamant that I had to keep proving myself in the Madison if I wanted to ride that event in the Olympics in 2008. A training camp in Perth, Australia, in the autumn of 2006 was, apparently, another rite of passage if I wanted to make it to Beijing.

The agreement before the camp was that I wouldn't be made to take part in the team pursuit training; I was about to start a road career with the number-one team in the world, and a good base on the road was essential for that. Dave Brailsford said this was fine. So, while the team pursuiters did a couple of hours on the road in the morning, I did four or five; while they did intensive run-throughs on the track in the afternoon, I waited in the center of the velodrome and jumped on to do motorpacing whenever they took a breather.

As I stood there watching, it became clearer to me why they'd stopped improving. Jonesy had a team of guys with massive aerobic capacities, real thoroughbreds who could go and go at 60 kph, but that was as quick as they got. To make matters worse, he was training them over a longer distance than the 4 kilometers they'd have to ride in competition—in my mind, a big mistake. He was then inputting all these data and technical information into computer programs and doing a minute analysis of everyone's position on the track as they moved through and off, yet the one thing that never seemed to occur to him was the simplest of all: He needed them to go *faster*.

I looked at him bashing away on the laptop, scratching his head, then burying it in his hands. I almost felt sorry for the guy. Then, just when the pursuiters finished one effort and I thought I could finally get back on the track, he'd keep them on the track, giving them the third degree about where they were going wrong with their technique. And that was when any sympathy I might have had turned to frustration.

That whole camp was tense. Jonesy was stressing out, and he wasn't the only one; we were all lodged in little houses in the middle of nowhere—young guys like Geraint Thomas and Ed Clancy, older guys like Chris Newton and Paul Manning, blokes who were tidy like Chris, lads like Andy Tennant whose rooms were a bombsite. Those houses were like tinderboxes—and sometimes the explosions were spectacular.

My relationship with Jonesy was the biggest time bomb of the lot, but initially we did a good job of avoiding each other. Then, from secondhand sources, I started hearing comments he'd apparently been making. Comments like "Cav's only interested in poncing around in his T-Mobile kit" and "If he says he wants to train, why isn't he doing the pursuit sessions with us?" This despite the fact that, right from Bordeaux the previous spring, I'd made it clear that the team pursuit didn't inspire or even interest me in the slightest.

It was all bound to boil over, and, finally, dramatically, it did one afternoon when the other lads were in their rooms resting and Jonesy and I found ourselves in the swimming pool. An uncomfortable silence was broken when he turned to me and asked what was clearly not an innocent question: "So, Cav, what do you want out of cycling?"

I frowned at him. "Er, I want to be a road pro, win stages at the Tour, and be world champion. . . ."

"Well, you're not hitting the numbers to do that."

"Hitting the numbers," always fucking "hitting the numbers." It was more than a mantra—it was every other sentence.

I took a deep breath. "Look, Simon, I'm riding on the track, I'm happy to do that, but all you're concerned with is the team pursuit. You're getting obsessed with it, Simon. All you need is four guys to go fast. At the minute, you're trying to create these diesel engines. You need sprinters. You need fast guys to do the team pursuit. You can't teach a diesel engine to sprint, but you can develop a sprinter's endurance. You can't train a diesel engine to have speed. . . ."

A quick explanation: The team pursuit is based on four riders taking advantage of each other's slipstream to propel the quartet as quickly as possible over 4 kilometers. In other words, the team rides in a rotating line with each man taking maybe thirteen- or fourteen-second turns on the front, when the leader is riding at maximum capacity and the other three are able to recover slightly as they draft on the wheel in front. In crude terms, my argument was that you needed men to ride *really* fast in their stint on the front rather than four men who could maintain a consistent pace for all 4 kilometers.

As I tried to explain this to Jonesy, I was getting louder and louder, more and more animated. "Look Simon, you're ignoring me because I don't want to do it, and I don't want to do it because of people like you. You need guys like me. You need fast guys in the team pursuit, or you need to get these guys training fast. You need to make them go overspeed."

Like our previous argument in Majorca, this was leading nowhere; we were never going to see eye to eye. Our latest spat further poisoned an atmosphere that was already turning toxic, so much so that one of the pursuiters, Steve Cummings, couldn't take any more and moved out of the communal accommodation into a house on his own.

After the row in the pool, I called Dave Brailsford to tell him what had happened. He said we'd discuss it when I got home. First, on our way back, there was a World Cup track meet to ride in Moscow. Ironically, Steve slipped in the toilets during a stop-off in Dubai, and I got brought into the second of our two pursuit teams. We actually did okay, not that Jonesy paid any attention to what was effectively a B team.

We got home, and, as promised, Dave Brailsford and I had our conversation about Jonesy. He asked me what I thought of Simon.

"I never want to have any contact with him again," I said. "I can say hello to him and perhaps be civil, but I really can't stand the man."

In the end, I didn't have to be civil: Within a few weeks, the coaching team was "restructured," and Jonesy left the Federation.

In the year and a half after Simon Jones left the Federation, the pursuit team's approach was revolutionized, and so were its performances. In the same way that the Australian team that won in Athens in 2004 had sacrificed technical perfection for speed, gradually, between the spring of 2007 and the Olympic final in Beijing in 2008, the pursuit team discovered that the only limit to its potential was how far and how fast the pursuiters could push themselves. The team's winning time in China was 3 minutes, 53.314 seconds—a massive ten seconds faster than it had managed in that World Cup meet in Moscow in December 2006.

The Simon Jones saga taught me a couple of very important lessons. One was that, whatever my strengths as a cyclist, they obviously expressed themselves in a way that someone like Rod Ellingworth could understand and appreciate but that was double Dutch to a lot of sports scientists. The reason was a secret ingredient that no computer or device could measure: passion. Passion was the difference between riding at 100 percent and 110 percent. Passion allowed you to suffer through pain. Passion was emotion, not science; racing, not performance. Passion was what separated me and dozens of more talented lads whom I was beating and would continue to beat.

The second lesson was even more fundamental: While it was essential to be self-critical, self-doubt was synonymous with self-poison.

"I want to be a road pro, win stages at the Tour, and be world champion. . . ."

"Stages of the Tour de France? What, you? Fat boy? With those numbers?"

Yeah, that's right.

STAGE 4: CHOLET-CHOLET (INDIVIDUAL TIME TRIAL), 29.5 KM

1. Stefan Schumacher (Ger), Gerolsteiner, 35:44 (49.534 kph)

43. Mark Cavendish (GBr), Team Columbia, 4:05

GENERAL CLASSIFICATION

1. Stefan Schumacher (Ger), Gerolsteiner, 14:04:41

98. Mark Cavendish (GBr), Team Columbia, 5:58

STAGE 5

Wednesday, 9 July 2008
CHOLET-CHÂTEAUROUX
232 KM

he most important ten seconds of my life. The next ten . . .
When most people think of a Tour de France sprint, the words and images that flash into their heads probably have something to do with speed, noise, color, danger, or adrenaline. But I don't think of any of that, at least not when I'm winning. I think of the silence.

You know those moments in sports films when the striker's through on goal, or the wide receiver's galloping into the end zone, watching the ball over his shoulder, or the baseball leaves the pitcher's hand—and the music and crowd noise suddenly stop and the film starts running in slow motion? Well, you may think those scenes are a cliché, but that's actually what it's like. In those moments—the speed, the noise, the color, the danger, the adrenaline—none of that matters. It's just you, the bike, the finish line, and . . . the silence.

How can you have silence when you also have tens of thousands of fans screaming on either side of the road? It's a good question, and not one I can answer; at every other time in the Tour, the crowd and its noise are the tailwind that whips you along faster than at any other race in the season. In those final few hundred meters, though, you notice the noise no more than you notice the air; maybe that's why, if silence is what it sounds and looks like, you feel as if you're riding through a vacuum.

I'd seen Thor Hushovd's lead-out man, Mark Renshaw, surge level with my right shoulder. I'd seen Hushovd on Renshaw's wheel. I'd swung left, across and past my teammate Gerald Ciolek. I'd trampled all over the pedals.

For the first time, 300 meters away, at the end of that vacuum, I had an unobstructed view of the finish line. Almost. Incredibly, just as he and his two breakaway companions were about to be swept up under the kilometer-to-go barrier . . . the Frenchman Nicolas Vogondy somehow located a few last droplets of energy and burst clear again. He hugged the barriers on the right-hand side, sheltered from the crowd, hidden in the shadows, clutching at the last available straws.

For a cyclist, "form" is probably a more mythologized state of physical euphoria than it is for any other sportsman, but for me, there are two, maybe three, seconds in every sprint finish when form doesn't matter. My kick is the fastest in cycling whether I'm on a good day or not; all that form changes is how long I can stay at top speed.

On this day, two beats of the pedals were enough to make me certain I couldn't lose.

My kick took me level with Hushovd. Usually, as long as you're sprinting parallel to another sprinter, you keep accelerating in case he surges again. Sense, rather than see, him slipping back and you know he's gone for good.

Now Hushovd was slipping.

My right side was clear . . . except for Vogondy, who could hear me coming like a death rattle. On my left was nothing. A vacuum.

I could hear one voice. My own. There were no more of those decisions to make, no more wheels to follow, no more risks to run—just me, a hundred meters of open road, the finish line, and a hundred photographers waiting to capture the moment.

Perfection.

Come on, Cav. It's coming, come on, it's coming, it's coming . . . fifty, forty, thirty, twenty . . . don't let them back in . . . just a few more revs . . . it's coming . . . one more effort . . . fifteen . . . yes, it is . . . ten . . . Oh, my God!

Oh, my God. Oh . . . my . . . God.

Five meters short of the line, I released my hands from the bars and brought them to rest on my helmet. Oh, my God, I'd done it.

My front wheel sliced through the finish line. And the silence ended. First came the noise, then the emotion. Six million volts of emotion—like an electric shock. For the last half of the race, throughout those last 50 kilometers, I hadn't entertained a single emotion, hadn't given a second's consideration to anything beyond what my body was doing and what it was going to do next. I was in the zone. Crossing the line was like turning on the power switch.

One of the first faces I saw when I crossed the line was Bob Stapleton's; his was always one of the first faces I saw when I crossed the line. Our team owner could have been sipping champagne in the hospitality area, which you'd think was the most natural place for a billionaire business-man to be. But no, Bob was always there, in the middle of the stampede of journalists, photographers, and soigneurs—inconspicuous, reserved, but as quietly delighted and excited as anyone. In age, demeanor, and occupation, Bob and I couldn't be more different, but we get on because we have one vital thing in common: passion.

I felt the Spaniard Oscar Freire give me a congratulatory pat, then the great German sprinter Erik Zabel. But now my emotions were running wild. I just wanted to see my teammates. Where were my teammates? I had to see my teammates.

Almost to a man, they'd crossed the line with arms aloft in jubilation. Now, one by one, they fought their way through the scrum to find me, hug me, and shout words that may have seemed incoherent at the time but that, in fifty years' time, I'll still remember. I later found out that Gerald Ciolek had hurt himself so much in the effort to launch me in the final kilometer that he'd had to go for a ride to warm down.

In a matter of seconds, chaos had broken out—a chaos that I'd helped to create by turning around and heading into the current of 180 riders, sucking the crowd of pressmen with me. Several of those 180, like David Millar, were happy for me; most were too preoccupied with their own fight for survival and the fight to muscle through to their team buses. One was furious—furious to have to battle through this crush and furious at the result; thus, Filippo "Playboy" Pozzato celebrated my first Tour de France stage win by reaching down for his water bottle and hurling it at a journalist.

There is a school of thought that says a rider aiming for the general classification in the Tour is better off doing without stage wins. The theory goes that stage wins are a handicap for general classification riders simply because the post-stage rigmarole eats big chunks out of your recovery time.

The first people I wanted to see after crossing the line were my teammates. One of the first people I actually saw, standing with my team soigneur, was an antidoping chaperone. These chaperones are under orders not to leave your side until you've given a urine sample. You have an hour after the finish to report to the cabin just beyond the finish line marked "anti-dopage."

The sixty minutes that followed my first professional win at the Grote Scheldeprijs had been the most euphoric, exciting moments of my life. What I'll most remember of that hour, besides listening to Melissa screaming down the telephone as she danced around the living room back on the Isle of Man, is that the Belgian journalists seemed almost as excited as I was; there was no 700-seat media center, no real protocol—just me, a tent, and a handful of mostly middle-aged men with bad haircuts and notepads. I could have talked all day, and they would have listened. I loved every second.

Was I less excited a year and a bit later at the Tour? I don't know. In the same way that the race is faster, fiercer, just altogether *more*, so is everything that comes next. There were more text messages, more phone calls, and certainly more microphones and television cameras. In cycling, anyone will tell you, it simply doesn't get any bigger than this.

The podium ceremony alone seemed as carefully choreographed as a West End musical. By this time, the antidoping chaperone was just one member of a growing posse of journalists and officials stalking me everywhere, and it was one of those officials' job to explain the podium protocol as I waited backstage.

There'd been interviews on the finish line, in the ruck, then more before the podium ceremony and a few more en route to the video room. At one time, apparently, stage winners would do a full-blown press conference in front of the accredited press pack in the main media center; now there were no more than a dozen in the video room and the rest watched and asked questions via a remote linkup. I'm a fickle bastard: Two days before, when I'd missed my chance in Nantes, I'd given more than one interviewer short shrift; now, by comparison, my answers were long and full of interesting nuggets.

Next stop was the antidoping booth. As always, I'd stopped only once on the stage, planning for precisely this eventuality; stop twice in the race and you might find that the plumbing's dried up, and before you know it, it's not just one hour of the evening that's been lost, it's two. The whole process is complicated and tedious enough without that added inconvenience: Drop your pants, lift your shirt, and turn 360 degrees so the antidoping officer can check for any hidden pouches or containers; wash your hands; pick a random flask with a sealed lid; break the seal; piss into the flask, which is then resealed by the antidoping officer; take the flask and pick a random container with two sealed bottles inside; open the two bottles and check for any signs of contamination; pour the required amount of urine into each of the bottles, which are then permanently sealed with a screw-type mechanism that can't be opened; hand over the bottles; watch the antidoping officer put them in a sealed plastic bag and then place the bag in a polystyrene box, which is also sealed. Oh, and I nearly forgot—you also have to sign a form to confirm that all the required hygiene conditions were respected and to specify any medicine you've been taking.

I left the antidoping booth, finally free of my chaperone, and walked straight into another scrum: autograph hunters. It's always the same; sign a hundred but don't get round to the last ten and you look like an arsehole. At the same time you're worrying about that, you're also worrying about the fact that you've been on your feet for over an hour, and if you're not careful, it'll be your legs that suffer tomorrow. You know it could make a kid's day, or even ignite a passion for the sport that might culminate, twenty years from now, in him doing exactly what you're doing now. But sometimes you walk on, guilt-ridden. It's just one of those things.

In the last hour of the race, I'd concentrated a lot, planned very little, and felt absolutely nothing. After that brief initial outpouring of emotion when I'd seen my teammates and Bob and my directeurs sportifs Brian Holm and Rolf Aldag, the last hour had been a relentless assault course of obligations. The previous year, at Scheldeprijs, the euphoria had been total, overwhelming, and unmitigated; now there was the rest of the Tour to contemplate—and the question of how I was going to recover.

I'd spoken to Melissa immediately after the finish, but now, in the team car that had waited behind to drive me back to the hotel, we had more time. She and her friend had seen me at the start village that morning, then headed straight for the airport to wait for their flight home. She'd watched the stage from a bar in the airport, which, in the space of a couple of hours, had become the newest outpost of my official fan club. The bar owner had uncorked a bottle of champagne to toast my win.

My memories of the rest of the evening are sketchy. It's funny—I remember time gaps and sprints and blowups from races going back ten years in brilliant detail, yet the more mundane aspects of life on the Tour tend to blend into one. The Tour organizers have a system whereby, over the course of the three weeks, every team gets its share of good and bad hotels, and one thing I do remember about that night was that we were in a hotel that could only be described as, well, shit. Two stars would have flattered the place.

Very little else stands out. The shower, the massage, dinner—give or take the odd phone interview or ten, the odd text message or fifty, it could have been just another day on the treadmill that is the Tour. There was champagne, sure, but then we always had one glass when we won a race, which had been practically every second day in 2008. At all other times, at races, alcohol wasn't allowed.

At one point during dinner Brian Holm wandered over holding his mobile phone. He crouched down next to my chair and passed me the phone. He said someone wanted to talk to me.

I looked at him suspiciously.

"Er, hello. Who's this?"

It was Sir Paul Smith, one of the fashion world's most famous menswear designers—a cycling nut, former aspiring pro, and Brian's mate.

It would be easy to say I went to bed that night wearing a huge, contented grin under a warm duvet of self-satisfaction, but the reality's different. Every night before going to sleep, I looked at the race manual and memorized the last 5 kilometers. Tonight I opened the book to Stage 6. Aigurande to Super Besse, 195.5 km through the Massif Central, with an 11-kilometer climb to the finish, of which the last kilometer looked brutal. It would be a day for surviving, not sprinting.

Tomorrow I'd wake up a Tour de France stage winner, the most talked-about 23-year-old in the race and in the sport. It didn't make a blind bloody bit of difference: I'd still have 195.5 km to ride before my next bedtime.

STAGE 5: CHOLET-CHÂTEAUROUX, 232 KM

1. Mark Cavendish (GBr), Team Columbia, 5:27:52 (42.45 kph)

GENERAL CLASSIFICATION

1. Stefan Schumacher (Ger), Gerolsteiner, 19:32:33

97. Mark Cavendish (GBr), Team Columbia, 5:58

STAGE 6

Thursday, 10 July 2008
AIGURANDE–SUPER BESSE
195.5 KM

Six stages and six evenings into the race, my teammate Kim Kirchen was leading the Tour de France. The Italian Riccardo Riccò had murdered everyone on the climb up to Super Besse, but Kim's 5th place was enough to take the yellow jersey from the German Stefan Schumacher, who'd fallen in the last kilometer. How do I know all of this? Well, besides the fact that even "Grim" Kim was smiling tonight, I caught the highlights on TV.

When Kim was crossing the line, I was where I am on stages where there are mountains to climb: at the back of the race, in the last group on the road, with fifty-one other poor buggers. I may be a much better climber than some people believe, but the parameters shift slightly when you're competing against the 180 best bike riders in the world. After a stage like today's—and indeed, after most stages—you won't catch me looking at the white results sheet that the directeurs hand out at the hotel; had I looked tonight, I'd have discovered that I'd finished 168th, and my fifty-one partners in suffering and I had completed the stage nearly eighteen minutes after Riccò.

I felt like shit. I couldn't help feeling that it had a lot to do with the post-stage palaver of the previous day. I had been dropped, on my own, early in the stage, and only a breathless pursuit with the French sprinter Jimmy Casper and the German Sven Krauss had brought me back to the gruppetto, my life raft for the rest of the day.

We were now a week into the race. By this point in the 2007 race, I had been waking up each morning and mentally ticking another day off the list, desperate for the pain to end. I'd finally gone home on the eleventh day. This year was different. Every morning I rolled out of bed and thought of the kilometers I had to ride on the day's stage—and not, today, of the five stages already under my belt or the potential sixteen yet to come.

I was right about the perks of being a Tour stage winner. There *was* respect in the other riders' eyes and in their actions. There were certainly lots of congratulatory winks and pats on the back and shoulder. As for my own feelings, well, the happiness, the excitement were all there, but, again, muffled under the knowledge that I still had a job to do, mountains to climb, and more sprints to win.

As I'd ridden to the start that morning, and on and off as I fought to hold those wheels in the gruppetto, there'd also been another thought nagging at my subconscious: I'd won a stage of the Tour de France, and the most precious person in my life hadn't been there to see or share it.

"I really miss Melissa. Really miss her. Really, really miss her."

It was January 2006, Majorca. As Simon Jones turned around and walked out the door, a thought entered my head that wouldn't leave. Soon it wasn't just a thought but a certainty. It was the surest thing that had ever crossed my mind.

A few weeks earlier, I'd announced to Melissa's parents and my own that, as long as they didn't have any objections, I intended to propose to Melissa—without having any specific timescale in my head for when the action might follow the intention. It could be a month, it could be a year. Now, though, more than a certainty, that thought had become an imperative: I really missed Melissa, and I wanted to marry her.

Suddenly, the previous few hours, the agony of the day's seven-hour session, Jonesy's comment, "That'll teach you for eating those chocolate bars at Christmas," were forgotten. I was going to propose to Melissa, and I knew exactly how and when I was going to do it.

I reached for my mobile phone to contact Ben Swift, a lad from Sheffield who was in the intake at the British Federation Academy after mine. He picked up straightaway.

"Swifty, I'm going to propose to Melissa. I'm going to take her to the place where we met and ask her to marry me. But I need you to do me a favor: I come home to Manchester Friday night, and I've got to stay in Manchester before I fly home to the Isle of Man on Saturday morning. I get back at about eight o'clock, so will you pick me up and take me to the Trafford Centre, because I've got to buy her a ring?"

Swifty said that was all fine. "Awesome," I said. "See you Friday."

Nothing could go wrong. I had everything planned, I knew what I was going to say, and where I was going to do it, and how Melissa would react. It was all going to be perfect.

Friday finally came. I was nervous but excited. The plane was on time, and even the wait at the baggage claim was shorter and less of a cattle run than usual. I gathered my stuff and headed for Arrivals, impatient to see Swifty and crack on with the plan.

The doors slid open. I scanned the faces in the crowd. "Where's Swi—oh, my life!" Melissa. Right there. And suddenly, I was standing there trying desperately to stop a look of horror from spreading across my face. Trying and not succeeding.

"Er, hiya, princess, what are you doing here?"

She could see straightaway there was something wrong, but she'd barely had time to open her mouth before I'd dropped the bags. "Wait here for a second."

"Marky, what's wro—"

I sprinted outside to find Swifty. Luckily I found him. "Swifty, mate, you've got to go. She's only bloody here!"

I was panicking. Instead of just forgetting the whole thing, or at least not dwelling on it, I ran back inside and acted as shifty as a shoplifter. Melissa's anything but stupid, and her mind was starting to race.

"Marky, what's wrong? What were you doing?"

"Never mind. It's nothing. How come you're here?"

"Well, I wanted to surprise you."

"Yeah, but you didn't need to. I was flying back to the Island tomorrow. . . ."

"But you're flying to Australia for another training camp next week. I thought we could spend an extra night together. I've booked a hotel and everything. I wanted us to stay somewhere really nice, but there was a big Manchester United game tonight, and all the best hotels were gone, so I've booked a Travel Inn. . . . Anyway, I thought you'd be pleased."

And so it went for the next ten minutes, all the way through the airport, in the taxi rank, then finally in the taxi. She was getting more and more confused and suspicious, and I was starting to get angry. When I snapped and told her to just "fucking leave it" because I wasn't going to discuss it in a taxi, she pulled out her phone and dialed my mum's number. "Adele, he's not even pleased to see me. He's acting weird. . . ."

All hell had broken loose.

We finally reached the hotel, paid the driver, and walked through reception to the check-in desk. Now we weren't talking. As I struggled through the lobby with my bike bag, Melissa snatched the key. By the time I'd squeezed inside the door, tears were streaming down my face.

I didn't have a ring, we were in Manchester and not Douglas on the Island . . . it was all wrecked. Ruined.

She gave me one last chance.

"Go on, then. So what is it?"

It was time to cut my losses. I got down on one knee, tears still streaming down my face.

"Well, it's not how it was supposed to be, but will you marry me?"

"What?"

"That's it. That was it. I was going to propose to you. . . ."

The only thing that went according to plan was her answer. She said, "Yes."

How often do people on television talk about sports stars as "special talents," "champions," "geniuses," or "freaks of nature"? Pretty often, right? Okay, now tell me, how often have you heard a commentator or journalist admit what everyone probably already knows, that as well as being supernaturally talented and determined or a bit of both, most top athletes are also incredibly selfish?

I mean what I say: Athletes are very selfish. I'm also not lying when I say that the real champion, the real special talent in our relationship, is the girl who's supernaturally selfless—the girl who's sacrificed whatever it took, whatever I needed to realize my dream. The real star of this story is Melissa.

Four years on from my proposal-gone-wrong-gone-right, we still joke that, knowing us and our relationship, it really couldn't have happened any other way. We've both lost count of the number of times I've missed flights. Or the number of times we've missed each other's birthdays. When I was winning my first Tour stage, she was stuck in an airport bar with a mate, in France but a hundred kilometers away from the race, which just confirms that if we were Romeo and Juliet, I'd probably have turned up under the wrong balcony.

Our relationship's maybe not always been traditionally romantic, but right from when we met that night in the Villa Marina in Douglas, we've been the best of friends, and occasionally argued like the best of friends. Right from the start, her family was brilliant with me. Within weeks I was round at their house more than my own. Melissa's parents own a microbrewery in Laxey, and her dad even sponsored me when I was a junior—or at least I'd do some work for him, and he'd overpay me.

With my mum and dad and Melissa's, it really is like having four parents and not two.

"Sacrifice" is a word you hear a lot in cycling—sacrifices in terms of diet, time for training, not going out—but over the years, she's made at least as many sacrifices as I. Perhaps that's one of the reasons why it's worked so well. I'd always warned her that if I got as far as I intended in the sport, I'd be away a lot, but how do you prepare a girl for being without the guy who claims he's the love of her life for 200 or 250 days a year, year after year?

Right from my junior days or my time with the Academy, she'd get upset when I had to leave. I'd always tell her, "Look, I promise you that it'll pay off in the end. I'm going to earn plenty of money. I promise you I'll give you a good life." Coming from a little scally who was earning three grand a year at the Academy at the time, this probably sounded about as convincing as Del Boy's "This time next year, Rodders, we'll be millionaires." But she didn't care either way. She'd tell me she wasn't bothered about money or material things. She just wanted to be with me.

Those years at the Academy ought to have been relatively easy on the relationship since we were spending a lot of our time in Manchester, not all that far from home. But the reality was often pretty testing. In theory, the off-season ought to have been completely dedicated to Melissa—the deserved reward for all her patience and support throughout the year. But at the end of the 2004 road season, the first with the Academy, instead of us going on our first holiday since we'd gone to India with Melissa's parents when I was sixteen, I spent the autumn traipsing round the Under 23 Six-Day circuit. It was Melissa who lost out.

Melissa's just as competitive as me, and fortunately, she's also just as much of a perfectionist. Her first job was with Isle of Man Newspapers, but she'd always wanted to work for an airline in its cabin crew, and of course she got taken on her first application. The airline was Euromanx. Within a few months of joining, she was senior cabin crew, and pretty soon after that she was a line manager and being prepped for senior management.

That airline was great to me. When I was world Madison champion in 2005, the owner of the company wanted to know whether it could sponsor me. I said the only help I needed was with getting off the Island. After that, when we used to go away, I would get free flights, and, ironically, Melissa would have to pay for her tickets, albeit at a special rate.

Has it all been worthwhile? You'd have to ask her that. She's always wanted to be independent, including financially, but at the end of 2007 and the beginning of 2008, she was working such long hours that we were barely seeing each other. It was the off-season, so theoretically the only time of the year when we'd share a lot of quality time, yet we were barely at home together any more than in the middle of the racing season. I could also see how tired and stressed she was getting, and it was breaking my heart. Eventually, I told her that if she carried on working, we'd be in danger of splitting up. She reluctantly agreed. It was a bittersweet coincidence when, within weeks of her leaving, Euromanx went bust and her old job disappeared.

Since the spring, before the 2008 Tour, she'd immersed herself in a new occupation: doing up the farmhouse we'd dismissed as an impossible dream when I'd first seen it on the Internet at the start of 2007. I'd just turned pro at that point, and, the ink still wet on my €40,000-a-year contract, I assumed that we could buy a house. Fat chance; I went online, saw a beautiful old stone farmhouse on a hill high above Laxey, looking out over the Irish channel and toward the Cumbrian Fells . . . then saw the price. So much for that idea.

I never imagined I'd win eleven races in my first pro season, never imagined my contract would be torn up midway through that season and replaced with something considerably more lucrative. I certainly never thought that in December 2007, the house in Laxey would still be on the market. And I never thought Melissa and I would be moving in the following April. Soon after we moved in, I left Melissa and an empty, undecorated house and set off for the Giro d'Italia; I came back three and a half weeks later, a double stage winner, to the house and the girl of my dreams.

She was my tenth teammate, and I was gutted that she hadn't been there to celebrate a victory to which she'd made a huge contribution.

STAGE 6: AIGURANDE–SUPER BESSE, 195.5 KM

1. Riccardo Riccò (Ita), Saunier Duval–Scott, 4:57:52 (39.38 kph)

168. Mark Cavendish (GBr), Team Columbia, 17:46

GENERAL CLASSIFICATION

1. Kim Kirchen (Lux), Team Columbia, 24:30:41

141. Mark Cavendish (GBr), Team Columbia, 23:28

STAGE 7

Friday, 11 July 2008
BRIOUDE-AURILLAC
159 KM

H oly fuck.

If I'd been asked for two words to describe today's stage, not for the first time in this book or in my life you'd have been owed an apology for my bad language.

But, really—holy fuck.

Stage 7 of the Tour de France was perhaps the hardest day I'd ever experienced on a bike. The roadbook said Brioude-Aurillac, 159 km, with five climbs in the Massif Central, none especially difficult. In Tour-speak, or rather according to the arbitrary classification of Tour climbs used for the King of the Mountains competition, category 4 climbs were usually small and relatively gentle inclines, generally between 1 and 4 kilometers. At the other end of the scale you had Pyrenean and Alpine "special category" climbs. Today's five never got beyond second category, which, in most people's eyes, qualified this as nothing more than a "transition" stage.

For me the stage was marked by several transitions: from apprehension to panic, to pain, to agony, to more agony, and finally, when it was all over, to an overwhelming sense of relief.

Ask most sprinters and they'll tell you that they have an intense dislike for climbs at the start of stages. We are handicapped by our weight and dense, fast-twitch muscle fibers, and for some reason those natural disadvantages are accentuated before the blood and adrenaline are fully pumping. Today's profile showed a category 3 hill, the Côte de Fraisse, after 11 kilometers; the prospect seemed about as inviting as cold porridge.

On most mornings at the 2008 Tour, I'd spent as long as possible safely tucked away in the team bus. Twelve months earlier, everything had been a novelty—the crowds, the color, the media attention. The five British riders in the race had developed a ritual of congregating in a small corner of the start village to drink coffee, read the morning newspapers, compare sob stories, and shoot the breeze. The start village was a packed fairground of food, hospitality tents, journalists, riders, and other distractions. This year distractions were not what I needed; the best place to avoid them was behind the tinted, one-way glass of our team bus.

Today I stepped out early, not to sign autographs or give interviews but to go for a warm-up on the roads fanning out of the start village. With Kim's yellow jersey the team's priority, and most of our men and resources focused on that, it would be essential for me to get over that first category 3 climb with the main peloton. Fail and I'd find myself racing against my most feared, most persistent, most detested opponent—the time limit.

There is a time limit in every Tour stage—no, in every cycle race. Calculated according to the stage winner's total time, the "comfort zone" can vary between 5 and 12 percent of that total time, depending on the winner's average speed and on whether the stage is classified as "flat," "rolling," or "mountainous." If it sounds complicated, it is; for safety and convenience, it's usually smart to assume that if you finish more than twenty-five minutes after the winner, you're dicing with possible elimination.

The start line that morning was like the photo finish at the end of a sprint. I looked one way and saw McEwen and Zabel, looked the other way and saw Freire and Hushovd. We all knew we had to be as close as possible to the front when the race hit the bottom of the climb, and, sure enough, the neutralized zone that day was like the Alamo.

The road was narrow, the climb steeper than I expected. After a brilliant first week in which we'd held the white, green, and now yellow jerseys and, more importantly, bossed the entire race, morale in the team was high. But today Kim looked stressed. I'd gently teased him about his refusal to sport the matching shorts that the team had custom-ordered for the eventuality of one of our riders wearing the yellow jersey. Kim simply didn't do "flash." He'd headed to the start in the team's normal, regulation black shorts.

I arrived at the climb in the first twenty positions. So far so good. A kilometer or two later, I was rapidly dropping backward but not, apparently, as rapidly as some of the other sprinters. Our directeurs sportifs had already spotted Francesco Chicchi losing ground, swaying through the cars. "Good job, lads," Allan Peiper chirped over the radio. "Chicchi's dropped. . . ."

It's a cruel sport, cycling. Chicchi was a fellow sprinter—by rights we were bound to the same unspoken pact, the same union. "Never attack a fellow sprinter. . . ."

Bollocks to that. I stepped harder on the pedals.

I was still clinging to the main peloton when we passed under the giant inflatable banner signaling the end of the first climb. Just. The armchair spectator may not see it, but it's never a surprise to a bike rider when the rear wheel of the man in front starts drawing away, slowly yet definitively, like a train from the station platform. When the fateful moment comes, when millimeters become centimeters become one bike length and then two, the rider has known for several seconds or even minutes that he's rattling like that train toward an inevitable conclusion.

Now, on the second climb of the day, like Chicchi before me, I reached that conclusion.

Perhaps it was a funny kind of karma; perhaps it was the crosswinds; perhaps I just had shit legs; perhaps whichever team it was that was battering at the front was determined to make these 159 kilometers a misery. Whatever the reason, after 60 kilometers I was in a group of twenty riders, hunched over my handlebars and thinking of only one thing: the time limit.

Who was that battering on the front? I made a few inquiries and discovered that it was David Millar's team, Garmin. I fucking knew it. We were both American teams, we'd both made a big deal of our strict antidoping politics, there was a healthy rivalry between us, but there was also one crucial difference: As far as I could see, our team rode just to win races, while they rode for that and to fuck other people up.

Garmin's tactics bemused me. They'd bemuse me even more later that day, after the stage, when Dave Millar said in an interview that they'd been trying to make the race hard for Columbia. A Garmin rider, Christian Vande Velde, was in 4th place on general classification, forty-four seconds from Kim, but surely they didn't think they'd be able to isolate him and take the yellow jersey on a so-called transition stage, however hard that was turning out to be. In any case there were two other riders and their teams between Christian and Kim's yellow jersey—Cadel Evans and Stefan Schumacher. To me, Garmin's strategy smacked of just wanting to get the team's faces and the corporate logo on TV.

The rest of the stage was one long, leg-ripping roller coaster through wind and fog, over climbs that were much harder than they'd looked on paper. I had never seen such a big gruppetto in the Tour. An Italian term that translates literally as "little group," the gruppetto is also variously referred to as the "autobus" or "laughing group." "Autobus" is the French name, and it may be no coincidence that French riders seemed to regard the autobus as somewhere to go when you wanted a free ride to the finish. The phrase "laughing group," meanwhile, comes from the idea that the last big group on the road is where nonclimbers assemble to banter and lark their way through the mountains. The second image is romantic but, as usual where romance is involved, slightly unrealistic; the task of avoiding the time limit is a risky and unpleasant business. This may explain why the senior pro who takes it upon himself to calculate the likely cutoff point and pace the group is often referred to as the "bus driver."

As usual on these stages, two races had developed: one, the real competition that would end with bouquets and excited applause and kisses from the podium girls; the other, invisible to the cameras, less competition than coalition, with the right to fight another day the common goal.

In race one, the Spaniard Luis Leon Sanchez was first across the line and Kim fourth. This meant Kim would keep his yellow jersey. Sanchez's average speed had been almost 41 kph, in crosswinds, on heavy, undulating roads.

In race two, the whole gruppetto—all sixty-one of us—made the time limit by six minutes. Only one rider didn't make the cut. It was Magnus Bäckstedt. He rode for Garmin.

That night, as usual, the first thing some of the team members did when we arrived back at our hotel was sink into one of the portable plunge pools the soigneurs had set up in the car park. The team had used these baths in 2007 and was repeating the experiment in 2008. The theory was that immersing your legs in cold water improved circulation to the muscles and helped to get rid of toxins. As usual, I walked straight past the baths and up to my room. The only thing I wanted to sink into was my bed.

That evening at dinner, all the talk revolved around the day's stage and its sheer, brutal relentlessness. The general perception was that, with the French Anti-Doping Agency taking over drug-testing duties and promising all manner of rigorous blood, urine, and even hair testing, the 2008 Tour would be the cleanest in recent memory. It followed that it should also be slower than the drug-addled races of the mid-1990s.

Brian Holm and Rolf Aldag had both been around in that era—the so-called EPO years. In the past year, both men had spoken openly about having used EPO, but I had never discussed it with them. Now, though, after that massacre, I was curious.

I told Rolf I had a question. "What was the Tour like on EPO?"

The resulting conversation was long, fascinating, and above all reassuring. Rolf said that in the mid-1990s, Tour stages had been exactly like today's, but the difference then was that *every* stage had been like today's.

EPO perhaps hadn't made the Tour faster, but it had made recovery easier, and as a result, the race had been more consistently savage. "Just you wait," he said. "Tomorrow will be better. Tomorrow will be okay. . . ."

That just about summed up the Tour; when you didn't win, or when it hurt, which was every day, you always had that hope to cling to—the same hope that gets people through every kind of suffering, every day, all over the world. "Tomorrow will be better. Tomorrow will be okay." They were the only mottos or mantras you needed to ride the Tour.

As for doping, well, the conversation with Rolf had confirmed to me that I should reserve judgment and concentrate on my own race. Beyond that, it had also cemented a bond with Rolf that I'd never anticipated when I'd joined his team just under two years earlier.

All my life, I'd been trying to make people laugh—often succeeding, sometimes not—but this was definitely one occasion when I'd rather have seen six poker-straight faces. The six faces belonged to my six new bosses, T-Mobile's six new directeurs sportifs, the six former pros Rolf Aldag, Allan Peiper, Tristan Hoffman, Valerio Piva, Jan Schaffrath, and Brian Holm. I hadn't cracked any jokes, and neither had they. So why, then, were they all smirking?

We'd been called in to discuss our objectives for the coming 2007 season and how the team was going to work under the new regime. Aldag and Bob Stapleton had recently been installed as the new management duo, and this get-together in Lugano, Switzerland, was going to be a key part of their bedding-in process—and mine as a rider.

I was desperate to make a good impression. Apparently I'd already failed.

"What do you want?" Rolf asked, still smiling.

"Er, what do you mean?"

"Which races?"

"Obviously, I'd like to do the big races, but I don't know. . . ."

"You don't know much, do you?" said Rolf, giggling with the other directeurs.

This wasn't going well. It was about to get worse.

Tristan Hoffman spoke next. A big, bracing former Dutch pro now entering his late 30s, he had a reputation for rarely taking anything seriously. Trouble was, his question sounded very serious indeed: "We hear you have a problem with the drink. That you're a bit of a party animal. Is this true?"

I was stunned. I told them no, I most certainly did not have a problem with drink—in fact, I barely ever drank at all. I pointed out that I'd won twenty-six races riding for Sparkasse. "I'm really professional. . . ." I protested.

The conversation moved on before I'd had a chance to argue my case. Those mysterious grins had disappeared but left all sorts of questions pinging back and forth in my mind. We went on to talk about race programs and training. The discussion lasted ten, maybe twenty, minutes. I left the room confused.

It was Roger Hammond's turn to go in next. He came out an hour later looking pale and exhausted. Seeing me, he shook his head in exasperation. "I've just been in there an hour, and fifty minutes were about you. . . . Max Sciandri's spoken to Piva and told him to watch out for you because you're a party animal. He's told them that you really like your alcohol."

My thoughts suddenly raced. To be precise, they raced back to my ride with Max after the Baby Giro earlier that year. I thought of the pep talk he'd given me about training and behaving like a professional. The only other time I'd seen him was at a birthday party for Dave Millar's sister, Fran, which happened to be in a bar. Now it clicked: Max had seen me drinking in a bar and somehow assumed that I must be some kind of raving boozehound.

It had all started so well with my first races as a stagiaire just a couple of months earlier, in August 2006. That summer, a management overhaul at T-Mobile had left me fearing that the whole deal would be off, especially when the manager of the German Sparkasse team where I'd spent most of the summer riding assured me that was effectively the case. I'd gone to Sparkasse the previous year with Ed Clancy after Rod had unexpectedly informed us, "Oh, yeah, lads, we're sending you to race in Germany, to get some experience."

Just over a year and twenty-odd race wins later, I was still with Sparkasse, still winning, still loving it as much as the team was loving me, but now here was the team's manager telling me I should forget my ambitions of a pro contract with T-Mobile. "Aldag says none of the deals signed before he arrived are valid. You may as well stay with us," he told me. I was incredulous—literally, in the sense that I refused to believe what he was saying.

"Well, I don't care, I'm still going to ride for a top team next year, whether it's T-Mobile or not," I replied.

It turned out that I was dead right: Sparkasse had simply invented a story in an effort to make me stay.

I got set to travel from my base near Dortmund to what was going to be my first race in a T-Mobile jersey, the stage-race Regio Tour, certain I'd need to impress the new T-Mobile bosses if I was to have any chance of securing a permanent deal. I'd trained hard all summer and had proved it by finishing 4th in a high-class international field in my last outing for Sparkasse the previous week. In what was my team's home race, the Sparkassen Giro, I'd been shoved in the sprint and come from maybe 12th position to finish 4th, no more than a tire-width from Erik Zabel, who was 3rd. Little did I know it at the time, but T-Mobile's directeurs had watched me closely that afternoon and liked what they'd seen; they'd liked it so much, in fact, that on the first morning of the Regio Tour, before I'd even pulled on the T-Mobile jersey for the first time, one of the team's then managers, Luc Eisenga, had called to tell me that the team was offering me a two-year contract. Luc said the offer was for €10,000 a year less than what they'd initially intended . . . but if that was still okay . . . ?

Still okay? I was bloody delirious.

My excitement may have gotten the better of me in that first stage. In the grand scheme of international cycling, the Regio Tour isn't exactly a big fixture, but to a German team like T-Mobile the race was important enough to make victory not just worthwhile but a near necessity. With experienced Tour de France stars like Michael Rogers and Giuseppe Guerini, we had a strong team and, in Andreas Klöden, a leader whom management would expect to be on the top step of the podium come the end of the race. The rest of us would be expected to get him there.

Within an hour of the start, strong crosswinds had split the race. Three of our riders made the break, but the two top dogs, Rogers and Klöden, were in the back group with me. Klöden rode on to my shoulder. "You have to ride to pull this back," he said. To me, it didn't make sense; we had three men in the front group to either thwart or take advantage of the split. But then, he was a Tour de France podium finisher and I was a little 21-year-old scally on work experience. I nodded and took myself to the front.

Maybe a few kilometers, a few minutes, went by. I pulled until I hurt. Then, out of the corner of my eye, I saw Michael Rogers.

"Why are you riding? We've got three men in the front group. . . ."

"Well, we were told to ride. . . ."

Mick told us to go back. Take it easy. I did as he said. A few more kilometers, a few more minutes, then someone else was tapping me on the shoulder. What now? It was Klöden again, scowling this time. "What are you doing? If I tell you to ride, you ride, okay?"

The race ended in a sprint—a sprint in which, Valerio Piva had informed me over the radio, I'd be leading out my teammate Andre Korff. That was exactly what I was preparing to do when, with around 3 kilometers to go, an Italian rider from the Naturino team leaned on my arm and left me with two options but no real choice: Either wipe out into a signpost and die or give him a gentle shove and hope he could stay upright. I took option two. The clatter of bikes and bodies was still ringing in my ears when I launched Korffy to a disappointing 2nd place.

The misunderstanding with Klöden and Rogers was cleared up that night. It had been just that—a misunderstanding. What had happened in the final 3 kilometers might be a thornier subject, not least because the entire peloton knew who had caused or at least been involved in the crash. Sure enough, the next morning, before the start of the second stage, I found myself besieged by Italian riders blaming me for the pileup. It took the intervention of Guerini and two or three other teammates to defuse what was in danger of becoming a very public and very heated row.

I'd always known that professional cycling was a school of hard knocks, and I'd finished my first day roughed up but also toughened up. The race continued in the same vein—hard and fast—but ended in triumph for both the team and its youngest member: Just as we'd hoped and planned, Klöden won the general classification, Rogers was 2nd, and I went home under a shower of compliments from the directeurs sportifs for all the time I'd spent selflessly driving on the front of the bunch.

My next race was a big one for me, if not for some of my teammates. In fact, it didn't take Einstein or a body-language expert to figure out that Matthias Kessler and Patrick Sinkewitz, at least, didn't want to be at the Tour of Britain. Fortunately I had enough motivation for about three riders. Our directeur sportif that week was Brian Holm, a wiry former Danish pro with a taste for funky haircuts and all things British.

On the first stage, as we approached the feed zone, a group of three had already gone clear, and Brian decided it was about time we chased. The whole team duly went to the front except me and Olaf Pollack, the German rider who was to be our first-choice sprinter that week. Within a couple of minutes, Brian buzzed in on the radio: "Cavendish, you fat fuck! When I say chase, you chase, okay?" He wasn't joking. It goes without saying that my first sprint that day was the one that took me through the peloton and on to the front.

Klöden pulled out of the race, ill, in the first 50 kilometers of that first stage. Pollack crashed, hurt his head, and told me to do my own thing in the sprint. I ended up finishing 7th—4th in the main bunch, behind the three men in the breakaway—and disappointed to have been blocked in the final straight. Brian sat down next to me at the dinner table that night; when he said 7th wasn't bad, I shrugged and puffed out my cheeks. He laughed and said he liked my attitude.

As the days went by, I could sense that I was fast earning my teammates' respect and, more importantly, Brian's. On the second morning, when the older guys had finished their breakfast, Brian came over again, just as he had the previous night. He pulled up a chair and motioned toward the window, to the rainwater cascading down the glass. I shrugged just as I had the previous evening: "Doesn't bother me," I said. Brian smiled.

I never did win a stage that week. I was 4th on Stage 2 and 2nd on Stage 4 to Birmingham, having spent the whole day in an eight-man break. The team was delighted with that performance, but I was mortified, not so much for myself, not even for my teammates, but for my mate from the British Academy, Geraint Thomas. There was an unwritten, unspoken rule that week that some of the GB riders would help me out in the sprints, with my T-Mobile team down to four riders, two of whom—Patrick Sinkewitz and Matthias Kessler—were no more than passengers. That day in the break, though, Gee helped me for no other reason than personal loyalty. By now everyone in the race knew I was a fast finisher, so it was inevitable that they'd try to get rid of me before the closing straight with repeated attacks, one of which, by the Belgian Frederik Willems, took him clear on his own. It was then that Gee moved into action—burying himself for no other reason than to reel in Willems and set up a sprint finish that I'd almost certainly win. When we didn't quite make it, Willems stayed away and I got 2nd. I felt bad for myself but absolutely gutted for Gee.

I finished the race with 3rd place in a bunch sprint in the Mall in London and, much more importantly, the green jersey. Awarded to the rider who'd totted up the largest number of the points available for finishing positions at the end of stages and in intermediate sprints, the prize was the direct equivalent of one of the holy grails of sprinting in road cycling: the green jersey of the Tour de France. Although I'd agreed to a two-year deal with T-Mobile at the Regio Tour, I'd only signed the contract that week in England.

As I left the podium, I happened to bump into the man who had started the ball rolling and first alerted T-Mobile to my potential over a year earlier—the former British Federation coach Heiko Salzwedel. I put my arms around him, then gave him the green jersey I'd just won together with a promise—that it wouldn't be my last, and that one day I'd give him a green jersey from a much more important race. I could see from the twinkle in his eye that I didn't need to elaborate.

So what exactly had Roger Hammond said to convince my new bosses that, when they talked about my program for 2007, they wouldn't have been better off pointing me in the direction of Alcoholics Anonymous's twelve-step program?

I later discovered that he'd simply told them the story of the Under 23 World Championships Road Race in Salzburg in September 2006, or rather what had happened immediately afterward. The race itself had been a tale of its own, and not one that particularly flattered me. I'd gone into that Worlds in good form, fresh from my good rides at the Regio Tour and the Tour of Britain, and convinced that, if I could beat Gerald Ciolek, who that season had become my rival in races in Germany and also the youngest-ever German senior road race champion, I'd be world champion. I had a brilliant Great Britain team and what I thought was an infallible tactic: Approach the one, key climb on the circuit in the first few positions, wait for the race to come back together on the descent, then smoke Ciolek in the final sprint to become world champion. What could be more straightforward?

It was all going beautifully. No, better than beautifully because on the final lap, Ciolek committed hara-kiri. As we neared the top of the crucial climb for the last time, a group of six or seven riders went clear and Ciolek gave chase. My jaw almost hit the tarmac: Ciolek, the favorite, the German wunderkind, my would-be nemesis, had just thrown away the world championship. On every lap, the bunch had splintered, then re-formed on the descent, and this time would be no different. Well, actually, it would: This time we'd hit the finishing straight and Ciolek's legs would be like two sacks of spuds after an attack that was as physically taxing as it was misguided.

The gap grew to ten, twelve seconds as we reached the top of the climb. Bothered? It was just a matter of time, a formality, they might as well give the troph—then, BOOM! A motorbike crashed in front of us and slid across the road. I stubbed my foot and broke my shoe. More to the point, the ten seconds of confusion as everyone swerved, slowed, looked for teammates, and set off again were fatal for our hopes of catching the break. Against all odds and all logic, Ciolek's suicide mission had paid off. A few minutes later he was world champion.

After the race, I'd gone back to Roger Hammond's flat in Belgium and Roger had offered me "one beer, just one, then an early night." I'd declined. Not only that but, that Monday after the race in Salzburg, I had told Roger that, never mind the fact that we'd just gotten off the plane from Austria, I was going to put a light on my bike and go out training in the dark.

That was the story Roger had told the directeurs. On hearing it, Roger said, the smirks with which they'd greeted me an hour or so earlier had been replaced by a look of mild and pleasant surprise.

That training camp in Lugano had been part planning meeting, part team-building exercise, with various "fun" activities like rock climbing designed to forge a spirit that I'd heard had been lacking in the team when everything had revolved around Jan Ullrich. Ullrich's involvement in the Operación Puerto doping scandal in the summer of 2006 had sparked the implosion that had resulted in his departure, the team's restructuring, and, almost, the cancellation of my stagiaire's deal. From what I'd seen in Lugano, there were still cliques, but the management wanted to see them disappear. They also wanted more dialogue with the riders through the winter and during the season; to this end, we were all assigned one of the directeurs sportifs as a liaison or mentor—and I was allocated to Brian Holm.

That winter, Melissa and I went to Florida, our first holiday for years. I also trained well while not making the common mistake of overcooking it in my effort to impress at the first real training camp with T-Mobile, which was to be held in Majorca in January 2007. Both Andreas Klier and I were arriving in Majorca a day early, so it made sense that we should share a room. Andreas was an experienced German pro whose interest in cycling was born out of a passion for racing and the traditions that, to fans of other sports, seem alien and mystifying. He loved the culture and folklore so much that he'd even uprooted himself from Germany to the home of blood-and-guts cycling, Flanders, Belgium. He was a man after my own heart, and although we hadn't spoken in Lugano, now we hit it off instantly.

I can't say it was an enjoyable ten days. Whatever skepticism my directeurs had about my ability and my attitude toward racing and training I'd started to overcome with my performances as a stagiaire, and Roger had done the rest in the now infamous meeting in Lugano. Now, though, I came up against a new obstacle—a young German coach by the name of Sebastian Weber, who, like me, had just started working with the team.

My experiences with Simon Jones at the British Federation had left me with very clear convictions about sports scientists. Consequently, to avoid wasting Weber's time and mine, I'd told him in Lugano that there was no point in our working together; in Rod Ellingworth, as far as I was concerned, I already had the best coach in the world. Weber clearly wasn't enamored with the idea, but he agreed that a good compromise would be him at least contacting Rod and finding out a little bit more about who I was and what I needed. From where I was standing, at that camp, it looked as though Weber ignored everything Rod had told him.

I've already talked about my hatred of fitness tests on a stationary rig or indoor bike. What I didn't know at that camp in Majorca was that the test I'd be made to do there would indirectly jeopardize the start of my first pro season.

I'd already warned Weber: I was always shit in lab tests, and this one wasn't going to be any different. Sure enough, I stepped off the rig at the end of my test, crimson-faced, drenched in sweat, having given everything but acutely aware that, of the twenty-nine riders in the team, I would probably have the worst results.

Another first-year pro might have panicked. Not me—at least not yet. In Andy Klier, I had a roommate whose contempt for crunching numbers matched my own; if I needed someone to reassure me that Weber had gotten it all wrong, it'd be Andreas. I knew he understood me, and he underlined that one night when he came into the room and announced that he'd just been talking about me with Rolf Aldag. He'd been asked what he thought about his new roommate, and Andreas had given a favorable verdict. Rolf had countered that I was fat; Andreas's last word on the topic had been that Rolf should look at the number of races I'd won while riding for Sparkasse the previous season.

Throughout the camp, on the road, I was in the slowest of three separate groups. There was nothing unusual about that, what with the directeurs conscious of the need not to abuse my youthful exuberance. Much more relevant, to my mind, was the day when we practiced sprint trains. Having signed me, my old rival Ciolek, Bernhard Eisel, and the Kiwi Greg Henderson, T-Mobile now had a glut of sprinters, and we all went head-to-head in lead-outs of around 3 kilometers, each of which would finish with a shoot-out between the two sprinters in the respective lines. In one of these "races," I was up against Eisel. When the last men pulled off, Bernie had a 10-meter advantage; when we crossed the fictional finish line, I was a bike-length clear.

That exercise alone seemed like a vindication. Again, though, as with Simon Jones over the previous two or three years, the disparity between what I could produce in a race scenario and in the lab was a source of constant irritation to some. Weber was one of those people. Toward the end of the camp, he presented us with the results of our rig tests. When he came to me, he looked and sounded disapproving.

"Unacceptable for a professional" was the phrase I seem to recall him using.

As I've already made quite clear, I was dubious about sports scientists, so it followed that I would be dubious about Weber. I also had the positive experiences of my stagiaire period to reassure me that I belonged among the professionals. Even without that, in Majorca, whether through explicit praise or other, subtler signals, people who knew from firsthand experience what it took to flourish as a pro—people like Brian Holm and Andreas Klier—ought to have set my mind at ease.

Outwardly, whenever Weber's name or his ideas came up in conversation, I was as cocky and dismissive as ever, even when he confronted me at the end of the camp. "Numbers don't lie," he said. It was like listening to Simon Jones.

My conscious mind wasn't paying attention, but somewhere, deep in my subconscious, an insecurity was stirring. "What's your first race?" he asked me. I told him I was due to ride the French one-day race, the GP L'Ouverture La Marseillaise, at the beginning of February in about a month's time. He sniffed. "With numbers like this, you won't even be able to hold on to the peloton. You're overweight, and you're not pushing enough watts."

Not even hold on to the peloton? I'd already ridden pro races the previous autumn and threatened to win more than once. Okay, so I was a couple of kilos heavier and slightly less fit, but that was normal—it was January. He clearly didn't know what he was talking about. Why, then, did I walk away from that conversation determined not just to prove him wrong but to prove him wrong on his terms? He wanted me to lose weight? Okay, I'd lose more than he ever thought was possible. He wanted more watts? Okay, I'd smash myself every day until I was putting out more power than he knew how to measure.

In an earlier chapter, I said I'd never had a true crisis of confidence. On reflection, now, I can see that, as I prepared to embark on my first full season as a professional cyclist, I was perhaps less sure of myself than I'd previously thought. It wasn't just Weber; Aldag had also said I was fat, and somewhere, deep in my memory, there was also the echo of conversations with Max Sciandri, Dave Millar, and Simon Jones. Maybe they were right, and I was the one who'd gotten it wrong. Maybe it would all be different now that I was a pro—a full-time pro, not just T-Mobile's equivalent of the office tea boy. Maybe those races that I'd ridden as a stagiaire in late 2006 had been unusually slow. Maybe Andreas Klier and another well-traveled teammate, Servais Knaven, were the ones who were deluded when, one evening in Majorca, they told me their cash would be on me to bring T-Mobile its first race win of 2007.

One thing I did know as I flew out of Majorca at the end of that camp was that I wasn't going to give Sebastian Weber the satisfaction of seeing me fail. I'd go back to the Isle of Man, train harder than ever before, eat less, and show up for the GP L'Ouverture La Marseillaise lean, serene, and ready to win—immediately.

It would take me three or four months to realize it, but before my professional career had even begun, that January, I'd already made my first, very costly mistake.

STAGE 7: BRIOUDE-AURILLAC, 159 KM

1. Luis Leon Sanchez Gil (Spa), Caisse d'Epargne, 3:52:53 (40.964 kph)

145. Mark Cavendish (GBr), Team Columbia, 21:53

GENERAL CLASSIFICATION

1. Kim Kirchen (Lux), Team Columbia, 28:23:40

48. Mark Cavendish (GBr), Team Columbia, 45:15

STAGE 8

Saturday, 12 July 2008
FIGEAC-TOULOUSE
172.5 KM

llan Peiper says that one incident from Stage 8 of the 2008 Tour de France summed up me and summed up my race. Allan, ironically, had been one of my biggest fans when I started my pro career with T-Mobile at the start of 2007. Why ironically? Well, Allan had left his previous employer, Lotto, the Belgian outfit, after controversial comments about the team's fondness for unwinding with a glass of wine or beer. A month or two later, at the end of 2006, one of Allan's first assignments in his new job at T-Mobile involved quizzing me about my taste for the same performance-impairing drug.

Allan, Rolf Aldag, Brian Holm—they all seemed cut from the same mold. All three had enjoyed successful if not prolific riding careers over the past two and a half decades, and all three still had the kind of athletic, sinewy physique that many current pros, me included, would need a lengthy stint on salads to achieve.

Like Rolf and Brian, Allan was a good communicator and good directeur—friendly and fair, firm but not authoritarian. In many ways, he was a typical Aussie—fast-talking, with a brilliant turn of phrase and an up-and-at-'em approach to racing, but with his neat, silvery hair, tanned complexion, and immaculately pressed shirts, he might easily have been mistaken for a French bank manager who spent summers on the Côte d'Azur.

Allan would be in charge at what was to be the first race of my first full season as a professional, the GP L'Ouverture La Marseillaise, in February. Between leaving the team training camp in Majorca in January and flying to Marseille, Sebastian Weber's comments had followed me on every training ride, every visit to the dinner table. I was overweight and I wasn't pushing enough power, he'd said. I wouldn't even be able to stay with the peloton, he'd insisted. Over the next four weeks, on every six-hour ride, on every day when my calorie intake barely crept toward four figures, those words had stalked me like a dark and menacing shadow.

It's difficult now to express exactly what I was thinking and feeling at that first race, La Marseillaise. What's certain is that I missed the key break and finished anonymously in the main group. This was nothing unusual or alarming—much more important, from my point of view, was that all the training and self-denial of the previous month had clearly paid off: I had good fitness, good legs, and I fully intended to demonstrate this at the Étoile de Bessèges, the four-day stage race set to begin the following day.

It was a short journey from Marseille to Pézenas, host town to the first stage. In the morning, as at every race, amateur or professional, our team directeur held a pre-race briefing to define our tactics. Today's stage, said Allan, would probably finish in a bunch sprint, and logic therefore dictated that we'd work for the team's faster finisher. The only thing that remained to establish was who that was. I looked around the team bus: Roger Hammond and Marco Pinotti—both quick but not that quick; Axel Merckx—couldn't sprint for toffee; Lorenzo Bernucci, Scott Davis, Frantisek Rabon—none of them; the German Andre Greipel—a chiseled hulk of a man, immensely powerful but not *fast*, not as quick as me, so no. So that left Cavendish—well, yeah, you'd think so, wouldn't you? . . .

Then Allan spoke: "So, you got that, chaps? We're working for Greipel, all right?"

The best I could do now was deliver Greipel with such speed and precision that he couldn't lose. Of course there was a risk to this strategy; the better I set him up, the more likely Greipel was to win, therefore reinforcing his credentials as the team's senior sprinter. But I had no other option: There's only one thing a cycling team with a budget of €15 million per year likes less than a fat, mouthy 21-year-old and that's a fat, mouthy 21-year-old who disobeys orders. As the peloton swung into the final 2 kilometers, and the sprinters' teams began to congregate up front, I was exactly where Allan and Greipel wanted me.

I slotted neatly into the conga line now being led by the Unibet team, a handful of positions from the front. Directly behind me was the Unibet sprinter Baden Cooke. Directly behind him was Greipel. We flashed under the red flag indicating 1 kilometer to go, then into the final 800 meters. The Unibet rider now in first position, Jeremy Hunt, glanced back, saw me on his wheel, and pulled to one side; as he did so, the wind hit me like the air from an oversized hair dryer. I kicked and kicked again, past 500, past 300, to the sign showing 200, then veered across the road, leaving Greipel a clear corridor to the line.

I turned around. No, it couldn't be, surely not: I'd dropped the bloody peloton. Trouble was, it was now too late to recover my momentum. I tried desperately to clamber on top of the pedals, but because I had slowed, the gear was far too big. The Italian Angelo Furlan whistled past me within a few meters of the line to leave me in 2nd place, cursing my own bad luck and wondering what the hell had happened to the team's so-called number-one sprinter.

Where *was* Greipel? My question was answered a minute or two later. I arrived at the bus, still breathless, took off my helmet, and climbed off my bike. I looked around and saw Greipel arriving. He didn't look pleased. In fact, he looked enraged.

"Cavendish!" he screamed, seemingly oblivious to the small crowd of spectators, riders, and managers within earshot. "You only sprint for yourself! You're selfish!"

"What are you talking about?" I said. "I was leading you out!"

"No, no, you only sprint for yourself. You selfish bastard!"

"I fucking led you out. Where the fuck were you?"

I daresay we'd still be swapping expletives if Allan hadn't been there to restore some order. As it was, I was summoned to the podium to collect my and the team's consolation prize—the jersey awarded to the best young rider on general classification.

Allan waited in the car while I collected the jersey. As we drove off toward the team hotel, I made my case to Allan and broached the question of why we'd been working for Greipel in the first place. Allan mumbled something about Greipel being German, the sponsor being German— "You know how it is, Cav . . ."—plus the fact that Greipel could point to several years of experience and even sporadic victories in the pro ranks. He spoke in a paternal tone: "Look, Cav, I know how fast you are, but you've got to ride for Greipel here. . . ."

"I did fucking ride for him," I said. "I didn't sprint from 500 meters for myself! Anyone in that race will tell you that."

Back at the hotel that evening, the inquest continued. My teammate Axel Merckx was one of the first people I saw. He immediately tried to put my mind at rest; Axel had spoken to Scott Davis, who in turn had spoken to his fellow Aussie Baden Cooke, the Unibet rider who'd been tracking my wheel when I'd accelerated with 500 meters to go. Cooke was adamant: No sprinter in his right mind would hit the gas so far out unless he was working for someone else. I then got a call from Andreas Klier—the teammate who'd made a private wager that I'd be the team's first winner of the season. I told Andreas about Greipel. He sounded sympathetic. The only thing that concerned me slightly was that there was no congratulatory text message on my phone from Rolf Aldag; Rolf always sent a congratulatory text message after a good result. Concern turned to mild alarm when, fifteen minutes after I'd finished talking to Klier, *he* sent me a text message: "I think it's better that you do what the directeur says." I could only assume that Klier had spoken to Aldag.

I didn't bother relating what Baden Cooke had said to Greipel. There was no point. I could also have gloated that Allan now seemed to believe my version of events and not Andre's, but again, what would that have achieved? The best option now was for me to avoid Greipel and for Greipel to avoid me. There was just one minor problem with that: Our malfunctioning partnership would be called upon again in what looked like another sprinter-friendly stage on day two.

So, here we are—roughly the same time, the same place, same routine for the pre-stage briefing on day two. Allan speaks: "So chaps, we're working for . . . Greipel again today. You got that?"

The briefing had been more or less the same, and the result was near enough identical; precisely where Greipel finished no one except him really cared—what mattered was that, despite more good work from the rest of the team, he didn't win, didn't even come close. This was all the more frustrating for me since, as both stages had worn on, I'd felt my legs become looser, the bike lighter, and the tarmac smoother under my wheels. I was experiencing the first flickers of a magical and elusive feeling that every trained cyclist knows simply as form.

Any decent doctor or old wife will tell you that the "in form" athlete is also an athlete who, for reasons never fully explained, is particularly vulnerable to illness and infection. Any cyclist, in turn, will tell you that there's nothing crueler than a bout of sickness to sabotage form, which has taken weeks and sometimes months of sacrifices to build.

On that second stage, I ended up lasting 20 kilometers before I flagged down Allan and told him I was ill. He told me not to worry. Back at the hotel that night, he even said I could stay with the team, rest, and maybe head out for the odd spin if I felt up to it. He said I had good form and it'd be a shame to waste it. As if he needed to tell *me* that.

The next day I managed 120 kilometers on my own. I felt sick, lethargic, empty. I flew home to the Isle of Man later that week, under orders to recover. But every time I could feel my strength, my energy, my motivation coming back, I'd take my bike from the garage, head out, then have to shamble back two or three hours later with my legs and my morale destroyed. I'd go to bed, recuperate a little, then restart the whole vicious cycle with my next training—or rather, draining—session. Days rolled into weeks, and still the pattern continued. At the beginning of March, I'd hoped to be fulfilling a childhood dream by riding my first real Classic—a Flandrian feast of cobbles and crosswinds ridden on an out-and-back route between the town of Kuurne and Brussels. As it turned out, the only dreams that day were the ones troubling my sleep as I lay in bed in the Isle of Man.

At first, when I'd left France, I'd assumed that I'd simply caught one of the endless bugs and flus that get passed around the peloton like a smutty joke. It had taken several recoveries and relapses and many more calls to my directeurs sportifs to convince me that something more serious might be up. Finally I went to see my local GP on the Isle of Man. I described my symptoms, when they'd started, how I'd felt brilliant those first two days at the Étoile de Bessèges, how I'd trained so hard for that race, my diet that winter, all the weight I'd lost . . . and as I spoke, it became obvi-ous: I'd undereaten, overtrained, overstressed, and overstretched myself. The reward had been an abrupt and spectacular spike in my form and fitness, then an equally steep descent into this pitiful state.

I now played the last three or four months back in my head. If only I could have relived them; given that opportunity, I would have respect-fully nodded at everything Sebastian Weber had told me in Majorca, then walked away and done my own thing entirely.

So: Stage 8 of the 2008 Tour de France. *That* story—the one Allan said "summed me up."

The race was now at the end of its first week and rapidly making its way south. The previous evening, the Tour had had its first doping scandal when the Spaniard Manuel Beltràn had been kicked out for a positive test for EPO. Now, at the start village in the little town of Figeac, the general mood was like the forecast for the rest of the day: gloomy.

For three consecutive days, there'd been lumpy terrain in the first quarter of the race—terrain that had me scrambling to stay with the peloton. The previous two stages had taken us through the Massif Central. Today it was the gentler hills of the southeast around Toulouse. To me, it all meant the same thing: pain.

When the attacks started as we approached the first climb of the day after 9 kilometers, I decided to adopt a novel tactic. Rather than position myself in the middle of the bunch and try desperately to hang on, I shot after one of the groups now launching themselves down the road and hoped I'd reach the top before, or at least not behind, the main peloton. As so often with these things, it was a great idea in theory that lost some of its effectiveness in practice: After a grand total of around 3 kilometers off the front of the peloton, I was swallowed up around a kilometer before the summit and spat out no more than a few hundred meters later. My sole consolation was that I wasn't alone; for the next 25 kilometers, I and around fifteen others found ourselves more than making up for the lack of a team time trial on the 2008 Tour route in a frantic relay that finally, thankfully, took us back to the main pack.

Before every Tour, even as early as the presentation of the route in a fancy Parisian auditorium the previous October, there are a certain number of stages you can tick off straightaway as "sprint stages" or "mountain stages." Or if you're me, "good" and "bad" days. Then there is a third category of stages that fall into a grey area—a grey area, as it happens, gently sprinkled with hills that I may or may not get over in a position or physical state that will allow me to sprint and, hopefully, win. Predictably, the problem with these stages is their unpredictability: Until the actual day, the last climb, the last kilometer, or even the last kick to launch my sprint, it's simply impossible to know whether the grey stages would be better left to other members of my team.

I can deal with not knowing. I, of all people, will always argue that cycling isn't an exact science. The problem is that these things take planning. On that eighth stage to Toulouse, for instance, we had a yellow jersey to defend and a decision to make about how many men and resources to devote to Kim and how many to me. There was also the question of equipment. At the start of the 2008 season, our management had realized that there were simply too many variations in technology and terrain for one type of wheel, or even one manufacturer, to cover all bases. Hence, Bob Stapleton had taken an unusual step: Never mind the money we could get from endorsing a particular company's products, we'd simply buy whatever wheels were most suitable for particular conditions on a particular day of a particular race.

So, there I was, finally back in the peloton, back in the hunt. Still 120 km and two and a half hours from the finish, rapidly getting wetter but feeling good. Good enough to take one hand off the bars and reach toward the microphone tucked under my jersey. "Allan, I'm coming back to the car for an 808 rear wheel."

The "808" was the model name of the deep-section carbon wheel, manufactured by the American company, Zipp, that I used for sprint finishes. Unsure of my own strength and the severity of the hills, I'd started the day with my lighter, shallow-rimmed "climbing" wheels—a pair of Zipp 404s.

There was silence for a second or two—the time it took Allan to relay my message to the mechanic in the backseat.

I waited.

Finally, there was a crackle, then the sound of Allan's voice.

"Er, Cav, mate, afraid we don't have any 808s in the car. . . ."

The first thing to say was that it was an uncharacteristic mistake. My team prides itself on its organization and professionalism, and that begins, rather than ends, with the backroom staff. The soigneurs, mechanics, and managers are the unsung heroes in what has been a huge success story since Bob and Rolf started running the team.

Right, now that's out of the way. Now I can be honest: I went apeshit. The excuse given was that it was a hilly stage and therefore far from certain to finish in a bunch sprint. Oh, yeah? So does that also mean you get rid of the smoke alarms in your house because there haven't been many fires recently? Am I being unfair when I say—and later said to the mechanic in question—that if I'm killing myself to get over a climb, if I'm willing to waste valuable energy to drop back to the car, change wheels, and chase to give myself and my team a shot at a stage win, the least he can do is provide the tools that will maximize my chances of succeeding?

As we all know now, all's well that ended well. After another couple of mishaps, I won my second Tour stage on the wrong, less stiff, and less aerodynamic Zipp 404 wheels, and the incident gave Allan a good story to tell whenever he's asked to describe what makes me different from most riders. Many, if not most, Allan would probably tell you, wouldn't have even bothered asking for that wheel change, and if they had and been told what I was told, they'd have shrugged or cursed under their breath or ranted to the nearest available rider about the "crap mechanics on our team."

My reaction was emotive, aggressive, but ultimately rational and constructive. Allan would also tell you that it erased any doubt in his mind about who was going to win that eighth stage.

It's funny how memory works. Writing this book, I amazed myself at the recollection I had of some races, stretching right back into my teens. First race as an Under 16? Easy—circuit race in Saltayre, near Lancaster: I attacked after 200 meters, lapped the field twice, and won on my own.

As the years and seasons tick by, no doubt some of these images might become a little foggier, but there are some races I'll never forget. The four stage wins in 2008—it goes without saying—but there may be one memory that trumps even them. They say you always remember your first love, right? I can guarantee that your first win as a professional cyclist is almost as special and every bit as memorable.

If you'd asked me back in February 2007 whether I'd win one professional cycle race—let alone four in a single Tour de France—I'd probably have hesitated. My instinct might have said "yes" but my body "no." As the weeks went by, as I lay in bed in the Isle of Man, trying to recover, a growing pile of emotional wreckage was starting to obscure that knowledge.

Finally, at the end of February, I'd been able to start training. At the beginning of March, I'd started competing. A minor Belgian one-day race, the GP Samyn, had been my comeback race. I'd finished, but with difficulty. Same thing next time out, in a stage race called the Three Days of West Flanders, then again in the Three Days of De Panne. De Panne was savage; I got my head kicked in—there are no other words for it. One stage was well over 200 kilometers—too far and too hard for me to finish in my still pretty precarious physical condition. But finish I did. Half dead.

Within the next fortnight, one of my teammates, Marcus Burghardt, would give the team a massive morale boost by winning the Ghent-Wevelgem semi-Classic ahead of Roger Hammond. My form and spirits were also improving. At the GP Pino Cerami, another of the hectic, hilly Belgian races that come thick and fast in March and April, I even finished in the front group. Two days later, I had the time of my life, recceing the final 130 km of the Paris-Roubaix route with the lads who'd been selected to ride that race the following Sunday. That day I did two training sessions—one to Roubaix with the rest of the team, then an extra 130 km when the cyclotourist who was supposed to lead me back to the team hotel from Roubaix casually slipped in, an hour or so after we set off, that my hotel was in the completely opposite direction. I ended up arriving back at the hotel with daylight fading and my fingers and thumbs bleeding from the battering they'd taken on the cobblestones that give Paris-Roubaix its nickname—"The Hell of the North."

The only "Hell" on my mind that night was how the hell my callused hands and aching legs were going to heal in time for my next race—the Grote Scheldeprijs in five days' time.

So where did we leave it? Memories, right? Memories of races. Why some races stand out as bold and solid as sculptures and others seem to fade away.

It maybe won't surprise you to learn that I often get flashbacks of sprint finishes, especially those that I won. There's a difference, though, between the memories that come spontaneously and those that have to be deliberately recalled and reconstructed. Don't ask me why, but that difference definitely exists: There are some races and some sprints that are still stuck in my body, under my skin, and others that survive only in my mind.

Weirdly, the eighth stage of the Tour de France is the only one of my four stage wins that fits into the second category. I say "weirdly" because it also happens to be the one that my teammates still talk about, laugh about, rave about. Me, I just don't remember it like I remember the other three.

One theory I have considered is that I don't remember it because I didn't *see* it very well. Ironically, given the roasting I gave our mechanic over the wheels, I also could have cost myself and the team that day by choosing the wrong lenses for my Oakley sunglasses. That morning the forecast had been pretty mixed, so it followed that I should go for a pair of lenses that catered to every type of condition. I chose "transition" lenses, the ones whose tint varies according to the light. Big mistake: As we came into the final 5 kilometers, the rainwater on the road created a glare that tricked my lenses into turning as dark and impenetrable as the eye masks they hand out on long-haul flights. I could have done without except that, when I'm sprinting, I'm so low over the handlebars—lower than pretty much any other sprinter—that on a wet day, spray from my front tire flies into my eyes and blinds me.

I ended up putting the glasses back on with around 2 kilometers to go. From behind the darkened lenses, I could see little more than flashes of color and action: Lövkvist taking over from Burghardt 2,200 meters out, a bridge with a kilometer to go, a corner at 800 meters—the kind of corner I'd usually attack at full throttle, but I crept around that day in the rain; Gerald Ciolek starting the lead-out at 500 meters, me three wheels behind, sprinting in the center of the road, winning, then seeing

Gerald's face after the finish. He was happy, but also, I sensed, wondering what it meant if he was burying himself for me and *still* finishing 2nd. After the stage, in the press conference, I didn't have to remind myself to talk up Gerald or say how proud it made me that we'd finished 1st and 2nd; deep down, without admitting it to anyone, I was thinking Gerald shouldn't have to ride another Tour de France at a teammate's beck and call.

Could two sprinters ever function harmoniously in the same team? If their names were Cavendish and Ciolek, then Stage 8 of the Tour de France proved that the answer was an emphatic "yes."

Okay, so now let's try the same question but change one of the riders: How about if their names were Cavendish and Greipel?

I daresay that Allan Peiper was asking himself the same thing on the afternoon of 17 April 2007. Allan picked me up at Roger Hammond's flat and we headed for a hotel near Antwerp, where the next stop on my comeback trail, the Grote Scheldeprijs, would start the next day. On the way, inevitably, the conversation turned to races in the previous couple of months and to Andre Greipel. I mentally chalked up a couple of brownie points when Allan told me I was looking "lean and fit."

We drove to Antwerp the next morning. Pretty early in a pro career, you can become matter-of-fact about even relatively prestigious races, but that apathy is never likely to affect me. The only thing I felt was excitement—and nerves. I'd set off for the race with Allan the previous day barely even able to pronounce or spell "Scheldeprijs," let alone talk about its importance; now, before the race, I had my teammate Servais Knaven telling me that he'd won here ten years ago and that, to local fans, it was like a Cup Final. Servais also said it was an ideal race for me. Within the space of a few minutes, I went from a feeling of mild curiosity to a chest-thumping adrenaline high.

I knew what Allan was going to say in the briefing: If the race came down to a sprint finish, which it did roughly every second year, our main man would be Andre Greipel. I didn't even flinch. I was learning fast that there were some things it just wasn't worth arguing about.

I can usually give you a fairly good idea of how I'm feeling and how the race will go within a few kilometers of the start. That day, just as I would in Stage 5 of the 2008 Tour de France, I felt amazing and made sure everyone in my team knew about it all through the day.

It was the kind of racing I loved—wind howling, breaks going, cobbles jarring, and a pace so fast that the soigneurs hadn't made it from the start in Antwerp to the feed zone in time to hand out our lunchpacks, or musettes. This actually played in my favor, as Rod had taught us at the Academy that the only people we should rely on for food in races were ourselves. Over the years, I'd devised my own personalized "meals on wheels" system, which meant that, while other riders would carry maybe the odd energy bar, then collect the rest of their food at the feed zone, I had everything I needed stuffed into my jersey pocket. My rule was that I needed one item for every 20 kilometers. I'd work back from a sachet of caffeine gel with 20 kilometers to go and 40 kilometers to go; normal gels at 60, 80, 100, and 120; and the rest would be energy bars. Each gel or bar would have a designated place in the three pockets in the back of my jersey: the middle pocket for the bars, the right-hand pocket for the normal gels, and the left-hand pocket for the caffeine gels. The logic was that not only did I more or less balance the weight, but more importantly, I wouldn't have to risk taking my right hand off the bars to reach for a caffeine gel in the last 40 kilometers, when I might be forced to brake and skid at any time.

The British Cycling Federation performance director, Dave Brailsford, is forever talking about how "the aggregation of marginal gains" is often the difference between good and excellent, winning and losing. That day at Scheldeprijs, as I watched panic turn to pandemonium when riders reached the feed zone and didn't see their soigneurs, I could see exactly what Dave B. was on about.

Earlier I mentioned the "magic" of form; unfortunately, while many riders have tried, it's almost impossible to convey just what a euphoric sensation it is to feel your body in a state of total grace, almost as if you're on a higher physical plane, where power and speed are effortless and pain . . . almost painless. I say it's impossible to convey; there may be no other cyclist in Britain who can talk with authority about winning sprints in the Tour de France but there may be hundreds of thousands, if not millions, who have experienced that magic. You can't buy it, but you can earn it; over several weeks, you build gradually toward it, yet it appears suddenly and disappears just as quickly; you can be fit or strong for fifty-two weeks of the year but, at the very most, if you're very lucky, experience two five-week bursts of "magic." As a professional cyclist, your whole life and training schedule revolve around making those five magic weeks coincide with the biggest races, your biggest objectives.

Now the magic had come from nowhere, as it always does. I'd spent the entire day near the front of the bunch, marking breaks, ducking and diving, yet my legs kept coming back for more.

Scheldeprijs finishes with three laps of a 20-km circuit; Servais Knaven had told me everything I needed to know. We entered the final lap, and Allan buzzed in for a few last checks.

"Cav, still feeling good, mate?"

"Amazing."

"Okay, everyone on the team ride for Greipel except Cav; Cav, just do your own thing, okay? So Greipel, you've got everyone working for you except Cav."

I felt a surge of adrenaline. Allan was giving me my first chance, my first real chance. In one sense I'd already won . . . but I could also lose: I may not have had the responsibility that comes when a whole team's at your disposal, but I did have the pressure that I'd brought upon myself with my none-too-subtle self-promotion.

It was easy, really: I just mustn't blow it. Yeah, right, easy—with no teammates to count on—really easy. With 3 kilometers to go, I was still coping well, on the Belgian rider Jos Pronk's wheel and even showing a bit of my mettle: at the 2.5-km mark, the road chicaned and Robbie

McEwen tried to muscle into the line. I held my ground. Robbie bounced off. Robbie McEwen is indisputably one of the best sprinters of the past fifteen years and not a man to be messed with on or off the bike. I barely knew him back then; when we talked about our little tussle later, he paid me a huge compliment: "My God, you showed some balls there. . . ."

I really thought it was all over for me at the 2-km mark. It would have been had it not been for Bernhard Eisel. Since that day, Bernie has given me many reasons to thank him, but nothing will ever make me forget the moment when, as I was on the way out of a corner with 2 kilometers to go—cut up, unclipped from one of my pedals, desperately out of position—Bernie nodded at me to follow his wheel. Bernie was rapidly dropping through the peloton, spent from his work for Greipel; yet for some reason, somehow, something possessed him when he saw me. "Come on, buddy," was all he needed to say.

Now it was all down to me.

One and a half to go. We're moving up, we're moving up. Inside the top twenty, top ten, Bernie, you're my hero. Who's that? Greipel. Concentrate, Cav. Keep moving. Past Greipel. Still top ten. Bernie's gone, but you're okay. Good, Cav, good.

One point two. One point one. Fuck. Oh, no. You're boxed in. How did that happen? You're boxed, you're boxed, there's nothing you can do. . . . You're going for a place here, 900, 800, you're still boxed, 700 . . . No! Quick Step! Weylandt! Get on it, Cav. It's Wouter Weylandt—he's leading out Gert Steegmans. Yes. You're on it, you're on it . . . Steegmans behind Weylandt, and Steegmans is going, he's going, he's going, he's gone, and now it's you and him, Cav, it's you, and your legs feel like a pair of rocket launchers, it's you and him, this is it, this is your chance, 100 to go, 50, here it fucking comes and here it is and here it fucking is and YES! YES! YES! YES! YESSSSSSS! TICK BOOM, TAKE THAT, YOU BEAUTY. . . .

I'd fucking won! I'd only gone and fucking won.

As ever, I came over the line screaming, punching the air, emotions all over the show, but really thinking just one thing: I wanted to see my teammates. Above all, I wanted to see Bernie. Ironically, the commentator on the live broadcast in Belgium had seen a rider in a magenta T-Mobile jersey come over the line in 1st place and shouted, "Eisel!" I later found out that nearly two million people had been watching the race on TV . . . on a Wednesday afternoon.

I saw Bernie. Hugged him. Hugged him so hard he almost needed neck surgery. I hugged everyone. I even hugged Greipel. That wasn't quite so heartfelt, and neither was the expression on his face when he told me, "Congratulations."

The next hour, two hours, three hours were great. As I mentioned earlier, at the Tour, a post-race press conference is normally the last place you want to be when you've just won, but that day the journalists were in danger of missing their deadlines, so long and so happily did I ramble on. Not that they minded—in fact, some of them looked as happy and excited as I did.

The text messages, the podium, the phone call to Melissa, the phone call from Aldag, from Brian—it was everything I'd expected and much, much more. A couple of weeks earlier I'd been lying in bed, despairing for my health and, to a certain extent, my future as a pro cyclist. Now I was standing on the podium with one of the greatest sprinters in the world, Robbie McEwen, on my right-hand side and 10,000 people in front of the stage, all thinking and saying the same thing: "So *this* is the new kid on the block. . . ."

There were so many things to do, so many people to talk to. Most importantly, there were people to thank. Above all of them, there was Bernie Eisel.

"Mate, I couldn't have done that without you. Thank you so, so, so much," I told Bernie as I did my rounds of the rooms that evening, telling everyone—even Greipel—how grateful I was.

"Don't worry, I was fucked anyway. . . ." He shrugged.

If I was almost overwhelmed, Bernie's reaction epitomized the bloody-minded generosity that, just over a year later, would keep me in the Tour de France.

STAGE 8: FIGEAC-TOULOUSE, 172.5 KM

1. Mark Cavendish (GBr), Team Columbia, 4:02:54 (42.61 kph)

GENERAL CLASSIFICATION

1. Kim Kirchen (Lux), Team Columbia, 32:26:34

143. Mark Cavendish (GBr), Team Columbia, 45:15

STAGE 9

Sunday, 13 July 2008
TOULOUSE–BAGNÈRES DE BIGORRE
224 KM

What does it feel like to win? Why do people want and need that feeling so badly? What makes it so beautiful and necessary that, on Stage 9 of the Tour de France, Riccardo Riccò was willing to take drugs, endanger his health, and risk a prison sentence just for a taste of that oh-so-special something?

I can only speak for myself, of course, and by now you might be taking with a grain of salt the opinions of a guy who seems to live his life on an emotional tightrope. Why would you take the word of someone like that for anything? Or the word of any 23-year-old, for that matter? And is it not just obvious, the more stories I tell, that, just as Lance Armstrong's manager said about him, my will to win comes purely from anger and resentment?

If you really are asking yourself that, then I must have done something wrong. By now, I hope you'll see that, with me, any anger or resentment that boils over in the heat of the moment has less to do with winning than with losing. When I say I'm a natural-born winner, that's not exactly what I mean; what I really mean is that I can't stand, can't tolerate, can't abide losing.

The nature of professional cycling is such that you'll always lose more than you win. In 2008, I won more elite races—seventeen—than any other rider but that still worked out to less than one win for every six days of racing. Most riders, and especially nonsprinters, are happy to finish the season with two or three wins.

Given what I've just said about hating losing, you might say I'm in the wrong sport. Maybe. But when I talk about losing, what I really mean is losing a sprint when I've been in position to win. And even then, the big issue isn't losing in the sense of missing out on the egotistical act of crossing the line in a blaze of glory. That's a shame, but that isn't what keeps me up all night.

I'm not exaggerating: When I lose a sprint, it stops me from sleeping at night, because of the guilt I feel at having let down my teammates. That guilt eats me alive. I can't stress this enough: It *eats me alive*. If you can call that feeling of shame and self-hatred a motivation, then I very definitely am in the right sport because a fear of those emotions allows me to do things that an SRM power meter or a rig test tells you I shouldn't be capable of. Every sprint I lose gets replayed over and over in my head until every little mistake has been deconstructed and mentally corrected for the next time. I said earlier that Simon Jones's perfectionism about the team pursuit became an obsession; what I didn't mention is that when it comes to losing sprints, I'm almost as bad. It's no coincidence that if I don't win a sprint and I'm to blame, 99 times out of 100 I'll win the next one.

Both Scheldeprijs in 2007 and the whole of the 2008 Tour perfectly illustrated my point about not losing being more of an incentive than winning. At Scheldeprijs, I simply couldn't allow myself to lose after what Bernhard Eisel had done for me in those last 2 kilometers. In the same way, halfway through the Tour, I looked at the faces in the team bus or at the dinner table and saw the physical and mental toll of hours spent not just finishing every grueling day but also acting as my personal butlers— driving at the front to pull back breakaways, chaperoning me through the bunch, fetching my water bottles. By Stage 9, Marcus Burghardt, the teammate whose commitment I'd questioned the previous year, looked ill, positively sallow. The guy was 150th on general classification, an hour and eleven minutes behind Kim, who was in the yellow jersey and had all sorts of pressures of his own to deal with. Every single thing that Marcus had done all Tour, he'd done for me, Kim, or the team.

You may say my motivation *can't* come solely from a selfless need to repay my teammates. You're right: There does need to be another driving force, a hunger, an element of ego, because otherwise you'd be nuts to take on the burden. If it's true to say that a Tour stage win can change a rider's life, then it can also mean thousands of pounds in bonuses for his teammates as well as a priceless sense of gratification. That's a lot to gain but also a lot to lose on a teammate's behalf.

Certain other riders who are far more talented than I am just don't seem to want this responsibility. I've often wondered about this in my old mates from the Academy, Ed Clancy and Geraint Thomas. Both are unbelievably talented, unbelievably loyal, unbelievably skilled, yet so far have achieved plenty on the track but much less than me on the road. This is partly because they're not out-and-out sprinters or mountain climbers or time trialists and therefore have to be a bit more creative when it comes to carving out their opportunities; basically, they have to win in breakaways. But that doesn't explain everything. Rod says I'm wrong—that I shouldn't expect other riders to have my drive, my need, that I'm almost unique in that sense. While I know what he means, it doesn't stop me from getting frustrated. I don't get annoyed for myself but because I'm desperate to see those lads fulfill their potential.

Gee rides for the South African–sponsored team Barloworld. Like Ed, he's one of the best team pursuit riders in the world. They both won gold medals in the team pursuit in Beijing. In 2007, when I'd already started winning races, I told Gee I'd love to have him with me at T-Mobile and that we could build a career together on the same team. I told him not to renew his contract with Barloworld until he'd spoken to me. A few weeks or months later, one day, matter-of-factly, he mentioned that he'd re-signed with Barloworld. When I asked him why, he said it was because he wouldn't be guaranteed selection for the Tour with T-Mobile. Good enough reason, right?

You see, this is where I struggle. Rod would say Gee is building a good career with Barloworld and that he's happy, which is true, but I still struggle. I said to Gee at the time, "Hang on, you say that you wouldn't be guaranteed a start at the Tour with T-Mobile, but do you think I was guaranteed to start the Tour when I joined T-Mobile? Of course I wasn't. On paper I didn't have a hope in hell of making the team. I had to make sure I was picked. . . ." What I didn't also point out, but I will now, is that it made no sense whatsoever to just "go" to the Tour; if I went, it'd be to pursue a dream, to win, to work to guarantee success. Why go with a modest team? Why not go with the best team? Again, Rod would say I shouldn't expect other people to have the same mentality as me. Unfortunately, that doesn't make it any easier for me to understand *why* their mentality isn't a bit more like mine, especially as we're talking about riders at least as naturally talented as me—if not more.

I suppose I make the same mistake as a lot of people: When I talk about talent, I instinctively think only in terms of physical potential. Now, Ed is a guy with phenomenal physical potential; in rig tests he's especially phenomenal. But he'll be the first to admit that he "can't" race on the road, although he's actually a lot better than he thinks. Part of his problem is tactical, so once, at the Academy, I thought I'd try to help him by teaching him how to play chess and, later, speed chess, in the hope that it'd improve his decision-making under pressure. Ed's a smart lad and a fast learner. He was such a fast learner, in fact, that before long he was beating me. Needless to say, that was when I stopped playing.

So Ed's problem clearly isn't intelligence or talent. What is it, then, if indeed it is a problem? I just ask myself whether Ed doesn't lack another type of hunger that Geraint possesses in spades—the ability to *suffer*.

Throughout this book I've made reference to pain. What I haven't explained so far is that there's a difference between hurting yourself and suffering. A track sprinter like Chris Hoy can hurt himself more than any road rider, but he doesn't suffer; for about one minute—the maximum duration of his full-on effort in a keirin or a team sprint or an individual sprint, Chris can go 110 percent into his reserves, but ask him to go at 80 percent for ten minutes and he can't do it. It's the same with Ed; as a pursuiter, he should be the opposite of Chris, but actually, I think Ed can hurt himself like a sprinter, though not suffer like a road rider. Ed thinks he can suffer, but I don't think he can. I hope he'll prove me wrong one day, but at the moment, I think Ed needs more hunger if he's going to succeed on the road.

To me, it's all interlinked—hunger, the ability to suffer, the hatred of losing—and the thread that weaves those things together is passion. When you have passion, the ability to suffer is automatic. Suffering can't be measured in the laboratory; it's not a physiological state you enter when you go over a certain heart rate or power output; it's not knowing your limits and pushing them—it's riding and hurting as much as it takes to get you over a mountain and inside the time cutoff in the Tour de France; it's riding and hurting as much as it takes to earn you the success that your passion makes you crave.

As for where my passion comes from, who knows? Part of it is the snowball effect of success, which makes you more and more motivated and more and more passionate the more you achieve. You start to develop an image of yourself as the "best"—whether it's in maths lessons at school or in the last 100 meters of a bike race. You succeed simply because you're passionate, and you become more passionate because you succeed.

And yeah, a big part of it is ego. I do crave that success for myself, not just for my teammates. I don't do it for the money or even the adulation; otherwise I'd have focused on the track, which is a much surer route to fame in Britain. I do it above all because I'm passionate about riding my bike and leaving my mark on races that, for generations before mine, have captured the passion and imagination of millions: the Tour de France, the Giro d'Italia, Paris-Roubaix, Milan–San Remo. . . .

I also do what I do, suffer like I suffer, because I know that, while losing is a nightmare, winning is an addiction. I love winning because

I love the pride that comes from knowing how much I've worked, how much my teammates have worked, how much I and they have sacrificed.

How Riccardo Riccò could have hoped to feel even vaguely similar to what I'd felt twenty-four hours earlier—while knowing that his were false sacrifices, that his was false suffering—I have absolutely no idea.

STAGE 9: TOULOUSE–BAGNÈRES DE BIGORRE, 224 KM

1. Riccardo Riccò (Ita), Saunier Duval–Scott, 5:39:28 (39.59 kph)
150. Mark Cavendish (GBr), Team Columbia, 28:11

GENERAL CLASSIFICATION

1. Kim Kirchen (Lux), Team Columbia, 38:07:19
151. Mark Cavendish (GBr), Team Columbia, 1:12:09

STAGE 10

Monday, 14 July 2008
PAU-HAUTACAM
156 KM

Have you ever experienced that feeling of waking from a nightmare and being so engrossed in your imaginary car crash, science exam, or God knows what other disaster that it takes a few seconds for reality and relief to set in? When you're a professional cyclist, and specifically a Tour de France rider, that waking fear can be a daily occurrence, with one very crucial difference—that very often you open your eyes to the realization that the true nightmare is the one due to begin in four or five hours' time. So it was that, on the morning of Bastille Day 2008, I woke to a mountain, or rather two mountains, of dread: the immense Pyrenean climbs of Stage 10 of the Tour de France.

They say the devil you know is better than the devil you don't, but I'm not sure that applies when it comes to dragging yourself and your bike over roads that were never made for cyclists. I'd ridden and suffered in the Pyrenees before, but how that was going to help me now, I couldn't quite see. The first climb on the day's route was the infamous Col du Tourmalet—the first Pyrenean climb ever visited by the Tour, ninety-nine years ago, 2,115 meters above sea level and 17.5 kilometers of guaranteed torture. The second was the even more ominous-sounding 15.8-km climb to Hautacam, the ski resort above Lourdes. No wonder I woke up nervous.

I said I'd suffered in the Pyrenees before; that's an understatement. In May 2007, my T-Mobile managers told me I'd been selected for the Tour of Catalunya but might as well have said they were sending me to a weeklong School for Suffering. Catalunya was part of the International Cycling Union (UCI) ProTour series of races—a new and controversial grouping of the sport's toughest and most prestigious events. ProTour races were different from the others in that the leading eighteen teams in the world were guaranteed and obliged to take part; it followed that the level of competition was also higher. When we'd originally discussed my racing schedule in the autumn of 2006, it had been agreed that Catalunya would be too hard and too hilly to take on so early in my pro career, but now my breakthrough in Scheldeprijs and two more wins at the Four Days of Dunkirk had forced a rapid reassessment. My directeur sportif at Dunkirk, Brian Holm, had told Rolf Aldag that he'd seen experienced, established members of the team flogging themselves on my behalf, in the pissing rain, with a commitment he'd rarely encountered.

Before skipping ahead to Catalunya, it's worth a short detour to explain how my ongoing power struggle with my teammate Andre Greipel had continued at the GP Denain, the day after Scheldeprijs. Denain is a fairly low-key, pan-flat French race that is made complicated by the fact that it's part of the French Cup—another season-long competition, a parochial and less glitzy version of the ProTour, featuring races that are open to teams of all nationalities but in which only French teams can score points that count toward a league table. All French races are chaotic and tactically disorganized; French Cup races are worse because the French teams don't give each other an inch.

There'd been shocking and brilliant news in the briefing that morning: If the race finished in a sprint, which it usually did, Cavendish and not Greipel would be the man. The other instruction was that we'd put a man in any break of four riders or more—in other words, in any break that had a chance of staying away until the finish. Any group with fewer than four riders would have almost no chance of outriding a peloton of more than a hundred; if a larger group went clear and we had a man in there, we'd have the option of that man collaborating with his breakaway companions, then hopefully beating them in the sprint, or of refusing to work with them, whereupon they'd be forced to call it quits. These were just commonsense tactics.

The race started, and with it the attacks. Lots of attacks—most of them brainless. I marked one or two of the breakaways, but mostly I just sat toward the back, soaking up all the plaudits from other riders for my win in Scheldeprijs. There was only one thing that was more out of control than the race, and that was my ego.

After a while, teammates started dropping back to ask me why I wasn't chasing. I explained: The breakaway groups that were forming contained riders from maybe two or three of the French teams, and we could rely on the French teams that weren't represented to chase them back. Soon I went back to the team car to tell Allan the same thing; I wasn't prepared to waste energy just for the sake of it. The previous evening, when I'd thanked him for handing me my first real opportunity to prove myself at Scheldeprijs, he'd said he was full of admiration for the way I'd seized that chance. Now I was trying to dictate to him how he should run the team. It was the equivalent of an 18-year-old striker who'd just scored his first goal for Manchester United trotting over to the touchline twenty minutes into the next match to tell Sir Alex Ferguson that 4-4-2 was the wrong formation.

Predictably, it all ended messily. We caught the break *on* the finish line, when the riders who had formed that break were spread across the road. The sprinters in the main pack, me included, were left to sprint in the only available space—up the gutter. I couldn't squeeze through. I finished 11th.

By now, the post-race routine was well rehearsed: I'd arrive at the team bus, climb off my bike, take a drink . . . then turn around and have to fend off Greipel. Today was no different.

"Cav, you don't do any work like the others. You save yourself so that you're fresh for the sprint. . . ." Greipel ranted.

"Oh, I get it," I said, smiling sarcastically. "So you're kicking off now. You think that's why I beat you yesterday—that I didn't do anything until the sprint, and you think I did the same thing today. Why am I going to waste energy chasing moves that are going nowhere? Just because you're fucking stupid, and you're going to chase, it's not my problem."

And so it went on. Again. For the third time this season—at the end of a race, in public. And just like the previous three occasions, it was left to Allan to step in.

This time, he said, I was in the wrong. "Cav, be quiet. I told you that you had to ride, and you didn't ride."

"Allan, I don't understand," I replied. "I'm going to argue with you when I don't agree. . . ."

Allan's last word on the matter was just that—final. "But Cav, I'm the directeur, and you have to listen to me."

On that, on reflection, he was absolutely right.

One of the outcomes of my successes in Scheldeprijs and at Dunkirk was a shift in schedule for both me and Greipel. He'd originally been penciled in for the Tour of Catalunya in Spain, and I was scheduled for the Dauphine Libéré in France, but my fast-rising stock had forced our directeurs sportifs into a rethink. I'd now do Catalunya at the end of May, and Greipel would be our sprinter at the Dauphine a fortnight later.

I've already referred to Catalunya as a weeklong School for Suffering, and I'd prepared myself for the agony with a week in the hills of Tuscany in Italy. Immediately after Dunkirk, when I heard I'd been picked for Catalunya, I'd phoned Rod Ellingworth to ask if I could spend a few days training with the new Academy lads, who were now based in Italy. Rod told me I was more than welcome. One epic 200-kilometer ride, in particular, turned out to be an unlikely morale boost: On the first of five climbs, the only kid in a pro-team kit (i.e., me) was dropped like a fag packet; on the second, I was better; on the third, I wasn't the worst; on the fourth, I was one of the best; and on the fifth and final climb, I was leaving the others behind. Five months into my pro career, I was already going longer and stronger, just like the races I was now riding.

Catalunya was always going to be a major test. Not only was it to be my first ProTour event and my longest pro stage race to date at seven days long, it was also to be my first real brush with some of the best climbers in the world on their terrain—the mountains, and more specifically the Pyrenees. A few weeks had been all I'd needed to figure out that on the plains and even short, steep hills of northern France and Belgium, I could more than hold my own. That was all well and good, but if I ever wanted to thrive on the sport's grandest stages—and in the Tour de France in particular—I needed a few lessons in how to survive the mountains.

The first stage was a team time trial. My teammates thought I'd be, well, shit—mainly because a lot of people still don't understand that a team time trial is really just everyone on the team taking it in turns to sprint, as in a team pursuit. Anyway, we finished well down the rankings, with me one of the strongest men in a mediocre team performance. Those sessions with Rod and the Academy lads seemed to have paid dividends; I confirmed that the next day, on Stage 2, when I amazed everyone, including myself, by winning a steep uphill sprint. You may remember the amusing subplot to that win from earlier in the book: Filippo Pozzato, our slanging match on the finish line, my "amateurish" descending, then my brilliant but foul-mouthed riposte: "Not bad for an amateur, am I? Now, fuck off!"

Not bad indeed. Stage 2 had featured two tough climbs, and I'd not just survived but won. Now I began the marginally more mountainous Stage 3 in the green jersey awarded to the leader of the points competition with renewed confidence and the renewed confidence of my teammates. That was the problem: So impressed had Valerio Piva and

Jan Schaffrath, my directeurs sportifs, been that on the last climb of the day, the Alt de Fores, they wanted the whole team on the front, reining in the climbers. The tactic was as old as the hills we were riding over; by setting a brisk but steady pace, my team could discourage the kind of constant, violent attacks that suited the climbers but would have me gagging and out the back.

The secret was finding a tempo that was not too fast, not too slow. Famous last words! We hit the bottom of the climb, and my team-mates surged to the front. Way too quickly. Before I knew it, I was disappearing out the rear end of the bunch as what looked like a giant, magenta-colored caterpillar—but was actually half-a-dozen of my team-mates—wound its way up the mountain. "Oi, guys, slow down! Slow down," I screamed, but by the time two of my teammates dropped back to rescue me, it was too late. Not only that, but the news had already spread through the peloton like a forest fire: Cavendish was struggling. Within seconds one of my rival sprinters, Baden Cooke, had ordered his teammates to the front of the peloton to up the pace and twist the knife. Remember what I said about me and Francesco Chicchi on Stage 7 of the Tour de France—the sprinters' union and all that? Told you it was a load of rubbish, didn't I?

I scraped through to the finish, hot and very bothered, something not helped by the fact that the green points jersey was the only one of the prize jerseys that had a short zip. Small mercies—I'd at least lost the jersey for the next stage; I'd need all the help I could get on what was a monster of a stage through the southern Pyrenees and finishing 2,000 meters above sea level. Again it was swelteringly hot, but I felt good. So good that I made it safely over the first climb and, in my relief and quiet delight, announced that I was going back to the team car to fetch water bottles for the whole team.

I headed back to the car. Took the bottles. Stuffed a few in my pockets, a couple under my jersey, and two in the bottle cages on my bike. It was around then that I noticed an unpleasant and familiar sensation: The road was climbing. On the route map it didn't say that the road should be climbing, not now, not already, but it definitely was. It was steep as well. And long. And I was weighed down with about five liters of water. And pretty soon, the full horror of what was happening started to hit me—at about the same time as the vision of the peloton inching up the mountain and out of sight.

Oh, fucking terrific. I had 130 kilometers still to ride, 35-degree heat, three climbs topping out at over 1,000 meters, and then the final, horrific slog up to Andorra. Plus I was alone—or nearly—because soon I'd clawed my way back to another rider who was gasping almost as much as me: the Belgian Dominique Cornu of the Lotto team. It's at times like these that you learn the first lesson of suffering in the mountains: Nationality, the logo on the other guy's jersey, whether you speak the same language—none of it matters one iota. The single important bond is the need to survive. To do that, you need to share the workload, with each man taking turns at the front and taking the brunt of the wind, share support, and even share food and drink. Now I glanced at Cornu, and he glanced back at me: We were both ready to be joined in unholy agony.

We reached the top of the evil, unmarked climb, then hurled ourselves down the other side at 70 or maybe 80 kph. We could see the peloton below us and were even edging closer when another disaster struck: I skidded on some gravel and went sprawling into a ditch. I stood up, dusted myself off, wiped the blood from my cuts, then hopped back on my bike and set off after Cornu. When I caught him shortly afterward, he asked me whether I was going to give up, as he was stopping. I shook my head: There may have been 100 kilometers to go, four mountains and an even bigger metaphorical one to climb, but quitting races wasn't my style. I was going to make it to Andorra or die trying.

I could go on and describe the full, excruciating torment of the next three hours, but, rather like the magic of form or the ecstasy of winning, a lot would be lost in translation. Suffice it to say that I'll never forget those three hours, and neither will our team mechanic Pedro. With our directeurs otherwise engaged behind the front of the race, it was left to him to follow and cajole me. I never pay any attention to the SRM meter that sits on my handlebars and measures the power going into each pedal stroke—but I did that day; together with Pedro, it was all that got me through. I decided on a target wattage and cocooned myself in the pursuit of that number. To my eternal gratitude and disbelief, a much more important pursuit ended when I saw, then finally rejoined, the gruppetto on the climb up to Andorra.

It was hard to judge which was more of a triumph: my win on Stage 2 or the test of physical or mental endurance that I'd passed two days later. The team, too, seemed undecided. Kim Kirchen was thrilled with me. Professional cyclists pride themselves on just how much pain they can endure, and anyone who rides over 100 kilometers of a mountain stage, most of them alone, can expect serious kudos. Winning a sprint, or even winning a sprint at the end of a hilly day like Stage 2, might prove my talent; finishing a brutal mountain stage had shown my resilience. A victory could bring adulation; survival brought something more valuable—admiration and respect.

After a mountain time trial on Stage 5, again up to Andorra, there would be more mountains, more suffering, and more confirmation of my growing stature on day six. That stage again started with a long climb. Again I was left behind, but this time at least I wasn't alone. I also had Jan Schaffrath imploring from the team car, "Don't give up. Whatever you do, don't give up!" It took a descent that would have made the skier Bode Miller wince to cancel our two-minute deficit and bring me back to the peloton.

It started raining. I remember that I was putting on my rain cape when I found myself riding next to David Millar. Funny—a year earlier, practically to the week, we'd been riding up a mountain in Italy, arguing about whether I'd ever cut it as a professional. As I recalled in the chapter dedicated to Stage 4, Dave had said much the same things as the former pro Max Sciandri a few days earlier, namely, that if I wanted to make the grade, I should eat better, train better, and generally liven up my act. I'd replied that I'd do all of those things *when* I started riding as a stagiaire with T-Mobile at the end of the year. But *only* then. In the end, we'd agreed to disagree.

Now Dave said he wanted to congratulate me for the way I'd ridden throughout the week. I thanked him and asked him if he remembered our conversation a year earlier. He said he owed me not just congratulations but also an apology—"a massive, massive apology." "I was so, so wrong about you," he said. "You told me that you'd step up, and you have. Cav, you were completely right, and you've been a phenomenon this season."

Comments like this could be as gratifying as any trophy or prize jersey or stage win. For the record, if Dave was impressed with me, then I was impressed with Dave; it's a rare sportsman who can overrule his ego and admit he was wrong.

On the same day, 6 kilometers from the finish line, bodies tumbled and I was caught behind the pileup. Within a minute or two, I'd shot out of what was now the third group back, joined the second group, then attacked again to catch the front group with 800 meters to go. Now I relied on the homework I'd done the previous night—to be precise, the mental note I'd made to go wide on the last, 90-degree left-hander with 300 meters to go, then launch my sprint as I swung back into the middle of the road. It worked brilliantly: The four or five riders ahead of me all overshot the bend, leaving me to blast through on their inside and take my second stage win.

Perhaps the most arduous but also rewarding week of my cycling career ended the next day with yet another hilltop finish that cost me victory in the green jersey competition. It didn't matter. I'd spent a week at the School of Suffering and passed every exam; I was now ready for the race where the best, toughest professional riders had all studied and graduated with honors. I was ready for the Tour de France.

The next day, I turned on the computer and wrote the e-mail reproduced at the front of the book. As you all now know, that letter requested a place in the Tour de France and a license to suffer some more—much, much more.

I couldn't have been happier when the request was granted.

When, several years from now, cycling fans and historians recall Stage 10 of the Tour de France, sadly it's not heroes of whom they'll reminisce but a cast of villains headed by the Italian Leonardo Piepoli. Like his younger compatriot Riccardo Riccò two days earlier, at Hautacam, the 36-year-old Piepoli seemed to confound gravity, logic, and our intelligence not just to win but to annihilate all opposition except his Spanish teammate Juan José Cobo. It was only several months later, when the French antidoping agency reexamined Piepoli's drug and urine samples that our suspicions about Piepoli's performance at Hautacam were confirmed. Like Riccò's at Super Besse and Bagnères de Bigorre, Piepoli's supersonic climbing had been fueled by a new, banned wonder drug called CERA.

That really was one of the tragedies of Piepoli's conniving, and indeed of all drug scandals—they overshadowed the real heroes. One such hero, without any doubt, was my teammate Bernhard Eisel.

Bernie is our team's equivalent of Prozac—he's permanently smiling and laughing, so more often than not, the rest of us also smile and laugh. I'm almost certain that the guy was born with a muscular condition that makes it impossible for him to look unhappy.

As I also mentioned earlier, Bernie had been signed to the team at the beginning of 2007, expecting to be the number-one sprinter in what was and still is the world's number-one team. I'd ruined that plan somewhat, but Bernie remained a highly talented rider who could win sprints and also wreak havoc on the cobblestones in races like Paris-Roubaix and the Tour of Flanders. On that tenth stage of the 2008 Tour to Hautacam, he was about to prove yet again that in the department of loyalty, there was simply no one better.

There was one good thing about that stage—the fact that it came immediately after a rest day. "Rest day" is a relative term at the Tour, as usually the twenty-four hours of "respite" are chockablock with media engagements, massages, sessions with the chiropractor, and—believe it or not—a short training session.

Having Melissa around that afternoon was a rare luxury. As I explained earlier, she'd left the race on the morning of my first stage win but had now come back for another flying visit. That afternoon we had a great time, just lying on the bed and chatting—and no, that's not meant to be a euphemism. Incidentally, on the same topic, after the Giro d'Italia, Riccardo Riccò was asked whether he'd "indulged" with his girlfriend on the two rest days of that race. Riccò had stared into the camera, given the watching public a weaselly smirk, and replied, "Let's just say that I did what I had to do. . . ."

Classy guy. He'll be sorely missed during his two-year doping ban.

What I said about my waking fear on the morning of Stage 10 was all true. The previous year, Catalunya had proved my durability as much to myself as anyone else, but it's a little like any scenario when you feel yourself driven to the brink of psychological despair, physical breakdown, or even, I suppose, death: Just because you've survived once doesn't mean that you'd relish the prospect of trying again, and neither does it guarantee that you'll make it through the next time. I'll talk later about how the mountains I'd encountered and overcome at the Giro d'Italia in May were steeper and harder than their equivalents at the Tour, but everyone in cycling knows it's the riders and not the route that make the race. The Tour was faster, more intense, more frightening than the Giro. The flat stages of the first week were *much* faster, *much* more intense, *much* more frightening. At the Tour, you were more tired when you reached the mountains. As I've explained more than once already, there was also just more of everything at the Tour—more adrenaline, more pressure, more fans at the roadside, more riders experiencing their "magic" moment of form . . . above all, there was just more *speed*.

Sure enough, the race started fast. Extraordinarily fast. To the spectator watching on TV, the best gauge of how quickly a peloton is moving is the helicopter shot from above: A slow-moving bunch is also a short, fat one; the quicker a peloton is moving, the more it resembles a long, skinny, venomous snake slithering across the earth.

In the first half hour of this stage, we had ourselves one very long, thin, angry, and above all fast-moving snake.

We sped past the 20-kilometer mark. To say you're "comfortable" in a group of 170 riders hammering along at a pace liable to set speed cameras clicking can only ever be somewhere between wishful and delusional. As I've said before, though, everything at the Tour is relative; I was as "comfortable" as I could hope to be on a 156-km stage, featuring two mammoth climbs, ten days into the Tour de France.

It'd take me several hours and the eyewitness accounts of numerous other riders to work out what happened next. Apparently, one of the police motorbike riders ahead of the race had seen a water bottle in the middle of the road and tried to kick it away but sliced his clearance in my direction. All I knew was that I ended up on the tarmac. And that it hurt. A lot. And that my bike was in bits. It was a bad time to have made my way to the front of the peloton, as now I'd have to wait for the entire race to swish past for my team car to arrive with a new bike. Not only that, but my teammate Adam Hansen had just punctured. This meant that our team car was even farther back, attending to Adam. On a day like today, the last thing I needed was a starting handicap before we even arrived at the mountains.

Usually, at times like these the race referees, or commissaires, who follow the race in the convoy would be sympathetic; it's widely accepted that a rider who has crashed or had a mechanical problem should be allowed to use the slipstream of the team cars lined out behind the bunch to help him regain touch. He just mustn't physically *hang on to* those cars. Here at the Tour, due to a political dispute between the Tour organizers and the UCI, the commissaires had been provided by the French Cycling Federation and seemed to view the Tour as their own personal three-week power jaunt. As I started to move up through the cars, the commissaires started to wag accusatory fingers at me. Fortunately, to a man, the directeurs sportifs in the team cars took no notice and raised no objections as I moved from bumper to bumper and finally back on the peloton.

I'd already accomplished a minor miracle. The peloton was still lined out, and by rights, I should have seen it for the last time shortly after my crash. The last thing I needed now, as I sat in last position, trying to catch my breath, was crosswinds. But crosswinds were exactly what I was about to get.

The wind started howling at 90 degrees to the road, and to counteract it, for shelter, riders moved alongside rather than behind the rider directly in front. The problem with this strategy was that there was only so much room for riders to fan across the road. The unsatisfactory outcome, as always, was that instead of one long line, the group now disintegrated into several short, diagonal rows, or "echelons." The other problem with this strategy was that the bloke at the very back—me—found himself riding harder just to stay in touch than the rider leading the remnants of the peloton, several hundred meters up the road.

The fall hadn't just hurt my morale. My body was a smorgasbord of cuts that needed urgent attention from the race doctor. Dropping back to the doctor's car in the midst of crosswind hell would have been akin to suicide, but as soon as the gusts eased, I went back to ask for dressing for a deep cut on my left arm and a painkiller. Usually, with the body under such intense stress, you ask for something to calm your stomach and help absorb the painkiller, but for some reason, this time, I forgot. We hadn't yet hit the foot of the Tourmalet, but my legs were already protesting, and so, suddenly, was my rear end.

At least today wasn't hot. And at least I had Bernhard Eisel. Was I glad to see Bernie. Usually, in stages like this, he'd be driving the autobus, seeing to it that not only he but also all of the stragglers made it to Hautacam inside the time limit. He'd forsaken that duty to wait for me. My rival for the title of worst climber in the Tour, Francesco Chicchi, tagged along. Not content with putting his own race in jeopardy or with pacing me all the way to the summit, Bernie now told me to take a drink, then hand him my water bottles. I looked at him, confused. He told me to hand them over. I then registered: He was insisting on carrying my drinks as well as his own just to save me the half kilo or so in weight that might be the difference between us sneaking inside the time limit and packing our bags that evening.

We asked for a time check from Allan Peiper in the team car behind. Fifteen minutes. Uh-oh. We reckoned that the time limit might be twenty-five minutes, half an hour at a push. That left us ten, or at most fifteen, minutes to play with. We would be hard-pressed not to lose all of that time on the climb to Hautacam, and before that, there were 18 kilometers of valley road into a headwind, where we'd be at a huge numerical disadvantage. There was only one way, one place to make the sums add up, and that was on the descent off the Tourmalet.

As an amateur, I used to like descending. Who wouldn't? There aren't many more satisfying feelings than bombing down what's effectively a giant toboggan run, a mountain vista unraveling in front of you, the wind whistling around your ears, the bike and your body in sync, on the edge of control. But that was then; since turning professional, descending had become my least favorite part of the job because of situations like this. Try taking a car to the top of a climb like the Tourmalet and racing a Tour de France peloton, and by the time you've reached the bottom two or maybe three minutes after the cyclists, you'll have an appreciation for how fast and how fearlessly pro bikers go downhill. Then imagine someone beating the peloton by two or three minutes—and your car by six minutes—not because it's fun, not because he can, but out of bare, brutal necessity. Imagine that and you'll just have imagined exactly what Bernhard Eisel, Francesco Chicchi, and I had to do that day.

This is what frustrates me about the general perception of sprinters. Some people don't understand—they think sprinters coast through every stage, then, on a few selected, relatively flat days, mosey up to the front of the peloton in the last kilometer and actually have to *try* for about 200 meters. They don't realize that on a flat day, climbers and all-rounders can spend the entire time coasting along in the peloton, whereas my stress levels are sky-high for the last 50 kilometers. I'm putting out 1,400 watts in the last 300 meters, but I'm doing 700 watts for the last 3 kilometers, which is akin to riding an individual pursuit on the track, having just done 200 kilometers on the road, with no break. That's a flat day. On a "medium," or "rolling," day, there's always a chance that it'll be a bunch sprint, so I'm constantly fighting to stay at the front and make it over the climbs, not only in the last 50 kilometers but throughout the stage. On a mountain day, then, I'm so ill-suited to climbing that I'm struggling to even make and stay in the gruppetto. Most pros in the peloton don't envy sprinters. It's nuts, the pressure we're under. It's nuts . . . and I wouldn't swap it for any job in the world.

We screeched into every hairpin, almost literally brushing the mountainside. The kick out of every corner was a bunch sprint—same power output, same heart rate, just 20 kilometers per hour quicker. We all reached the bottom, exhausted from the effort and the stress, then had to start all over again with what would effectively be an 18-kilometer team time trial through the valley, into the headwind. Chicchi would sprint on the front for twenty seconds, then it'd be my turn, then, finally, Bernie would hit the front and stay there for two whole minutes while Chicchi and I gathered our forces for the next desperate thrust.

The gruppetto was now about a minute away. The front group, the real race, was much, much farther up the road, but one TV motorbike was still hovering close by to capture what was in danger of becoming the "other" big story of the day—Cavendish missing the time cut. Any attempt we now made to shelter in the cars would be caught on screen and the message relayed to the commissaires.

Cav, just a bit more, a bit more . . . but my arm's killing me, and my leg and my stomach . . . No . . . blank it out . . . a few more efforts . . . get in the gruppetto, then you'll be all right . . . gotta survive . . . gotta stay positive . . . gotta keep pushing . . .

The voice in my head was interrupted by Allan Peiper's from the team car. "Come on, guys, it's touch and go whether we make this time limit. . . ."

I love Allan, love him to bits, but how was that comment helpful now? "Allan, fuck off!" I spat.

As he drove off, I realized I'd been out of order. I'd apologize later that evening.

We skirted Lourdes, hoping for a miracle, then round the back of the town and on to the climb. The crowds were now three or four deep at the side of the road, a lot in Lycra, having ridden here, and a lot in the latter stages of inebriation. Some strange law of geology or road-building dictates that the first kilometer of a climb is often the steepest, and Hautacam was no different. The pedals were hardly turning. I realized why: I'd changed my bike after the crash and been given a rear wheel with twenty-three teeth on the biggest sprocket. It should have been twenty-five; the gear was too big, too hard to push. Apparently there were no wheels with a twenty-five sprocket in the car. Again, as on Stage 8 to Toulouse, I was furious. These were exactly the kind of simple organizational errors that could cost us races or riders in the Tour de France, and that Bob Stapleton wanted eradicated.

A kilometer from the top of the climb, we still didn't know whether we were going to make the time limit. Bernie had led me all the way up the mountain. I couldn't tell you much about the crowds, the weather, or the atmosphere that day simply because my head was drooped over the handlebars, my eyes were glued to the asphalt, and my senses were completely numb. At one point on the climb, riders who had long since crossed the line started passing us in the opposite direction. Their team buses were all waiting in a car park back at the foot of the climb; those guys would be watching replays of Piepoli's big charade on the TVs in their team buses by the time we made it to the summit.

This was turning into the first really bad day of the Tour for the team. Up ahead, Kim had lost the yellow jersey to Cadel Evans. Now we were also in danger of losing two riders. The gruppetto would have meant certain salvation—today's laughing group was sixty strong—and the Tour organizers always bent the rules when a group that size was at risk of elimination. But two riders—well, what were two riders? Even if one of them was a double stage winner.

We crept around the final bend, lurched up the final ramp to the finish line, still not knowing. The giant stopwatch above the finish line said 34 minutes and 55 seconds had passed since Piepoli had crossed the line. . . . Was it too much? As I collapsed into our soigneur's arms, I didn't even have the energy to ask.

The next person I saw was Dave Millar. Suddenly, I remembered the Garmin water bottle I'd seen lying close to the spot where I'd fallen a few hours earlier. "Dave, your team's a fucking bunch of menaces," I snapped.

That would make it two apologies I'd owe that night—one to Allan Peiper and one to Dave Millar. To Bernie Eisel, quite simply, I'd owe my thanks for keeping me in the Tour de France.

STAGE 10: PAU-HAUTACAM, 156 KM

1. Leonardo Piepoli (Ita), Saunier Duval–Scott, 4:19:27 (36.08 kph)

169. Mark Cavendish (GBr), Team Columbia, 34:55

GENERAL CLASSIFICATION

1. Cadel Evans (Aus), Silence-Lotto, 42:29:09

158. Mark Cavendish (GBr), Team Columbia, 1:44:41

STAGE 11

Wednesday, 16 July 2008
LANNEMEZAN-FOIX
167.5 KM

Maybe I was one notable exception to the rule, but there can surely be few environments that require a young man to grow up as quickly as the rough-and-tumble world of professional cycling. The traveling, the hierarchies, the responsibilities—as a 21- or 22-year-old rookie, you don't have to visit a velodrome to find yourself on a fast track to maturity.

"Immature" or "arrogant"? Which of those adjectives have I seen used to describe me more often? I now do my best not to look at Internet forums, but sometimes I can't help myself. Melissa's the same—except, if anything, she gets more upset. A lot of the comments that you could qualify as "professional criticism" just make me laugh: I call myself "fat," but that's a tongue-in-cheek way of conveying that I'm not as superhumanly skinny as some of my peers; when armchair fans employ the same term and really *mean it*, I just think it's risible. The personal stuff is much more offensive. When I hear that I'm a "jumped-up little shit," it's not the insult that bothers me so much as the fact that its author is basing that assessment on two minutes of edited TV coverage when the microphone's been thrust in my face seconds after the end of an ordeal like the one I just described at Hautacam. Sometimes I watch myself in interviews and *do* think I've come across as a jumped-up little shit . . .

but that's not *me*. I just wish people wouldn't assume that a person's behavior in the highly unusual circumstances of the end of a stage is a reflection of how he conducts himself for the other twenty-three hours, fifty-eight minutes, of the day.

Returning to the original question, I agree that I am sometimes immature. I would also argue, though, that, between me pulling out of the 2007 Tour after one week and passing the same milestone in the 2008 race, I'd evolved as much as a person as I had as a rider. "Don't change," my team manager Bob Stapleton is always telling me, no doubt with half a thought for the marketability of a rare sportsman who speaks his mind. "You've got nothing to worry about" is usually my reply.

One thing that hasn't altered in my two and a half years as a professional cyclist is that, as far as I'm concerned, there's a certain kind of "PR" that could easily stand for "pointless rubbish." Professional cycling's business model relies on quantity and quality of publicity to give one or more corporate sponsors brand visibility in return for the budget with which the team manager pays his overheads and wage bill. One way to guarantee a sponsor this visibility is by winning races; spouting platitudes to the media may be another . . . but it's not in my repertoire. I made a promise to myself when I turned pro that I'd carry on wearing my heart on my sleeve, and that's exactly what I intend to do.

The question is, can you be tactful *and* direct, diplomatic *and* honest? Over a period of twelve months since that 2007 Tour, I was beginning to learn that not only was this possible, it might also be in my interest. I was now one of the team's undisputed leaders and, as such, needed my teammates' full commitment. There's an old saying that it's better to be respected than liked, but I've never seen why the two should be mutually exclusive; in fact, I'd discovered, it was when affection and respect were blended together that they formed the most potent mix. The Kiwi rider Greg Henderson reaffirmed this to me during the Tour of Qatar at the start of the 2009 season. "The reason people will give everything for you, Cav, is that you don't go round with your nose in the air," he said.

You may argue that, on the evidence of the past few chapters, there's no one less qualified than me to talk about the importance of diplomacy, but the truth is that even I now appreciate how vital it can be to cultivate goodwill in cycling. To read accounts of the Tour in the 1960s, '70s, and even as recently as the '80s, you'd be forgiven for mistaking the professional peloton for a mobile mafia with wheels greased by cold-blooded "bosses" and their bad-tempered cronies. The peloton may not have had a "*padrino*," or a godfather, but it always had a "*patron*," or a boss. The French five-time Tour winner Bernard Hinault was probably the most famous *patron* of any age; the implication was that whatever Hinault said usually went, and if it didn't, there'd be hell to pay.

It may be different now, but more than in any other sport, a cyclist's ability to play politics can determine the outcome of his career. In football (soccer, I mean, but the same applies to American football, I'll bet), it's hard to imagine a scenario in which it pays to be friends with the opposition; by the same token, the sport's history is littered with examples of players who have traipsed from club to club, falling out with managers and teammates at each one, yet who have still enjoyed a prosperous career. In cycling, this simply can't happen: Burn bridges with your teammates and you can forget about winning races, which in turn means you can forget about scoring a lucrative move to another team and, possibly, forget about your pro career altogether. Burn enough bridges with other members of the peloton and, in place of your race number, you may as well stick a target to your back.

My difficulty with all of this is that politics requires pragmatism, not emotion. Sometimes, and especially when my legs and head are still throbbing with adrenaline during or immediately after races, my emotion is a wild animal running amok. But I'm lucky that the more I race and the more the other riders get to know me, the more people realize this. The other British riders in the peloton, for instance, just roll their eyes; they know what I'm like. That's not to say there's no genuine sentiment underlying what I say on the spur of the moment, it's just that between

2007 and 2008, I'd slowly come to appreciate the value of a mysterious quality called tact.

Occasionally, when I look back at interviews I've done or things I've said, I'm nothing short of horrified. That's the case when I think back to one of the first races after the 2007 Tour—the Tour of Britain. On the first day, I'd won a 2.5-km prologue time trial around the Crystal Palace in south London to take the yellow jersey, then defended it with another win the following day in the next stage, this time in Southampton. Just to bear out what I said about the other British riders knowing that, with me, it's all about taking the rough with the smooth: Having been expertly set up by my T-Mobile teammate, Roger Hammond, I'd come across the line whooping, "I love you, Roger," at the top of my voice.

The next stage, heading into Exmoor and finishing in Taunton, was to be decisive in the battle for overall victory in Glasgow four days later. With a course as hilly as the one that week, I was never likely to be a factor in that battle, but I still set about defending my yellow jersey by sending my teammates to control the race in the first half of the stage—which was what they did until a small climb signaled the start of hostilities. As I rapidly lost contact, I couldn't help noticing how many riders from small, semiprofessional British teams were disappearing up the road along with my chances.

I finished that stage in 34th place, just over ten minutes behind the leaders, tired and frustrated. On my way back to my T-Mobile team bus, I rode past the car belonging to the Great Britain national team and spotted the familiar face of John Herety—one of the coaches who had interviewed me for a place at the Academy in late 2003. I also recognized a journalist from a British cycling magazine sitting next to John in the passenger seat. This ought to have been my cue to save whatever I was going to say for later that evening and the team hotel; instead I thoughtlessly mouthed off about how "the British riders have no respect for the yellow jersey. . . ."

I can't stress this enough: Looking back, I'm horrified. I can't imagine what I was thinking. Maybe that my team had been setting the pace on the front all day and that, to show their appreciation, everyone else in the race should have respectfully clapped us in to the finish; or that, as the new darling of British cycling, I should be allowed to coast all the way to Glasgow in the yellow jersey, applauded and adored by a doting public. Whatever I was thinking, it was immature garbage that completely ignored the fact that cycle racing may be political and it may be tactical, but the clue is still in the name—cycle *racing*.

When I make comments like I did that day, I can hardly complain about the way I'm sometimes portrayed in Great Britain, on forums and in the press. There have been other times in the past two years, however, when I've felt aggrieved about my treatment in the UK and haven't always found it easy to rise above the provocation. The Ghent Six Days track meet at the end of 2007, when I partnered Brad Wiggins, was one such occasion. It came at the end of a brilliant but exhausting first pro season for me and, more to the point, after a two-week holiday with Melissa in Thailand, dodging monsoons. I'd warned the organizers months earlier that I wouldn't be fit, that they shouldn't expect miracles, and they said they wouldn't; if only certain members of the British press had also heeded the message. Brad and I gave one journalist unprecedented, behind-the-scenes access that week—even inviting him into the cabin where we changed and prepared for races—and were disgusted to return to the UK and read a report from the same journalist rubbishing our performance and completely ignoring the fact that we'd gone to Ghent that week to fulfill an obligation to the organizers—which was all they'd expected or wanted. It was typical: We'd gone to Belgium and been treated like kings, then come back to Britain and faced only scorn and criticism.

That week in Ghent was a reminder that I couldn't and shouldn't bank on fair treatment from the media, least of all in Britain. One of the things that makes cycling unique and uniquely appealing among modern mainstream sports is its intimacy; in very few other sports can fans watch at such close proximity to the stars, and in very few other sports are those protagonists so amenable. In central Europe in particular, cycling's popular, some say working-class, roots have ensured that, while large corporations may pay our bills and their logos adorn our jerseys, they haven't yet and never will corrupt the sport's soul. I may be biased, but as far as I can see, cycling has avoided the kind of glamorization and sterilization that have taken a lot of the passion from soccer and Formula One. The passion, the intimacy, the intensity—it all means a better deal for the fans and journalists already drawn to the sport; unfortunately, that passion, that intensity, and that intimacy are so ingrained in the fabric of the sport that they're sometimes taken for granted.

If they'd pissed me off in Ghent, the English media angered me again early in 2008 at the Tour of California. That race was one of the most important of the season for our team, with our administrative base in California and our Californian team boss, Bob Stapleton, hunting for a new sponsor. The race was also set to be a huge story in the cycling community: Arguably the biggest and certainly most outrageous personality to grace professional cycling in the past twenty years, the 41-year-old Italian sprinter Mario Cipollini, was making a shock comeback three years after his last competitive outing.

I watched professional cycling with only a passing interest in Cipollini's peak years, the mid-1990s, but I knew all about his 200 professional wins, his playboy lifestyle, and his repeated public utterances about how much or little pre-race shagging sessions diminished his performance on the bike. If, as he claimed, an orgasm was both ideal preparation and the only off-the-bike experience comparable to winning a sprint, it was also clear that three years out of the sport hadn't dimmed his spark or lightning speed on the bike. Even in my first pro races in 2007, I'd never allowed myself to be bullied or gently eased out of position by more established sprinters, but, in those first couple of stages with Cipollini, I found myself wanting to politely smile, move aside, and wave him through. On Stage 2 to Sacramento, I almost gifted him unintentionally with a stage win by powering away from the rider I was supposed to lead out, my teammate Gerald Ciolek, and failing to realize that Gerald had purposely let me go. I looked around to see a huge expanse of daylight, but by then it was too late and I was too spent to regain momentum. The Belgian superstar Tom Boonen powered past me in the dying meters, Cipollini was 3rd, and I could only hold on for 4th.

Cipollini and I found ourselves side by side again three days later. This time the race was a time trial around the town of Solvang and the context much more relaxed; neither of us was a contender for this stage or the overall standings, so we could afford to take things easy. Cipollini, it seemed, was taking things rather more easily than me—so much so that, having set off a minute after him, I caught him midway along the route. As I drew parallel, I grinned and, seeing him grin back, thought I'd have a bit of fun by unclipping one foot and pedaling with one leg. Again, as he saw me, he smiled and I smiled; in a sprint it may be different, but here, today, two of the biggest egos in the peloton could afford to take the day off together.

We shared a giggle about the incident again at the finish line, and that would have been the end of it had a reporter not been earwigging close by. The next day, before the penultimate stage, the same journalist quizzed Cipo about the incident; despite having laughed with me the previous day, now Cipollini suggested that my antics in the time trial had been disrespectful. "Cavendish's results speak for themselves, but he's still a *bambino*," he said. "If he'd turned pro in the 1980s, the sheriffs of the group would have ruined him already."

I didn't blame Cipollini for the apparent U-turn. He hadn't minded sharing a private joke—as long as "private" was what it remained. You could say this was petty pride—that everyone understood I hadn't *really* been strong enough to pass him with one leg, that I hadn't *really* been taking the piss, that he shouldn't take himself so seriously—but I knew the journalist had put words into his mouth. More than any lesson that I needed to learn, the whole episode simply highlighted yet again that, while it was okay to be spiky, spontaneous, candid, and even controversial—and all of those qualities might even help to raise my profile—I was still at the mercy of the media and however they might choose to represent me.

Over the last three days at that 2008 Tour of California, if you include the storm in a teacup over Cipollini, I ended up being punished for three mistakes . . . only one of which I'd actually committed. On that penultimate stage finishing in Santa Clarita, I thought I'd brought the team its first win of the race, only for the Brazilian rider Luciano Pagliarini and his team to claim that I'd been illegally assisted by a team car after a crash on the first of three finishing circuits; crudely put, they said I'd held on to the car. The complaint was upheld. In reality, all I'd done was benefit from the unwritten, universally accepted rule that states that if a rider loses contact because of a crash or puncture, he can draft behind his own or other team cars as he makes his way back to the peloton. Three months later, I was half amused, half appalled to see the directeur sportif from the Saunier Duval team who had officially reported my "crime" in California overtaking me on the hardest climb in the Giro d'Italia, the Passo Giau, with one of his riders attached like a sidecar to the outside mirror.

My only real gaffe in California came in Solvang, neatly sandwiched between the time trial and my disqualification in Santa Clarita. Again the media were involved. This time, though, the only person I had to blame was myself. The journalist in question, this one from *Procycling* magazine, had heard me speak in less-than-enthusiastic terms about Andre Greipel's sprinting the previous autumn and now asked me what I made of Greipel's four stage wins in the recent Tour Down Under in Australia. The question may have been laced with mischief, but there was no need for me to rise to the bait. I did so, completely belittling Greipel and his achievements by belittling the riders whom he'd beaten in Australia. "When Andre was winning the sprints," I said, "you have to remember that Graeme Brown was second and Matt Hayman was third . . . you know what I mean?"

He knew exactly what I meant—so did the readers, so did Brown and Hayman, and so did Greipel.

The funny thing about Greipel and me is that, off the bike, we always got on fine. At training camps—pretty much the only time of the year when riders would linger after dinner for a beer and a chat—I would socialize with Andre almost as much as with anyone else. If anything, at our camp in Majorca in January 2008, our rapport had improved *because* we now hardly ever raced together. After we'd started the 2007 season as the two sprint prongs of what was essentially T-Mobile's B team, I'd rattled off six wins before the 2007 Tour and six between then and the end of the season. The issue of our incompatibility suddenly became irrelevant; as my status had changed, so had my race program, and Greipel and I now frequently found ourselves competing in the same jersey, at the same time, on different sides of the continent or sometimes the world.

The 2008 Giro d'Italia, or Tour of Italy, was to be a big test for several reasons. For one, I still hadn't won a stage in a three-week major tour—Giro, Tour de France, or Vuelta. Until that happened, I could win as many stages of as many smaller races and beat whomever I liked, but my credentials as a top sprinter would still be open to debate. The same applied to my ability to survive mountains that came not in two well-spread installments, like at the Tour, but scattered all through even the "easier" stages at the Giro. The other challenge was going to be Greipel, who had also hoped the Giro would mark a definitive breakthrough but now found himself grappling with the idea that his main purpose in Italy would be boosting the stock of another sprinter. Three weeks before the start of the race in Sicily, the team's directeurs sportifs had said that he could take his place on the start line in Palermo on one condition: He would have to lay his personal ambitions to one side and support me. Greipel had given his word.

The race was due to start with a team time trial of 28.5 kilometers around Palermo. A team time trial is always a delicate exercise—basically a longer version of a team pursuit, with more men, and on the road rather than the track. The principle and technique are much the same in both disciplines: Get your team of riders from one point to another, as quickly as possible, in a rotating formation whereby, at any one time, only one rider is exposed to the wind and all of his teammates shelter on each other's wheels. I'd grown up riding and watching team pursuits with the British Federation, even if I didn't particularly enjoy them. In fact, I'd ridden and seen so many of the bloody things that I could easily have written a small coaching manual on the topic.

Unlike some of the other teams, and particularly Garmin, we'd done next to no practice drills. I hoped we could compensate with a bit of savoir faire and common sense so was at pains to press home one key point in our pre-race meeting. Forget all doing equal turns, I told my eight teammates—the weaker riders could swing onto the front and stay there for only a few seconds if they wanted, *as long as they maintained the pace.* I'd seen it so many times before—riders' pride clouding their judgment, their feeling embarrassed to take shorter pulls than their teammates, the pace dropping, and the team's performance suffering as a consequence. "No fucking h-e-r-o-i-c-s!" I said, pronouncing every letter for added emphasis. "If you do shorter pulls, or even if you do nothing, no one will think any less of you. Just no heroics . . ." As I repeated the mantra, my eyes scanned those of all of my teammates; I knew immediately who wouldn't pay a blind bit of notice to what I'd just said. Lo and behold, the next afternoon, just as I suspected, Greipel was one of three or four whose ego-aggrandizing efforts broke both my golden rule and the team's momentum.

Stage 2 was uneventful, mainly because I was never going to be a factor on a steep, uphill run-in. Stage 3 looked sure to end in the first bunch sprint of the Giro, and if you didn't already know it, with a bit of background info you might have guessed it if you'd seen Greipel remonstrating with our directeur sportif Valerio Piva outside our team bus at the start in Catania. Even from my vantage point inside the bus, it was obvious that Greipel was complaining, and it was obvious what he was complaining about. "He's not happy 'cause he has to lead me out," I said, nudging

Brad Wiggins and pointing to the confab still rumbling on outside. Later that day, it was I who was grumbling when, out of position, with Greipel nowhere to be seen, I could only manage 9th place in the bunch gallop.

Now day four arrived. Despite my mistakes on the previous day, I'd felt good—and, with my form still building in a crescendo, I expected to feel even better today. The only potential hiccup was a steady, 8-kilometer climb 20 kilometers from the finish. With this in mind, in the briefing that morning I told my teammates that I needed their total, unqualified commitment. "Look, I'm really up for today, but I really need every one of you around me," I said. "I need to start that climb at the front, and I need *everyone* around me. I will get dropped on that climb, but I won't be dropped so much that I won't be able to get back to the bunch. If I fuck up, I won't be able to live with myself . . . but I won't fuck up."

I was as good as my word, and so were they—Greipel included. We were like an armored tank, chugging up the climb, then dropping down the other side, onto the back of the bunch, then to the front. The German rider Tony Martin took me to around 12th position with around 700 meters to go, at which point I screamed the order to hit the gas. Tony dropped me off at 400 meters, right on my rival sprinter Daniele Bennati's wheel, and I was too quick for the Italian in the sprint.

It was arguably the biggest win of my career up to that point. It was also my first in a major tour and the last time Andre Greipel or anyone else would challenge my position as the team's number-one sprinter. Or so I thought. A few days later, on the morning of Stage 12, what should have been a straightforward briefing was interrupted by Greipel declaring that today, *he* wanted to be our sprinter.

Valerio came up with the perfect solution: Andre could be my sweeper—in other words, he could take my back wheel in the sprint. That way, he could stop opponents launching themselves out of my slipstream but also use that slipstream to follow and perhaps even beat me, if he had the speed to do so. This suited Andre, and I was secure enough in my own ability for it to suit me. In the event, it didn't really matter—I lost out to Bennati in a photo finish, and Andre trailed in way down the field.

The next morning, Valerio was explicit: "Andre, you've had your chance and not taken it, so now you're riding for Cav."

The result? Andre did an excellent job, and I won my second stage, thus becoming the first Briton ever to achieve that feat in the Giro.

By the time we reached Stage 17, I ought to have been back in the Isle of Man, savoring my achievements. The plan before the Giro had been that I'd pull out after twelve days, before the Dolomites. As the race went on, however, the more mountains we climbed, the more I suffered, the more I wanted to suffer and the farther I wanted to ride; every night, after the stage, Valerio would come into my room and ask whether I was ready to go home, and every night I'd tell him, "Just one more day." "Taking one day at a time" may have been a cliché, but it was also the secret: Don't look at the number of stages already completed, don't look at the number of stages to come, just open the roadbook, calmly digest the task at hand, and worry about how much it hurt later. This approach had gotten me through to the final week of the race, and by now, it seemed like a shame not to continue all the way to the finish in Milan.

Stage 17 was to finish in Locarno, in Switzerland. It was also to herald the beginning of the end of my power struggle with Greipel—not that any such eventuality seemed even remotely likely at the time. Any kind of positive outcome at all had seemed pretty unlikely when we were struggling to haul back the Russian rider Mikhail Ignatiev in the closing kilometers. By now, though, the errors of the first week were a fading memory and our confidence was surging almost as powerfully as the train we formed on the front of the bunch. We duly caught Ignatiev just inside the 5-kilometer mark; the stage, this stage, was now set for my third sprint exhibition of the Giro.

At the 2-kilometer banner, we occupied the first six or seven positions in the peloton—an embarrassment of riches. With 800 meters to go, I actually thought we might have committed too late, as Tony Martin was on the front and we still had Greipel to come before my coup de grâce. At 700 meters to go, I screamed at Andre to jump because Tony was visibly slowing. At 600, I screamed again. And again at 500, 400, 300, until, finally, *finally*, on the last corner, with 250 meters to go, he kicked with me in his wheel. I was sure that we were moving too slowly, that Erik Zabel or Daniele Bennati would dive-bomb out of that final bend, but I also knew that overtaking Andre in the last 100 meters would be akin to poaching his goal under the crossbar; as it turned out, to my surprise, with 50 meters to go, there was still no one except Andre in my field of vision, and I knew then that the win was safe. The photograph of Andre crossing the line with arms held high, and me just behind in the same pose, in 2nd place, was the stuff a team sponsor's dreams are made of.

Our embrace amid the post-stage commotion was, if anything, even frostier than the one we'd shared at Scheldeprijs a year earlier. If Andre mumbled a "Thanks," I didn't hear it. The next person I saw was Max Sciandri. This was ironic—in the spring of 2006, Max and I had been riding up a climb just a few hundred kilometers south of here, airing our conflicting views about whether I'd ever make the grade as a pro, and now here I was winning two stages at the Giro and gifting a third to a teammate. Max and I had patched up our differences and become close friends in the meantime, but I could tell from his expression that he was at least mildly surprised, maybe completely mystified, by what I'd just done. "It's a big thing to give away a stage in the Giro," he said, sounding a little like a parent debating the best uses of a kid's pocket money. "It's the kind of thing you might do to reward someone who's been working for you for ten years, but, you know . . ."

He didn't need to go on. I knew.

There was something funny about the atmosphere in the bus that afternoon. Somehow, it almost seemed as though we hadn't won. We arrived at our hotel, back over the border in Italy, went up to our rooms, unpacked our laptop computers, and started reading the quotes from Andre's press conference. And that was when the trouble started.

One of the questions, maybe the first, had focused on my role in the sprint. How did he feel about me "gifting" him with the stage?

"What gift? I won the stage because I was the fastest," Andre had replied, stone-faced.

In fairness, at that point, he may not have seen the action replays. He also didn't have eyes in the back of his head. He perhaps couldn't know what was patently obvious to the journalist asking the question, namely, that in those last 150 meters, I hadn't been so much sprinting as patrolling his back wheel. In any case, he'd apologize as soon as he saw me back at the hotel and watched the highlights on TV, wouldn't he? Wouldn't he?

Er, actually, no, he wouldn't. Neither that night nor the following morning on the bus, when he at least recognized the need to diffuse some of the tension. "Guys, yesterday was the biggest win of my career, and some things I said after the finish got taken out of context. . . ." he mumbled, his speech sounding more like self-justification than an apology. Or a thank-you. That's exactly what I told Rolf Aldag when he called to check that harmony—or at least some semblance of it—had been restored.

It had now been fifteen months since the first of our disagreements at the Étoile de Bessèges. Despite those arguments, I felt that Andre was basically a good bloke who, to give him his due, had a winner's mentality similar to my own. That was what made it hard for us to get along; while we both wanted to be acknowledged as the best rider in the team, if not the world, there was only room on that pedestal for one of us, notwithstanding the fact that Andre's outstanding power made him one of the fastest finishers on the planet.

In the most sensitive possible terms, this was the news I tried to break to him that evening when, again to his great credit, he came to my room in the hope of clearing the air. It was all quite emotional. And, I suppose, dramatic. In short, he admitted that he'd read interviews I'd given, admitted that some of my comments had upset him, and also that it was hard to revel in my success when gnawing at his consciousness was the hunch that it could and maybe should all have been his. As he sat on the bed, emptying his heart, welling up, it seemed obvious that just over a year of childish squabbles was tapering toward a truce, or at least something close to it. Before I knew it, we'd shaken hands, and a smile had settled on Andre's lips and mine. Just a few months on, we now celebrate each other's success with the same vigor as our own.

The Giro had marked my coming-of-age in so many ways. By now, with just three days and two mountain stages to go, I was about to chalk up my first complete major tour. That in itself was almost as much a badge of honor as my two stage wins, but perhaps most gratifying was the way that, over the three weeks, I'd sensed my profile growing among the Italian fans. In Belgium, I'd noticed, they loved every cyclist; in Italy, they loved, even worshipped, a winner.

Physically, I'd surprised even myself by making it through the mountains. Brad Wiggins had explained to me that in the third week of a major tour, the body and its muscles went into survival mode—rationing their resources, solidifying, and generally becoming leaner and meaner. I was too tired to notice the benefits in the time trial that brought the race to a close in Milan, but I would in just over a month's time . . . I would at the Tour.

Andre Greipel wasn't the only beneficiary of my newfound diplomacy. If anything, in my first few months as a pro rider, my contempt for Sebastian Weber dwarfed even my dislike for Greipel. At least I could relate to Andre, inasmuch as we were both bike racers and we both wanted to be winners. Weber, on the other hand, had demonstrated to me that he knew sod all about cycling at my first-ever training camp with the team in Majorca in January 2007. "You won't even hold the peloton" had been his prediction for my first pro races in France at the start of that season. He may have been talking nonsense, but something had still possessed me to overtrain and undereat in my effort to prove him wrong.

Since that spring, Weber and I had had very little contact. To be precise, we'd had very little contact since I'd recovered from my overexertions in February and March and won at Scheldeprijs, twice in the Four Days of Dunkirk, and twice again at the Tour of Catalunya, doing things very much my own way, i.e., ignoring Weber and his graphs and diagrams and scientific claptrap. After my wins at Catalunya, he'd called to congratulate me, and for once I hadn't appreciated someone blowing sunshine up my arse. "I told you," I'd said tersely. "These are the lines that mean something to me—the finish lines, not the graph lines."

For months after that—in fact, for well over a year—my opinion about Sebastian didn't alter. Meanwhile, he carried on working with the riders who could make use of his analytical skills and left me in peace. This was the difference between Sebastian and Simon Jones—and it was also the reason why, a year or so after our initial clash, almost without me realizing it, my respect for Sebastian was growing. In short, Sebastian had understood that we had different ideas about training and racing and that, if I was winning races, what wasn't broke clearly didn't need fixing. With Jonesy, on the other hand, it had always been his way or the highway.

Sebastian and I ended up bonding at the 2009 Tour of California over, of all things, herbal tea. After the prologue in Sacramento, as I hung around for the presentation of the best young rider's jersey for my stage, I copped a whiff of a sweet cinnamon smell and followed the scent all the way to the vapors rising from Sebastian's mug. "Ah, that smells good," I cooed. "I don't suppose you could get me a cup, could you? I can't move from here until the presentation's over. . . ." A year or so earlier, he'd have looked at me as though I'd just asked him to shine my shoes. Now he said, "Sure," and returned a couple of minutes later with a steaming-hot, spicy-smelling mug.

Every morning in California, I was going for physiotherapy on the pelvis, which, I think, has been slightly displaced by years of riding counterclockwise around a velodrome, my whole body twisted toward the inside of the track. We have a physio who travels with the team at major races, and in California he happened to be rooming with Sebastian. One morning, I was lying on the bed, receiving my treatment, when Sebastian casually asked whether I'd like a box of the cinnamon tea I'd sampled a few days earlier. "Nah," I said, "you keep it for yourself—I could just have a couple of bags."

He insisted: "Nah, Cav, you take the whole box."

Again, a year or even a few months earlier, I'm guessing the only reason he'd have given me his hot drinks would have been in the vague hope that I might burn my mouth.

Did the end of hostilities with Greipel and Weber mean that, at the grand old age of 23, I was already mellowing? Mellowing, perhaps not—not yet—but maturing, almost definitely. As spiky as I still am and will continue to be, I've always been willing to give people a second chance—provided they know that's also their last chance. That quote from Johan Bruyneel about Lance Armstrong—"He's always drawn his motivation from anger and resentment," the little black book that Armstrong keeps in his head—all that still applies to me, but it's only half the story. The truth is that I don't *like* conflict, especially when it's with people from my own team. I don't like it, and I don't always need it, but, fortunately or not, I seem to thrive on it.

Part of maturing was also knowing when it was in my interest and the team's for me to maintain and finesse certain relationships. Since the first summer of that first 2007 season, I'd become one of the team's undisputed leaders, and that status brought responsibility. One such duty was acknowledging how valuable a rider like Greipel could be to our squad of twenty-nine when we were racing different programs, or even when we were together at the same race. From a purely selfish perspective, I could see now that there might be days when I didn't want the mental pressure or the physical strain of sprinting and preferred to pass the buck to Andre—who would very gratefully and capably take it off me.

On the bike, I never stopped learning, never stopped growing, in that twelve-month block between the 2007 and 2008 Tours. The Giro had been the successful culmination of a year's hard study, but, even there, like at other races in the spring of 2008, the most valuable experiences had maybe been the ones when I'd finished beaten and dejected. The Belgian Classic race Ghent-Wevelgem springs to mind. I'd lined up for that race with my form and morale soaring after a couple of stage wins in the Three Days of De Panne, and the bookies had clearly taken note, installing me as the first British favorite for any Classic since the late Tom Simpson forty-odd years earlier. I daresay that I deserved and would have lived up to my billing had I not let complacency creep in and skulked about, twenty positions back, while my teammates continually tried to drag me to the front in the last hour of the race. With a kilometer to go, I was poorly placed but still unflustered . . . then the Spanish rider ahead of me jerked inside the 1-kilometer-to-go banner and blocked my path. I ended up not even sprinting. Half an hour after the race, I was to be found in my usual post-defeat position, sitting alone and in silence at the back of the team bus, a towel over my head, wondering how I could have been so selfish when my teammates had worked so hard on my behalf.

As ever, I made amends at the next available opportunity, defending my title at Scheldeprijs—the race that meant so much to me after I'd won for the first time as a pro there in 2007. It was good to know that other sprinters also made stupid mistakes: After finding myself obstructed again in the last kilometer, this time by a rider from the Dutch Skil Shimano team, I was able to squeeze past and win, thanks to Tom Boonen's premature victory celebration. Boonen might think that he had the last laugh after I slipped and face-planted on the podium that evening—but at least I'd succumbed on my way to collect first prize.

The final five months of 2006 had been my official "apprenticeship," or "stage," as a professional cyclist, fast followed by a six-month baptism of fire ending with the 2007 Tour de France, and now a coming-of-age that would hopefully end with stage wins at the 2008 Tour. First, though, there was just time for me to head to the British National Championships and leave a few hours later, not knowing whether to laugh or cry at the way I and the other pros riding for major European teams had been targeted by the domestic pros. Even with dozens of the British-based pros ganging up to chase, someone like David Millar was strong enough to break free, as he'd shown when he won in 2007. Me, I may have been the best sprinter in the world, but in every other department I was average at best. It was hard, frustrating, infuriating, but I had seen it before, and

I'd see it again even at the Tour—there were people who'd rather see someone else lose than win themselves.

And to think that I was the one they called childish.

STAGE 11: LANNEMEZAN-FOIX, 167.5 KM

1. Kurt-Asle Arvesen (Nor), Team CSC–Saxo Bank, 3:58:13 (42.19 kph)

130. Mark Cavendish (GBr), Team Columbia, 22:14

GENERAL CLASSIFICATION

1. Cadel Evans (Aus), Silence-Lotto, 46:42:13

156. Mark Cavendish (GBr), Team Columbia, 1:52:04

STAGE 12

Thursday, 17 July 2008
LAVELANET-NARBONNE
168.5 KM

S peak to anyone who followed professional cycling from afar in the years when I was falling in love with the sport and, at least now, in hindsight, they'd tell you that it was an era dominated by drugs. I was 12 years old when some French customs officials opened the trunk of the Festina team car on the eve of the 1998 Tour de France and with it a Pandora's box stuffed with EPO, human growth hormone, and assorted other banned substances; since that day, pretty much, as far as the general public is concerned, cycling's come to mean doping, and doping to mean cycling. Unfortunately, it's not as though the idiots who thought they could beat the system haven't given them ammunition.

In July 1998, I was a 12-year-old little scally interested in only one thing: bikes. Bikes, not cycling. You may not make the distinction, but to me "riding bikes" was what I did, what I loved, what I couldn't live without, whereas "cycling" was something else. Cycling was what you read about in the magazines, a spectator sport popular in faraway countries (well, if you live in the Isle of Man, even Belgium seems a long way) whose stars were Italians, Spaniards, and French blokes with obscure-sounding names. Cycling was the Tour de France, Paris-Roubaix, the Giro d'Italia. I'd seen the pictures in *Cycling Weekly*, I knew the names, but that wasn't why I handed over my twenty quid or whatever it was at the newsagents. My mate Christian Varley, he was into cycling. Me, I was all about the bikes—or rather the adverts that told me how many papers I'd have to deliver before that stem/those handlebars/those wheels I wanted could finally be boxed up and put on a ferry to the Isle of Man.

Varley was pretty much my only source of information when it came to the pro road scene. This in itself didn't exactly make Christian an authority on what it took to make it as a pro, but neither did it prevent him from telling me that what it took was drugs. And I listened. I listened because Varley had read the magazines—he knew. "You know, Cav," he'd say, "if we're gonna be pros, we'll have to take drugs." While I didn't question him, when you're 12 years old, no matter how much you want to be a pro bike rider, it somehow doesn't seem that relevant. The words would go in, I'd nod sheepishly, then ten seconds later, it'd be "A quid says I'll beat you to the top of this hill."

But as the years went by, I started getting more and more into cycling, and cycling got more and more into drugs, or so it seemed. The year after Festina, the legendary Italian climber Marco Pantani was kicked out of the Giro d'Italia on the penultimate day, and scandals seemed to start coming monthly, weekly, and sometimes daily. Meanwhile, I just carried on racing, winning, loving it, none the wiser. A lot of people in the know will tell you that in those years, there was even a drug culture in the junior and amateur ranks in continental Europe, but no such notion ever crossed our minds. Danes, Dutch, or Belgians—or whoever they were—if they were cheating, all I can say is that it wasn't working because I was a fat banker with an addiction to cream cakes, and I was still giving them a kicking. To me, it never appeared in the least bit unusual that I never took a dope test until I was well into my late teens.

Ignorance was bliss, even later at the Academy. Sure, once a month we'd have to go do a blood test with Dr. Rog—Roger Palfreeman, the Federation doctor—but we didn't think anything of it. Of course, we knew that one of the reasons you get blood-tested in cycling is to screen for the signs of doping, but we certainly didn't have anything to hide. Dave Brailsford or Rod never gave us the third degree about doping, and on reflection, it was probably better that they didn't.

This was a lesson that Roger Hammond had taught me when I joined T-Mobile: Ultimately it was safest not to even think about doping—and I don't mean to *think* about actually doing it but not even to contemplate the issue at all. Roger was twelve years older than me, but he'd also grown up racing in England, totally sheltered from and naive to whatever unsavory practices were apparently de rigueur in more established cycling countries in Europe. Roger had turned pro, grafted for a few years in minor Belgian teams, and as the tests improved, the dopers became more isolated, the races slower, so Rog had started to get results. In 2005, he'd achieved his big break and joined the same team as Lance Armstrong, Discovery Channel—and it being cycling, people had started asking questions. Rog told me that even before that, when he joined one team—not Discovery—the first thing one of his teammates asked him was "What are you taking?" When he replied, "Nothing," far from being amused or impressed, his teammate was almost disgusted. In this gentleman's eyes, Roger was being unprofessional by not taking drugs and maximizing his ability to win races for himself or the team.

In 2005, still a teenager, more bored than curious, I'd already broached cycling's sixty-four-million-dollar question with a teammate at Sparkasse: "Are you taking drugs, and if so, what?" He was an older guy who'd been around the block a bit. I'd already informed him that I didn't take anything at all and that, to be characteristically blunt, I "didn't know the first fucking thing about doping." He took that as his prompt to assure me that he didn't take anything either, but, in case I was interested, the drugs of choice were EPO and human growth hormone; he added that if I was going to turn pro, I needed to know about these things. I listened, a bit like I had with Christian Varley years before, then, partly out of curiosity, partly out of mischief, inquired where I could acquire such "essentials" if the need or desire arose. Apparently "he knew some people. . . ." When

I replied with words to the effect of "thanks, but no thanks," his final advice was that if and when I finally turned pro, I should "go one way or the other—either take drugs or don't, but don't lie to yourself. . . ." My curiosity both satisfied and killed, I responded by changing the subject.

What almost no one outside the British Federation knows is that by this time, I might already have been serving a two-year ban for doping. There'd been no big spiel about doping when we'd joined the Academy the previous year, but one thing we did have to take on board was the start of out-of-competition testing and a "whereabouts" system. This meant we had to go online and fill out forms telling UK Sport where we would be at different times of the week so they knew where to find us if they wanted us for a dope test. We could give three addresses—our home address, in our case the house in Fallowfield; a training address where they could find us for one hour a week, so in my case the Manchester velodrome on a Tuesday morning; and any "exception," which for me at that particular time meant the Isle of Man. There was no obligation to fill in the training venue or the "exception," but for the sake of one example, I knew I'd be in the Isle of Man for a week before Christmas 2005, so I noted it down. Might as well be as helpful as possible, I thought.

So there I am back home before Christmas—it's a Tuesday—and my phone rings. The velodrome. I take the call. "Cav, where are you? There's someone here from UK Sport wanting to test you. . . ."

I had no idea what was going on. I'd filled in the forms, done everything I was supposed to, but what I hadn't realized was that the "exception" didn't change my training venue; in other words, they'd still expect me to be at the velodrome on a Tuesday even though I'd be on the Isle of Man. *Boom!* That'll be one missed test, one strike, thank you very much. Three missed tests and three strikes equals a positive test and a two-year ban.

I was fuming, but at least I'd learned my lesson. Or so I thought. The next April, Ed and I were bundled off to Germany and Sparkasse, and in the chaos of last-minute packing, I forgot to fill in my whereabouts form.

Wouldn't you know it—the day after I left, the testers finally found their way to the Isle of Man. *Boom!* Second missed test.

By now, Rod and Dave Brailsford were going apeshit. I was lucky that they did because for the next year and a half, until the first missed test was wiped from my record, they wouldn't leave me in peace; another oversight on my part would have been a disaster for the Academy, the Federation, and potentially their Lottery funding. For me, it could have meant an indelible asterisk over everything I achieved for the rest of my career. Just ask the British 400-meter runner Christine Ohuroghu; she missed three tests in 2005 and 2006, served a one-year ban, has since won gold medals at the Olympics and the world championships, and still has people calling her a "tarnished champion." As a cyclist, guilt already comes by association with a sport that the media have successfully—and unfairly—labeled as one of the most drug-riddled sports of all. As far as the press is concerned, a cyclist who comes into the pro ranks having already served a doping ban couldn't look more suspicious if he arrived brandishing a smoking gun in bloodstained hands.

If nothing else, the whole episode was an important reminder—and not the first or last—that however much I wanted to avoid doping, by choosing cycling I'd chosen a sport in which avoiding the issue simply wasn't an option.

By the time I started riding as a stagiaire for T-Mobile at the end of 2006, my naïveté about doping would have made even most armchair fans wince. One important lesson I *had* absorbed was that you could never accuse someone of cheating without proof or assume they were winning because they were taking drugs. As it was, after that first season at the Academy, I returned to the Isle of Man to find that Christian Varley had spent the six months since he'd left shamelessly peddling lies about just what was the secret of my rapid progress. I'd be out for a ride and every time it'd be "Ah, so how's it going at the Academy, Cav? Christian said they're trying to get you to dope. . . ." I don't know whether my predominant feeling was anger or disbelief. It beggared belief—there was nothing, *nothing* Christian could have mistakenly confused with doping—no injections, no pills, nothing—in a coach with unbendable ethics and a bunch of lads who had no interest in or curiosity about doping, and certainly no knowledge of where to buy performance-enhancing drugs or how to use them.

It would be far from the last time that I'd have to defend myself against baseless accusations. I'd never been fitter or thinner than when I turned up at the Sparkasse Giro in Germany in 2006, just before the start of my stagiaire deal, and I'd never seen my old teammate from the Academy, Tom White, looking less svelte. Tom was now riding for a South African–based team, Konica Minolta, and we hadn't seen each other in months. Professional cycling's a macho sport, but it can also be a bit like a school playground, with its petty jealousies and bullying. Hence, Tom went up to Ed in the middle of the race and openly accused me of doping. He said, "Cav's body shape's changed. He's never been that lean before. He's doping. . . ."

Ed was gobsmacked. "Er, no Tom," he said. "Cav's body shape's changed because he's been doing shitloads of training. . . ."

But Tom was having none of it—he was adamant that I was using drugs.

What can you do? I just laughed when Ed told me the story. And I felt bad for Tom. But again, the episode demonstrated how a ridiculous claim founded on nothing other than supposition could easily snowball and damage a reputation—or a friendship, in this case mine with Matt Brammeier. All it needed was for Tom to tell Brammy about his "hunch," for Brammy to confuse gossip with gospel, for me to find out, and my relationship with my former best friend was suddenly ruined. Finally, almost two years on, Brammeier and I are on good terms again.

Varley's and Tom's accusations were symptomatic of the widespread assumption that the sole route to success in cycling took in a detour to the medicine cabinet. On the eve of my first race with the world's number-one professional team, I may have pretended to be immune to such cynicism, but a conversation I had with Rod after the Circuit Franco-Belge hinted that hadn't been entirely true. It was only my third or fourth race as a T-Mobile stagiaire, and while I hadn't exactly taken the pro scene by storm, I had seen enough to know that I could compete without any artificial help. This prompted me to explain to Rod that when I was growing up, I'd always heard that I'd have to dope when I turned pro but that, in the space of a few weeks, I'd realized that simply wasn't the case. Rod was taken aback; had I ever thought any differently? he asked. I replied to him that, yes, to be honest, I sort of had.

"Cav," he said, "I need you to promise me something. I need you to promise me that if ever you decide you're going to take drugs, you'll tell me straightaway. I won't judge you, but I need to know straightaway so that I can disassociate myself from you straightaway. I don't want anything to do—"

I didn't let him finish. "Rod," I said, "you have nothing to worry about. I'm never going to take drugs."

Clean or not, there was simply no escape from the shadow of doping. I had joined a team, T-Mobile, whose leader, Jan Ullrich, had been kicked out of the previous summer's Tour de France for allegedly working with a Spanish doctor under suspicion of giving blood transfusions, and the whole management structure had been overhauled as a result. Out went the old pros who had been running the team; in came a California businessman, Bob Stapleton, who'd never ridden as a pro but whose zeal for bike racing was the equal of anyone's in the peloton. In, too, came probably the strictest antidoping philosophy of any team.

All of this brings us quite neatly to my old T-Mobile teammate Patrick Sinkewitz. Where do you start with him? Maybe by explaining that after pulling out of the 2007 Tour on Stage 8, I'd gone to Munich to pick up the Audi we'd all been promised at the start of the season, driven up to meet Melissa in Brussels, and was in the middle of our own little romantic road trip when I received a call from Roger Hammond. He'd called to say that Sinkewitz had tested positive for testosterone in an out-of-competition control before the Tour. I came off the phone, and my first words to Melissa were "That's it. We haven't got a team."

Sinkewitz and I had never been mates. He'd practically ignored me when I'd joined the team as a stagiaire the previous year. The first time he'd really made an effort with me was at the Tour a few days before his positive test, when he could see I wasn't too enamored with finishing "only" 9th and 10th in Stages 3 and 4, and he'd made a brave attempt at cheering me up. He said I should be pleased because he'd never had two top tens in Tour stages in his life. It didn't make me feel any happier, but I suppose I at least appreciated the concern.

Sinkewitz followed the stupid decision to take drugs with another stupid decision. Over the next few weeks, he gave interview after interview describing in minute detail not only how he'd bought the testosterone gel that had caused his positive test on the Internet but also how, until the 2006 Tour, certain T-Mobile riders had been doped under the University of Freiburg and the previous management regime. He could just have saved it all for the police and their investigation, but, oh no, Sinkewitz wanted to twist the knife. He said it was his way of helping the sport; I say that, from where I was watching, it looked suspiciously as though a lawyer had told him he could have his sentence reduced if he cooperated with the police. That would have been fair enough, but Sinkewitz then had an attack of verbal diarrhea and blabbed to every newspaper, magazine, and TV station about a system that he'd been quite happy to abuse until a few weeks earlier. Every time I watched or read one of his interviews, I felt like crying. He wasn't thinking of the consequences, of how cycling was already an easy target, especially in Germany, and of how he was almost singlehandedly endangering the jobs of dozens of people—riders, mechanics, and masseurs—who'd had nothing to do with what had gone on in the 1990s and the start of the current decade. It hadn't occurred to him that, yes, he might get his ban reduced from two years to one but that, if he wasn't careful, he'd have no sport to come back to. It seemed to me that he felt like the martyr sacrificing himself on the altar of his sport. There was just one problem with that, Patrick: You took drugs, and we didn't.

Thanks to a lot of hard work and some skillful negotiation by Bob, somehow the team finished the 2007 Tour and finished the season. But Sinkewitz had left us holding a ticking time bomb. It finally exploded in mid-November, when I was riding the Ghent Six Days with Brad Wiggins and the news filtered through that T-Mobile was ending its sponsorship. The contract was due to expire at the end of the following year, but company directors in Bonn had decided that the association with the team was doing their brand more harm than good—and certainly more harm than they could justify for a tariff of over ten million euros a year. My reaction was the same as it had been when Roger had called about Sinkewitz in July: "That's it. We haven't got a team."

For ten days I really thought it might all be over. I'd won an almost unprecedented eleven races in my first season, I was 22 years old and hot property—but you try looking for a team in late November, when the squads are full and the budgets for the following season already spent. In our conversations that autumn, Brian Holm said Bob was spending more time in the air between California and T-Mobile's headquarters in Germany than on the ground and that he was barely sleeping. Fortunately, or rather, deservedly for Bob, it all paid off: T-Mobile was so desperate to divorce its image from the team that it agreed to fulfill its financial commitment for 2008 provided that its brand disappeared on anything and everything connected with the team. Bob could rely on a large chunk of T-Mobile money, but the team would now carry the name of his California-based management company, Highroad Sports.

Almost immediately, operation airbrush began: A full DIY kit arrived in the post—black stickers, white stickers, long stickers, thin stickers. Bob wanted every trace of a T-Mobile logo, every hint of magenta, the T-Mobile company color, to disappear from the frames of our Giant bikes.

The new season would start in a few weeks, and we'd have new bikes with a new color scheme, but that didn't matter: The corporate cleansing had to start straightaway.

Naturally, I was delighted that my future and the team's now seemed secure. My only regret was that the end of an era for T-Mobile also meant the end of the road for a lot of good, hardworking people whose link with the team had been through the company itself. They were now losing that link, and in some cases their jobs. They were all completely blameless, yet more innocent victims of a few imbeciles' stupidity.

What Bob Stapleton did that winter to save our team merely confirmed what I'd already suspected about the guy: He had a love for cycling that kept him striving long after most people would have thrown in the towel. Bob's a businessman, cycling-mad but a businessman nonetheless—an entrepreneur who only found his way into the sport and the team when he sold his telecommunications company, Voicestream Wireless, to T-Mobile in 2000. What makes Bob unique is his passion; his scrapping to keep his dream of a successful, special, clean team alive was the direct equivalent of me pushing so hard to get over the Col de la Colombière in the 2007 Tour that I was almost keeling over—or of my teammates grinding so hard to put me where I want to be in the last kilometer that it almost brings tears to their eyes and mine.

Bob wanted our new team Highroad to be even stronger and more united than what we'd created the previous year with T-Mobile—and even more ethically transparent. In 2007, the Slipstream team had employed an independent company called the Agency for Cycling Ethics (ACE) to add an extra layer of blood and urine controls to the testing provisions made by the Union Cycliste Internationale (UCI), the World Anti-Doping Agency (WADA), and the riders' national antidoping agencies. The idea of a team paying for additional, independent dope tests was rightly seen as quite groundbreaking, so it was no surprise that the move had brought Slipstream some excellent publicity. More importantly, it was widely agreed that, with the addition of the ACE testing, it had become almost impossible for the team's riders to cheat. Bob now wanted a similar ethical warranty for our team, so he contacted ACE. Very soon they had an agreement: ACE would collect and analyze an average of thirty blood or urine tests per rider per year. In return for this extra "seal" of authenticity on our performances, we, the riders, now signed new contracts pledging 3 percent of our salary to finance ACE's testing.

ACE set to work pretty early at our training camp in California in February. That was also where the problems started. We had our first ACE blood and urine tests at that camp, and I was amazed to note that the needle being used to take blood samples was like a spear; the cheaper the needle, the bigger and thicker it usually is, and these were huge. Fortunately, I have big, bulging veins that are nearly impossible to miss, even with a needle like that, and when it came to my turn, my blood disappeared up the vial as usual.

If it had just been the needles, I'd have bitten my lip, but then there were the urine tests. These days, the dope-control booths at major races are set up like forensic laboratories, and I daresay the procedures are nearly as tight. I only wish I could tell you that the ACE procedures were the same, or even similar. Unfortunately, I'd be lying: Here there was no undressing, no hand-washing, no glass screen—just an ACE employee, a pot to piss in, a toilet cubicle, and an instruction along the lines of "Bring it back when you're finished."

I went to see the boss. "Bob," I said, "I've got a problem. I've just gone in and I've taken a piss in this pot, with no one else in the room, and they're using these big syringes to take our blood. We're paying 3 percent of our salary. . . ."

Bob tried to placate me. He said what ACE was doing was important and expensive. I wasn't convinced. I wondered what ACE's motives really were, whether anyone there really cared about ethics in cycling, as it said in the name, or whether they just saw the problems in cycling as a license to make a buck. We were paying the agency hundreds of thousands of euros out of our own pockets, but for what? I certainly hadn't seen anything in California that made me think its input was going to benefit us or the sport.

The ACE testing carried on through the spring. I never worry about my test results—why would I?—but I started to hear murmurs among the other riders and managers of ACE not storing samples properly, of weeks going by without anyone sending us test results. Then the 2008 Tour came. One day, we were told that ACE was in the hotel to do a blood test. At the Tour, you're trying to squeeze in as much sleep as humanly possible, so we practically rolled out of bed and into the room where a girl from ACE was waiting to do the testing. I was up first, so in I went and held out my arm. Out came the usual javelin, er, I mean needle, and into my skin. I watched the vial. Nothing. I looked again. Still no blood. I looked down at the needle wriggling around under my skin, then up at the girl and her flustered face. No one had ever missed my vein before, but that's what she'd done. She looked embarrassed; the girl wasn't even a qualified nurse, so I tried to be sympathetic. "It's okay," I said. "Why don't you just try again?"

Deep breaths all round. She unwraps a new needle. Needle touches the skin, skin flexes, then breaks, needle disappears, and we all wait. And wait. There's no blood, so she starts wiggling the needle again, and I can see my skin stretching, stretching, stretching, and I'm hot, no, I'm cold, sweating, and the skin's stretching . . . then, BOING, out comes the end of the needle in a different place from where it went in, and now I'm screaming—"Get the fucking thing out!"—and teammate Thomas Lövkvist's screaming at this girl because he's watching, and he's Swedish, and this girl's Swedish, and now I'm lying on the bed, feeling sick, and someone's gone to get the doctor, and I don't know what's going on anymore, and everyone's screaming. . . .

It was all over in a few minutes—the team doctor, Helge, arrived, and I was okay—but it's not an exaggeration to say we'd narrowly avoided disaster. From my point of view, it was the last straw, or rather the last syringe: I wouldn't let anyone from ACE go near me with a needle for the rest of the season. With all the problems we'd experienced, I don't think there was ever any question of the team carrying on with ACE

My first win in a major tour, in Catanzaro, on Stage 4 of the 2008 Giro d'Italia. © GRAHAM WATSON

Disbelief and delight mingle in my reaction to my first Tour de France stage win in 2008, in Châteauroux. Six million volts of emotion—like an electric shock! © GRAHAM WATSON

My second Tour stage win,
in the rain in Toulouse. Notice
my teammate Gerald Ciolek
looking mightily impressive as
he finishes second. After this
victory, it dawned on me that
Gerald was too good to ride
the Tour as my deputy.

The ultimate cliffhanger:
Heinrich Haussler and I throw
our bikes over the line in the
2009 Milan–San Remo.
My speed was enhanced by
aerodynamics, as in the sprint
I tucked in tighter than the
significantly taller Haussler.

Bob Stapleton congratulates me after one of my two stage wins at the 2009 Tour of California. A few years ago, Bob was a businessman selling his wireless communications company for billions of dollars. Now he's my team manager, my mate, and one of my biggest fans.

© TIM DE WAELE/TDWSPORT.COM

Emotional? Me? I've cried a few times in my career, but never as hard or as happily as in San Remo that March day in 2009. © GRAHAM WATSON

With sprint legend and five-time Milan–San Remo winner Erik Zabel in Qatar. Erik's experience helped guide my plan for San Remo and many victories since. © GRAHAM WATSON

You never get tired of it: spraying the bubbly stuff in Riomaggiore after winning Stage 13 of the 2009 Giro d'Italia. It was my third stage win in the race, after which I withdrew to prepare for the Tour. © GRAHAM WATSON

My victory salute in Stage 3 of the 2009 Tour de France was a premeditated gift to our new team sponsors, mobile-phone giant HTC. Just under an hour earlier, a combination of crosswinds and my teammates had blown the Tour apart in the Camargue. © GRAHAM WATSON

For a sprinter, there's nothing lovelier than the green jersey. Here, I'm pulling it on after winning Stage 11 in the 2009 Tour, reclaiming it from Thor Hushovd. Three stages later, it would all come to tears. © GRAHAM WATSON

A civil exchange of opinions between Hushovd and me in Besançon at the 2009 Tour. An hour or two later, Hushovd's claim that I'd obstructed him in the sprint for 13th place was upheld, and my hopes of taking the green jersey home were as good as gone. © TIM DE WAELE/TDWSPORT.COM

Had I known the size of my cushion over my opponents on the Champs-Élysées in 2009, I'd have slammed on the brakes and let my teammate Mark Renshaw come through for the win. As it was, Mark and I synchronized celebrations of my sixth stage victory of the 2009 Tour. © GRAHAM WATSON in 2009. In the event, the decision was taken out of our hands, as ACE went out of business.

The concept of independent testing is a really good one, so I was very much in favor when Bob informed us that he'd asked Don Catlin to design a testing program for us in 2009. Catlin is one of the most respected experts in the antidoping field, not only in the United States but worldwide. That said, at our training camp in California at the start of 2009, I kicked and screamed about having to attend a team seminar with Catlin for the simple reason that, as I argued to Rolf Aldag, a rider who doesn't dope doesn't need to know how he's not going to test positive. In the end, I was glad I went; not only was I an awful lot more impressed with Catlin than I had been with ACE a year earlier; I also left that meeting with a strong faith in the system of repetitive testing and long-term profiling that is now the present and future of testing in cycling.

The tragedy in our sport now is that suspicion is almost as much of a problem as doping. People became so used to lies and cheats that they're ready to interpret any gesture, any comment, any decision you make as evidence that you're cheating. For that reason alone, in 2008, it would have been almost inconceivable for us to break off the agreement with ACE halfway through the season. It was ironic: Bob had called in ACE to give a message to the team that doping wasn't an option and to tell the press and public that they could have confidence in our results. Ultimately, we found ourselves in a position where it was the ACE testing that the riders didn't trust, yet admitting that would have left us open to even more speculation and cynicism than if we'd never employed an independent testing agency in the first place.

The sad reality is that the public has been let down so many times that people watch professional cycling with almost the same detachment with which they watch a Hollywood blockbuster: It's entertaining, sure, but, in real life, no one can really cartwheel over that burning bus, no one can really outrun those dozen police cars . . . and, in the same way, they assume no one can really win four stages of the Tour de France at 23 years of age. This attitude is so embedded, even among fans and journalists who are aware of the progress our sport has made, that I'm pleasantly surprised when self-confessed skeptics in the media, in particular, look at my results at the 2008 Tour and think or say nothing other than *"chapeau."*

If only everyone had such faith in my ethics and my performances. When I pulled out of the Tour a few days later on Stage 14, exhausted, the foreign press immediately insinuated that I was really just getting out before the dope testers could get me, or that I'd already been notified about a positive test and I was sneaking out the tradesman's entrance. I discovered this only much later, when Brian Holm told me that those fifty voice-mail messages he'd left on my phone when I switched it off for a week after the Tour were because he'd feared the worst. Even Dave Brailsford had been bombarded by journalists. It was the same a few weeks later when, for exactly the same reason—tiredness—I opted out of the British team for the World Championships in Italy. My announcement just happened to coincide with the news that a number of suspicious samples from the Tour were being retested with a new method to detect CERA—the drug Riccò had taken. Some newspaper in Belgium then reported that some of the samples *apparently* belonged to riders who had "pulled out of the World Championships at the last minute," putting me right in the firing line. They were right about three things—the German Stefan Schumacher had been a late withdrawal from the Worlds, they did retest his blood, and he did test positive. The new method also nailed Schumacher's Gerolsteiner teammate, Bernhard Kohl, who'd finished 3rd in the Tour, and the winner of Stage 10 at Hautacam, Leonardo Piepoli. Three months on from the Tour, the only repercussions all of this had for me was that the sport I love got dragged through the mud yet again.

Doping had never interested me, never really affected me, never really upset me . . . until the 2008 Tour. I was on a plane from Manchester to the Isle of Man at the end of the 2008 season, casually chatting to the guy sitting next to me, explaining that I was a professional cyclist, when the conversation turned to doping. I told him about how often we're tested, about how we have to account for our whereabouts, and his eyes nearly popped out. What I hadn't yet calculated was that I was tested *fifty-nine times* in 2008! Then you get Rio Ferdinand saying that some Manchester United footballers were tested "three or four times last season"—as if that's a lot—or Sir Alec Ferguson saying it would be "a nuisance" if his players had to provide information regarding their whereabouts. I don't want to point the finger at any other athlete or any other sport, but I would say that cycling seems to be the only one whose governing body, the UCI, will maximize the chance of exposing scandals—scandals that will damage its sport—by maximizing the number of tests, maximizing the effectiveness of those tests, and maximizing its transparency about antidoping practices. I can't help but notice that in other sports, it's when the Olympic Games come around, and it's WADA and not the governing bodies doing the tests, that you suddenly start seeing doping cases.

Riccardo Riccò and Bernhard Kohl brought discredit upon the 2008 Tour and, by indirect association, discredit and suspicion upon me. In a way, though, they were still shamefaced contributors to one of the most positive, downright beautiful developments my sport has ever seen. For years we'd heard that the dopers are always one step ahead of the testers, and they obviously believed they were when they dosed up on the new wonder drug, CERA. That's always what's annoyed me most about riders who take drugs—not only are they getting an unfair advantage, they think they're smarter than the rest, and smarter than the testers.

In 2008, I had another, much more personal, reason to feel not merely aggrieved but positively disgusted with these riders, and in particular Piepoli. My suffering to make the time limit at Hautacam, Bernie Eisel's suffering, the anguish that caused the rest of the team . . . it had all been accentuated by Piepoli's cheating. Quite simply, the 1 or 2 or 3 percent that he gained from his magic potion that day could have equated to the minutes and seconds that might have cost Bernie and me the time cut and our place in the Tour. As it was, I simply never recovered from the beating we took that day; I would quit the Tour on Stage 14, but in a certain sense my journey ended that afternoon at Hautacam.

The other, direct consequence for me was that I walked into my press conference after Stage 12 in Narbonne and found myself facing questions about Riccardo Riccò, his positive test for CERA, and his ejection from the race that morning. An American journalist took the microphone. He clearly wasn't interested in my feelings on becoming the first Briton ever to win three stages in a single Tour de France.

"Mark, after Riccardo Riccò's positive test for CERA this morning, can you tell us why we should believe that your wins in this Tour de France have been achieved clean?"

Right down to the forty-second pause that baffled a few journalists but allowed me to gather my thoughts, I'd still respond now exactly as I did then.

· "I am in a sport that I love. I believe in hard work, and that to get the best out of yourself takes hard work. I don't want to tarnish the sport I love, and I know that the majority feel the same way as me. Cycling is not just a job but a passion, and people that resort to doping don't have the passion I have. That's not just the case in cycling, but in every aspect of life. The tests are catching people, and for me that's a good thing."

STAGE 12: LAVELANET-NARBONNE, 168.5 KM

1. Mark Cavendish (GBr), Team Columbia, 3:40:52 (45.77 kph)

GENERAL CLASSIFICATION

1. Cadel Evans (Aus), Silence-Lotto, 50:23:05

147. Mark Cavendish (GBr), Team Columbia, 1:52:04

STAGE 13

Friday, 18 July 2008
NARBONNE-NÎMES
182 KM

Questions about Riccardo Riccò's positive drug test hadn't been all that had threatened to ruin my mood after my Stage 12 win—my third of the Tour and the one that took me past the Yorkshireman Barry Hoban's twenty-nine-year record for stage victories by a British rider in a single edition of the Grande Boucle.

Three or four things stand out about the stage start that day. One was the commotion around the Saunier Duval team bus as the French police arrived to hand Riccò notification of his failed test and lead him away. The second was trying to fight my way through the crush of reporters, fans, and rubberneckers gathered to see the little twerp on his way as I rode to the start—and nearly being wiped out by a TV cameraman. The third was the reaction back on our bus—or rather lack of any reaction, because we'd all seen this coming four days earlier, after watching the highlights of his Stage 9 win—and above all the insult to physics and our intelligence that was his attack on the Col d'Aspin. My mate David Millar hit the nail on the head when, in reference to Riccò, he told the press, "When you see things that appear too good to be true, it usually means they are."

Above all, we were just too immersed in our personal battles to care. Cycling may be a team sport and the Tour a collective effort, but as the race groaned toward its third week, we were all ready to lock in to the "survival" mode that Brad Wiggins and I had discussed at the Giro. You often hear people refer to "Planet Tour"—the world to which the cycling family decamps en masse for three weeks every July, and which exists in its own solar system and sphere of consciousness. What no one tells you is that when you're a rider on that planet, it's not the Tour that dominates your thoughts—the whole Tour—it's your *own* Tour, and to a slightly lesser extent that of your team. In the evening, after stages, different-colored sheets of paper showing the standings in all of the race classifications are handed around—one for the general classification, one for the King of the Mountains, one for the points competition, one for the best young rider's classification—and you ignore them all except the one that relates to you and your personal aims. For me, that meant the points or green jersey competition—although with four places and forty points to make up on the leader, Oscar Freire, even my interest in that race within a race was fading. All that remained were a couple of stages that, on paper at least, lent themselves to sprint finishes, starting with today. Beyond that, way beyond—too far to contemplate for the moment—lay Paris.

As I've already mentioned, as part of my pre-stage routine I always took one last, careful gander at the single A4 page in the Tour roadbook mapping the final 3 or 4 kilometers of the route. On the morning of Stage 12, while the melodrama starring Riccò unfolded a short distance away, I'd absorbed and memorized everything—but stalled on the roundabout that the sketch said we'd have to negotiate 3.5 kilometers from the finish line. As anyone who's seen TV pictures of the Tour taken from a helicopter will know, a peloton will often split into two lines and take to either side of the roundabout before those lines reconverge into single file as the road continues on the other side. When the route enters and exits the roundabout at the same angle, you can go either way and it will make no difference. But even though this map showed the road as a straight line dissecting the roundabout on either side, past experience had told me you couldn't always trust the drawings. That was why, every day, I'd ask the soigneur who'd be waiting for us with towels and drinks on the finish line to reconnoiter the last 5 or 10 kilometers of the route and call the directeurs sportifs with feedback as he made his way there.

The message that came back during the stage from the soigneur, via our directeurs sportifs, put my mind at rest. He'd checked, and the roundabout was exactly as it appeared in the roadbook—straight in, straight out, and utterly straightforward. Good. That was at least one less problem. Now we just had to get there.

In truth, for all my homework on the route (which, in any case, I did for every stage, even mountaintop finishes, because you never knew what might happen), I'd warned my teammates that I didn't fancy sprinting on this stage. Not that I was resting on my laurels, but I *had* already won two stages, and both my legs and head were balking at the prospect of another final 50 kilometers on the edge. As always, though, as the kilometers went by, as the adrenaline started kicking in, I became absorbed in the hunt. Two hours into the stage, the sun was blazing, the wind was gusting at our backs, the average speed was a supersonic, record-breaking 59 kph, and I was in the mood to make a bit of history of my own.

Five kilometers from Narbonne, I was still well placed and my teammates were where they'd been all day and practically all Tour— hammering on the front. We hit the roundabout. I chose the left-hand side. Hugged the inside. Kept going, going, past the apex, going, going . . . and going and going and going until, finally, I intersected with the rest of the peloton at practically 90 degrees to the main current of riders and forty positions farther back than when I'd entered the roundabout. Sixty positions from the front, out of contention, and fucking furious.

The single thing, or rather rider, that saved me that day was Adam Hansen. Adam, a.k.a. the Terminator, had already taken his final turn on the front and was dropping back through the mass when he spotted me floundering in the second third of the bunch. It was Bernie Eisel at Scheldeprijs in 2007 all over again: Almost as though the sight of me struggling had sent him into a trance, Adam forgot everything, somehow numbed himself to the pain, and over the next kilometer and a half acted as my taxicab to the final corner with 1,100 meters to go, the top fifteen positions, and, most importantly, Gerald Ciolek's wheel.

After the finish that afternoon, before the victory celebrations could begin, I wanted to speak to the soigneur who had fobbed me and everyone else off with his dud info about the roundabout. It was obvious to us all that everything he knew about the last 5 kilometers of that day's route he'd learned from the roadbook. Conveniently, he was waiting for me beyond the finish line—the first face on the TV pictures, just how he liked it. I wasn't going to begin my rant in full view of the cameras, but neither was I going to let this go. Later I sought him out and said my piece: "If I'd lost that stage, you'd have lost your job, so you've got me to thank—no, you've got *Adam Hansen* to thank for your job right now."

By that time, my directeur sportif Brian Holm had already unleashed his own tirade, which had been met with the response "Well, he still won, didn't he?"

This had incensed Brian even more; yes, I'd won, but in order for me to do so, Hansen had done the work of two riders in order to compensate for a member of our backroom staff completely deserting his duties. And, no, you could never breathe a sigh of relief when disaster was averted and victory snatched from the jaws of defeat and, in this case, professional self-sabotage. At the Tour there might always be consequences to pay the next day; who, for instance, could know whether that final 1-kilometer sprint that Adam had conjured from the depths of exhaustion wouldn't have flooded his muscles with toxins that couldn't be flushed out in time for him to make the time limit the next day?

As had been the case in Stage 8, when I'd had to sprint on the wrong Zipp wheels, and at Hautacam, where I'd had the wrong gears, what annoyed me most about the incident was that details like this could be the difference between me winning and losing. Attention to that detail was one of the reasons why I'd been able to win three stages in the Tour and, by now, almost thirty races since turning pro at the start of 2007.

In order for my diligence to pay off, I needed all of the other team members, mechanics, soigneurs, coaches, directeurs sportifs, and doctors to do their bit as well. As I mentioned in Stage 8, the cumulative effect of lots of little improvements—or the "aggregation of marginal gains," as the British Federation performance directeur Dave Brailsford puts it—had been the cornerstone of the British team's domination of the international track scene.

The same idea had always been second nature to me, although it's true to say that as my responsibilities had grown, so had the extent of my meticulousness. This was another area in which I was very much on the same wavelength as Rod Ellingworth at the Academy. In 2008, Rod was still "only" the coach of the Under 23s at the Academy, but that hadn't deterred him from mentioning one or two things that the world's number-one team was doing wrong when he paid us a visit on the day of the first time trial of the Tour in Cholet. Kim Kirchen would wind up the winner of that stage after the German Stefan Schumacher's positive test for CERA, and like most riders on the Tour, Kim had warmed up for his ride on a stationary bike outside the team bus, facing the crowds milling around the start area. Rod had seen this and been quietly shocked—so shocked that he'd called over our team manager, Bob Stapleton, and asked why on earth his best time trialist and main hope for the overall classification was warming up where he could be—and was being—continually disturbed by TV crews, members of the public, or even members of his own team's staff. That was typical Rod: He didn't give a monkey's about whom he was talking to—if he saw something that flew in the face of common sense or what his experience had taught him, he wouldn't hesitate to point it out.

Rod and I agreed that, much more than most track disciplines, road racing was a lottery, but one in which you could significantly increase your chances by making sure you were well prepared. More than that—I'd always maintained that I *had* to look for my advantages in some pretty unlikely places because I simply wasn't physically gifted enough to get by on innate ability and a few mere fundamentals—a healthy diet, rigorous training, and a light bike. For the very same reason, now that I'd taken my place among the world's top riders, there could be absolutely no question of me easing up or becoming sloppy. Some of my rivals could booze, splash their cash, party, and still wing it on their natural talent; me, the day I stopped dotting the *i*'s and crossing the *t*'s would also be the day I'd stop winning.

Already in my pro career, there'd been numerous occasions when I could pin down a tiny detail or piece of planning without which I'd have been scrapping for a podium place rather than holding the bouquet. One such occasion was the prologue at the 2007 Tour of Britain, where I'd practiced the first corner maybe thirty times, clinging to my team car, then letting go around the bend to simulate race pace. After that I'd completed ten or twelve circuits of the full, 2.5-kilometer course. When the results were all in, my old foe from the British Federation, Simon Jones, who was commentating on Eurosport, said on air that he couldn't fathom how a rider with low power output could have gone so fast.

The final stage of the Tour of Denmark, immediately after the 2007 Tour de France, was another good example of the same painstaking preparation. It was to be an important day for me and the team, what with the race finishing in our directeur sportif Brian Holm's old home-town, Frederiksberg, and me battling to overhaul a two-point deficit in the points jersey competition. The stage finished with eight circuits of central Frederiksberg and would also almost certainly end in a sprint; the one issue that still needed to be worked out was the gear to use on a gently rising, 300-meter final straight. On the first lap, it struck me straightaway that this, more than finishing speed or perhaps even positioning, might be the decisive factor. It also occurred to me that the road was wide enough for me to drop behind the bunch each time that we approached the 300-meter straight, rehearse my sprint, settle on a gear, then move comfortably back up to the peloton. And that was what I did, lap after lap after lap until, on the final circuit, I started the last corner in a smaller gear than all of my opponents and scuttled easily past as they tried to grind their way to the line. Again, it may be that I was the fastest rider in the field that day; what I know for a fact is that I was the best prepared.

I think it's already pretty obvious that I was neither exaggerating nor indulging in false modesty when I told our soigneur that he was indebted to Adam Hansen for saving his job in Narbonne on Stage 12 that day. What I didn't mention, and perhaps should, is that it had also taken my most agile and tactically accomplished sprint of the Tour.

In common English parlance "switching trains" is what you do when there are leaves on the line on a damp November morning. In sprinting, the expression refers to a maneuver that may be lower on frustration but is somewhat higher on risk; in fact, if you were to trace the metaphor back to its more conventional locomotive context, if you really wanted to make a comparison, I'd say that what I attempted and pulled off in those final 500 meters in Narbonne was somewhat similar to the kind of train-switching that Matt Damon's character has down to a fine art in the Bourne trilogy.

At 800 meters from the finish line, I was moving up the right-hand side in a first-class carriage behind my engine driver of choice, Gerald Ciolek. Immediately to our left were the Crédit Agricole threesome of Mark Renshaw, William Bonnet, then poised in last position, and Thor Hushovd; to the left of them, much farther to the left, on the other side of a wide boulevard road, I could just about make out three white-and-blue Quick-Step jerseys. And that was when instinct took over.

Melissa will never forget those next three or four seconds, even if I do. Having whistled past the Crédit Agricole lads' right shoulders, abandoning Gerald's back wheel, and jagging across the road at a 45-degree angle, I was now edging 70 kph, and Melissa was already composing a text message threatening me with preemptive divorce if I ever repeated the same stunt. As ever, though, from where I was stomping on my pedals, now on the far left of the road, on the back of the Quick-Step train, there was no time for thought or any kind of conscious risk evaluation. I'd seen a faster, better route, and I'd gone for it. No doubts, no questions, no hesitation. All that remained was for me to press the accelerator with 300 meters to go, tear past everyone, and start celebrating 10 meters short of the line.

The next morning the photo of me striking my victory pose would adorn the front pages of the *Guardian* and the *New York Times*. I was, said Bob Stapleton, the third cyclist in history to make the front page of the *NYT*. The first two had won ten Tours de France between them; they were the Americans Greg LeMond and Lance Armstrong.

If by this point papers from all over the world were full of articles debating exactly what it was that was making me so irresistible, Stage 12 had pundits raving about the agility and instinct that, they presumed, came from riding Madisons and points races on the track. No doubt this was partly true, but there was certainly a big difference between sprinting up a straight road on a bike with gears and brakes and bombing around a velodrome on a machine with neither of the above at even higher speeds. On the road, though, my nose for the right line or position had also been honed by necessity. Sprinters fell into two categories, the first of which included riders like Tom Boonen or Hushovd or the Italian Alessandro Petacchi, who generated speed by generating indecent amounts of power and who could hit the front and wind with 400 meters to go and still hold on. Robbie McEwen and I belonged to the other subset—the speed merchants who'd learnt to dart from wheel to wheel like a bumblebee buzzes from flower to flower, in search of the nectar that sprinters call shelter. For me, this applied not just in the final kilometer or even 10 kilometers of a race but from the moment the starter squeezed the trigger or waved his flag. Rod Ellingworth will tell you that he's looked at data that show that I consistently have to produce far fewer watts, that is, expend much less energy than other riders throughout a race, partly because I have an efficient natural pedaling technique and partly because

I have a knack for finding the smoothest-moving nooks and crannies of the peloton. Rod would also argue that this in large part explains why, unlike a lot of other young riders, I rarely, if ever, run out of gas in races of 200 or 250 kilometers.

It's not a question of having one secret weapon but of doing my best to assemble a full artillery. My team was far and away the most important component of that and would prove it again on Stage 13 to Narbonne. The helicopter shots that day showed not so much a line as a huge, Columbia-colored stain at the front of the pack, like a puddle of blue ink. The previous day had been hard and hot, and by now there were too many aching limbs in the peloton for the usual bun fight to be in the first big break of the day in the first hour. Two riders attacked in the first kilometer, and everyone was quite happy to let them frazzle before the inevitable Columbia charge would bring them back with around 10 kilometers to go, which was exactly what happened.

With 3 kilometers to go, the peloton vortexed. In simpler terms, a rival line first drew parallel to, then ahead of, our train on the opposite side of the road, and we spiraled backward. By now, you know what happens next—all that changes is the teammate who gives me the kiss of life. Today it was Marcus Burghardt. Having just put in the mother of monster turns on the front—one among many in the mother of monster Tour performances—Marcus saw me thrashing about in the belly of the bunch, nodded to me to move onto his wheel, then flew up the side of the road to leave me in a perfect position with 1,500 meters to go. Marcus had no more to give and I had no more teammates in sight, but from there I might just about be able to take care of myself.

I said I had no secret weapon. I lied. For "secret," though, read "very sparingly used" and "for emergencies only." Emergencies like the one that began to unfold when, about 400 meters from the line, the bottom left-hand corner of my left eye was suddenly flooded with the dark green of a Crédit Agricole jersey, and before I had time to react, William Bonnet surged past my right shoulder with Thor Hushovd on his wheel. For every "What's Cavendish's Secret?" piece in the French press, there was another one pondering "How Do You Beat Cavendish?" The answer was to overpower and outlast me from 300 or 350 meters out. Thor Hushovd had either been reading the papers or drawn a similar conclusion on his own. As I explained in the first few passages of this book, when another sprinter decides it is time for him to go, then it is time for you to go as well, whether you like it or not; now, at the 320-meters-to-go mark, Hushovd had thrown off the shackles and I had no choice but to go with him.

Without my "secret weapon," I might barely have crept inside the top ten that day. That's because, within a few seconds of starting my sprint, I could feel the strength seeping from my legs and my front wheel slowing. My secret weapon was my second kick; I'd not needed to use it before in this Tour—I'd not needed it many times in my career—but with 150 meters to go and Robbie McEwen having swung across from the right-hand side and onto my wheel, I simply had no choice. Double kick, sixth gear, turbo boost, secret weapon—call it what you want; when you watch the replay of that sprint, there's a precise moment, roughly 100 meters from the line, when, rather than sucking the rider behind me along, my rear wheel seems to be blowing everyone backward. It was no coincidence that the "double kick" would bring me my biggest victory margin of the Tour—an abyss of three or four bike-lengths.

Is there a secret behind the secret weapon? Genes, perhaps, plus determination—that and all the racing I'd done on the track, in Madisons, points races, and scratch races. Those events weren't a steady buildup lasting several hours followed by one big sprint finish—they were punctuated by constant accelerations at uneven intervals, when you never knew when you might need to eke out a bit more speed to win a sprint or follow an attack. This was why I could move almost seamlessly from a block of track racing to road races and compete straightaway; whenever I swapped from the road to the track, on the other hand, it would take me days and sometimes weeks to refamiliarize myself and my muscles with the kind of multitiered sprinting speed that I needed to be a regular winner.

The trouble with the double kick was that, as far as my legs were concerned, it was like riding an extra 50 kilometers at the end of the stage. If it had taken 15.8 kilometers of climbing and a cheat in Leonardo Piepoli to leave me reeling on the ropes at Hautacam, it might just be that the effort of those last 320 meters here in Nîmes, and especially the last 150, was the one that had knocked me to the canvas.

Stage 12 had nicely exhibited how attention to detail could win or lose races, as could hair-trigger reactions in the final kilometer; the next stage had showcased my double kick. All four of my stage wins to date, and indeed every single thing I'd done since the Tour had left Brest two weeks earlier, had demonstrated beyond any doubt that I was so good because I wasn't one rider but nine—all of them identifiable by the Columbia sportswear logo on their jerseys. Yet again, on that thirteenth stage, as the temperatures inched toward the mid-30s (C), I'd felt not just grateful but humbled and embarrassed as my teammates went back and forth from the team car with water bottles. Had I been observing this from afar, I'd have been in awe of every one of them—George, Kosta, Bernie, Gerald, Marcus, Tommy, Kim, and Adam—and in awe of a sport and an event that demanded such selfless solidarity.

My teammates weren't only my water, or my shelter, or even my encouragement to make it over a climb—they were the fun in an event that could fast turn unpleasant if you dwelt on the negatives. You only had to look around the peloton at the wan, sunken faces of some of the other riders to see that. The overwhelming tiredness, the niggling injuries, the overcooked pasta in the crap hotels, the homesickness, a moody directeur sportif—if one of these didn't get to you, then another would. The only remedy was a sense of fun, enjoyment, and play, and nowhere was that more evident than in our team bus on the way to stages or at the dinner table at night. My exchange with George Hincapie as soon as we saw each other on the bus after the first, backbreaking stage in the Pyrenees couldn't have summed it up better.

Me: "How many major tours have you done now? Like thirty-six, or something stupid . . . ?"

George: "Nineteen."

Me: "You must be fucking nuts."

There was a serious point lurking in the laughter that came next—namely, that you had to smile, otherwise it *would* drive you nuts. I'd had the philosophy ever since I'd started riding as a kid: This was too difficult, too painful, a sport if you didn't squeeze out as much fun as possible. And to me, fun is what it had always been, partly because back home on the Isle of Man, there were always people to go riding with, mates to take the piss out of, and partly because there was something in my makeup that meant I bloody loved it—even when it *was* hard and it *did* hurt like billy-o. It was the same with anything, I'd decided—the more you enjoyed yourself, the better you'd perform. Having fun and giving fun were also the closest I came to a purpose in my life.

Of course "fun" or "passion" was never going to satisfy the anoraks who wanted facts and figures and muscle biopsies to account for my sprinting prowess. In fairness, there *were* scientific factors that played a major part, one of them being a capacity to generate power and therefore speed that was disproportionately high in relation to my frontal area. In plain English, that meant that while I produced slightly less power than the Tom Boonens or Thor Hushovds or Andre Greipels of this world—say, 1,400 watts in a sprint to their 1,800—I was a lot shorter and managed to get a lot, *lot* lower on my bike when I was sprinting. I was therefore a *lot* more aerodynamic. And the best of it was that, while I could work on increasing my power, there was absolutely sod all they could do except get a fraction lower at the risk of, you guessed it, losing some of their wattage because the position was too uncomfortable.

My team, my directeurs, my eye for detail, the best equipment, the legs, the bike handling, the instinct, the passion—they all added up to a simple and honest if arrogant-sounding response to another question that I and other riders and pundits were now being asked on a daily basis.

The question was "Is Mark Cavendish the fastest sprinter in the world?"

The answer, thirteen stages into the 2008 Tour de France, could only be "Yes."

STAGE 13: NARBONNE-NÎMES, 182 KM

1. Mark Cavendish (GBr), Team Columbia, 4:25:42 (41.10 kph)

GENERAL CLASSIFICATION

1. Cadel Evans (Aus), Silence-Lotto, 54:48:47

144. Mark Cavendish (GBr), Team Columbia, 1:52:04

STAGE 14

Saturday, 19 July 2008
NÎMES–DIGNE LES BAINS
194.5 KM

I t's one of the great tragedies of the Tour de France that, at any point in a rider's three-week, 3,500-kilometer journey through one of the most naturally beautiful countries on earth, the only landscape and landmarks that exist in his consciousness are the ones that feature in two dimensions on the pages of the Tour roadbook. Châteaus, rivers, towns, and monuments all flash past like a tourist-board slideshow—and leave an even less lasting impression. If a Tour rider were to compile a guidebook based on his experiences, the criteria for inclusion would be "Does it have a road?" "Are we going over it?" and "If so, how much will it hurt?"

Stage 14 perfectly demonstrated this unfortunate reality. The stage village that day hugged the walls of one of the most famous Roman amphitheaters in the world in Nîmes, but my teammates and I were too busy going through our pre-race rituals behind the tinted glass of our team bus to pay any attention. I've often argued that you have to be pretty comfortable with your sexuality to choose a sport in which shaved legs and Lycra are the norm—and that's particularly true on our bus when everyone's stripping down and applying all sorts of muscle rubs and antichafing creams in the hour before a stage start. Put it this way: The last time I saw so many dangly objects, there was a tree and it was Christmas.

Looking around the bus now, you could tell we were heading toward the third week of the Tour. I saw the same eight faces that had lined up at the team presentation in Brest, but in every one, there was a subtle difference, a slight change, or maybe just an accentuation of something that was already there. That was it: In the same way that the speed, the noise, the difficulty were just *more* in this race, so here, after two weeks, everyone was somehow *more* himself. We hadn't become nine different men in the space of a fortnight, but people were right when they compared this race to an emotional roller coaster; since leaving Brest, we'd not so much ridden through France as embarked on a journey through our own and each other's emotions.

At the end of every stage, we'd all pile onto the bus and tell our stories, and every one would be different. Each of us was the star of his own personal daily drama. Some plots were etched in facial features—like the blood vessels in Marcus Burghardt's eyes, which seemed to grow redder and more prominent with every stage that he spent flaying himself on my behalf, while other tales of triumph and despair played out behind an uncomplaining, inscrutable mask like Thomas Lövkvist's. Tommy was our silent warrior, his mood as steady and steadfast as his position on the bike. There was some debate over whether his bike was even fitted with gears; every time the terrain changed, while the rest of us would be frantically flicking at our gear levers, Tommy knew only one technique, and that was to push harder.

Eisel was even cheerier, Kirchen even drier, Siutsou even more the archetypal East European—they were all just *more*. My roommate Adam, George Hincapie's main rival for the title of nicest man on the team, was even nicer than usual. Adam had started the Tour apprehensive and still largely unheralded at this level, but thanks to his fabulous contribution to my stage wins, no one had boosted his profile more in the first two weeks of the race. He was loving it—and it showed in everything he did, however quiet and soft-spoken he remained.

Adam was desperate for me to win that fourteenth stage. I would have been, too, but within a few kilometers of the start in Nîmes, and possibly even earlier that morning, I'd quickly realized that my legs were losing patience with their daily beatings. I mentioned in the previous chapter that one of the perils of the "double kick" was a high toll of tiredness the next day, and, sure enough, now I was being asked to pay the full tariff. I'd warned the guys in the briefing that morning that I was unlikely to make it over the category 3 climb 15 kilometers from the finish in Digne with the main group and that, consequently, they should concentrate on teeing up Gerald Ciolek. "If I'm still in touch, I'll let you know on the radio and we can change the plan," I'd said. Adam had insisted that he should stay with me, but I'd been equally adamant that it was a gamble not worth taking. The hometown of Nostradamus may have been on the route that day, but it didn't take a soothsayer to work out that my great Tour de France adventure might just be entering its final act.

My prediction turned out to be as accurate as the one on Stage 5 with which I opened this book. This time, there was no trip back to the team car that wasn't enforced, no order to the directeurs sportifs to place bets with Unibet.com; if they'd wanted to make a bet on my race ending in Digne, in any case, all the evidence they needed could be found at the back of the peloton, where I spent the entire day straining to stay in touch. As it happened it wasn't so much the climb that did for me as the mad dash to the bottleneck at the base of the hill. It was one bunch sprint too many. Earlier in the week, I might have clung on, but now my legs had given up. The Spaniard Oscar Freire would win the stage and a tired Gerald Ciolek finish well down in the same lead group while I struggled home over three minutes behind.

If you watch the couple of TV interviews I did on my way back to the bus that afternoon, you can see the weariness in my eyes and detect it in my voice, but there's also a hint of sadness. I can only think that my subconscious was in on a secret—because it didn't occur to me there and then that my Tour could be over. My teammates would have told you that it didn't occur to them either; that afternoon, everyone was exhausted, and the somber mood on the bus ride to our hotel was merely a reflection of that.

It was when we arrived back at the hotel that the team doctor, Helge, called me into the small room at the back of the bus used by the soigneurs to store and prepare food. He moved deliberately and spoke quietly—as people always do when they're about to break bad news. I braced myself, not for the surprise but more for the inevitability.

Sure enough . . .

"You know what I'm about to say, don't you?" Helge said.

I might have croaked a "Yes," I might have just nodded. Whatever my response, it was followed by an eruption of tears.

I didn't want to leave the Tour de France. There were all sorts of good reasons for leaving, far fewer for staying, but I still didn't want to leave. It wasn't the prospect of more stage wins or even reaching Paris that would make it so hard to quit; while I very much hoped there'd be other years and other opportunities to target those milestones, what I'd never be able to accurately re-create were all the emotions I'd shared with my teammates since we'd left Brittany, and which the other eight would now share without me in the last week of the Tour. It was hardly surprising that Brian Holm's last words to me before I left would be "Whatever you do, don't watch the race, and especially not the bunch sprints, because you'll regret it. . . ."—not that I'd be at all tempted.

On the night of that fourteenth stage, some could perhaps have guessed, but none of my teammates actually knew that I wasn't starting the next day. I don't know whether I was embarrassed to tell them—whether I was hoping for some miracle rejuvenation—or whether I didn't want to give them any more food for anxious thoughts on the eve of the first Alpine stage of the race to Pratonevoso. Whatever the logic, I waited until breakfast the following day. Alas, there had been no sudden, overnight renaissance, and there'd be no Mark Cavendish on the start line in Embrun that morning.

In truth, there were worse times and places to abort this particular mission. Stage 15 would take the race over the third-highest mountain pass in Europe, the Colle dell'Agnello (the race was due over the highest, the Col de la Bonnette, in two days' time), and into Italy. Of the seven stages remaining, only one looked certain to end in a bunch sprint, and that would be on the last day in Paris, on the Champs-Élysées. Besides that carrot, in racing terms, the only conceivable benefit of staying on would be a bit more attrition on my CV and the badge of honor that was finishing the Tour. The risks were both more numerous and more laden with consequences. In under a month, I'd be in Beijing, riding an Olympic Madison that I'd been working toward for over three years. Without that to consider, I'd have done my best to press on, but now, in terms of my form, time spent just surviving would be wasted time in terms of the sharpness I'd need in China. Far better to quit while I was ahead, rest for a week, then refocus. It was a painful choice but also the right one.

That morning, in Embrun, our team press officer had alerted the media to my abandonment and said I'd be available to answer questions at the team bus before the start of the race. It was pouring with rain—another reason to be grateful—so I chose a sheltered spot, on the steps of the team bus, to talk about what had been over the past two weeks and what would hopefully be in the next month taking me through to Beijing. A crowd of perhaps two dozen journalists and cameramen had gathered—all of them keen to find out whether I appreciated what I'd achieved. I told them that my fellow sprinter, Thor Hushovd, had asked me the same thing in the race the previous day; just as I had with Thor, now I shrugged and said it'd probably take a while to sink in. Only months later, while writing this book, would I realize that not only had preoccupations with the Olympics hastened my withdrawal from the Tour, they would also mean that the "sinking in" would never take place.

One of the soigneurs drove me over the Agnello and to the feed zone, where he had to stop, and I hopped into one of the directeurs' cars with Brian Holm. To the casual spectator, that stage to Pratonevoso was the most riveting of the Tour so far, with attacks, collapses, and every other key ingredient of a classic Tour stage. To me, it was a peculiar feeling to be witnessing it all from behind a car windscreen. For the previous two weeks, one race had existed in my eyes and mind and above all my legs, and now I was seeing a different Tour. It was a Tour I hardly recognized. A Tour in which I felt a spectator, or at worst an intruder. A Tour in which I'd been left behind like a memory.

I flew back to the Isle of Man the following day, the Tour's second rest day. Melissa picked me up from the airport and drove me straight to her parents' pub in Laxey. My "hero's" welcome amounted to a kiss from my girlfriend and my pet golden retriever bounding toward me across the pub car park with red, white, and blue ribbons tied around her neck. Or at least that was what I thought was the extent of it; had I been a little less weary, a bit more lucid, or just a bit less delighted to see Amber, I might have looked around and realized that the dog had been sent as a cunning decoy to divert my attention from the familiar cars that would have given away the surprise. I pushed open the door to be greeted by balloons, posters commemorating my stage wins, and of course, most importantly, the family and close friends who'd perhaps celebrated and savored my achievements more than I had. Melissa told me she would have organized something bigger, only she knew I was tired and wouldn't want to be hounded. My dad had agreed, but, not that I minded, it was he who ended up hounding me more than anyone.

I said I didn't follow the last few stages of the Tour on TV. That's not strictly true. When I heard that Marcus Burghardt had won Stage 18 in Saint-Étienne, outsprinting the Spaniard Carlos Barredo after a long breakaway, not only did I make sure I caught the highlights, but I was probably more emotional watching Marcus win than I'd been after any of my own stage wins. As I've already stressed more than once, Marcus had barely budged from the front of the peloton since the start of the Tour—a fact borne out by an independent analysis that gauged the visibility each team's sponsor had obtained during the Tour and found that Burghi's towering, six-foot-two frame had appeared on screen more than that of any other rider except the eventual winner of the Tour, the Spaniard Carlos Sastre. The difference was that Sastre had been pursuing personal glory all along, whereas everything Burghi had done until that eighteenth stage, he'd done for a teammate. It just went to show that, while Sastre was the rider who'd have a yellow jersey around his shoulders in Paris that Sunday, and while the pundits were pretty unanimous in pronouncing me their other "star" of the Tour, in many ways, unacknowledged by the watching public and press, Marcus Burghardt had eclipsed both of us.

I may not have been watching my teammates every day, but I was in contact with them throughout that final week, usually via text messages. George Hincapie was determined that I should fly back to Paris to celebrate with them on the final day, but to me, it didn't seem right; the applause on the Champs-Élysées was a privilege reserved for those who'd earned it—the reward at the end of a journey that I hadn't completed. George would have none of it; no doubt exaggerating, he said that if I didn't show up, the rest of the team would opt out of their lap of honor of the Champs in protest at my absence.

Melissa believes in karma; she'd say that would explain the catalog of mistakes and misfortune that befell us that Sunday—that, just as I'd tried to tell George, I was never supposed to be in Paris that afternoon. The complications started even before we set off, when Melissa went to London for a hen weekend and we had to coordinate flights for me to meet her at Gatwick on Sunday morning. That plan was destined to fail as soon as I arrived at the airport on the Isle of Man at five o'clock that morning and found that fog had delayed my flight. No matter—I called Melissa and told her she'd have to go to Paris on her own and I'd swap flights, go to Manchester, then fly from there to Paris. I'd ask Bart, the team soigneur, to pick her up at the airport, and I'd join her later. With a bit of luck, I might still just about make it to the Champs-Élysées in time for the race.

The hours ticked by. The delays got longer. Eventually, around lunchtime, the fog lifted and I boarded the plane for Manchester, at about the same time that Melissa was starting her descent into Paris. Now she was the one waiting around as Bart showed up an hour late. We were finally reunited at eight o'clock, three hours after the end of the race but just in time to join the team for the start of a celebratory dinner in a restaurant in central Paris. At least, that's what we would have done had we been able to find the restaurant. We sat down to our starters at ten o'clock. Knackered. After a few drinks, a few laughs, and a brief visit to the Garmin team's end-of-Tour party, I'd been awake twenty hours and was desperate to fall into bed.

Had the 2008 Tour de France changed my life? It may not have felt like it in the days and weeks that followed, but in some tangible respects, there was no mistaking that some things were different. On the Isle of Man, I've always been just one of the lads, and that hadn't changed. There was more interest, more flickers of recognition, when I went to the supermarket—even a giant poster at the airport welcoming tourists to "The Home of Mark Cavendish"—but the Island was probably where life looked most like it had a month or two earlier. It was when I went back to Europe, and particularly the Dutch and Belgian post-Tour criterium, or circuit, races that kicked off in the week after the Tour that I really got a sense of the shift in perception. The sole purpose of these races is to showcase the heroes of the Tour, who are unsurprisingly happy to bask in the adulation of tens of thousands of fans in return for substantial appearance fees. From my point of view, not only was the money a welcome bonus and the fast, nervous racing ideal preparation for the Olympics, but in the echoing voices of the fans as they cheered my name lay the most vivid confirmation yet of how wide and powerful the Tour's impact could really be.

With success, clearly, came popularity, and for a cyclist, with popularity comes money. In no other sport is a rider's earning potential so closely tied to his ability to generate publicity for a corporate sponsor, and after a Tour in which I'd proven my ability not just as a sprinter but as a moving billboard for the Columbia brand, a reevaluation of my market value by both me and my team was inevitable. I'd signed my first pro contract for €40,000 a year at the end of 2006, then renegotiated and re-signed for another two and a half years in June 2007 when the victories started flowing. Now the sponsor, our manager, Bob Stapleton, and I all wanted to make sure I remained with the team beyond the end of 2009.

I could have left Columbia at the end of 2008. Two teams had tabled bids equal to exactly double the salary Bob Stapleton was offering—and that was before I'd even needed to haggle. Ask almost anyone in professional cycling and they'll tell you that it's a short career, that the hundreds of thousands or even millions you can earn as a top pro won't last forever, and that, therefore, the best offer is also, always, the biggest one. More than one person did tell me this when I confided in them that summer, and every time I listened respectfully and politely declined their advice. I presented Bob with the minimum figure that it would take for me to stay, and he said I had a deal. My new contract would keep me with the team until the end of 2010 with an option for 2011—in other words, Bob could decide to either keep me or let me leave.

Why didn't I go elsewhere and double my money? Simple—for the same reasons that I'll now honor my contract with Bob rather than join Team Sky, the much-trumpeted, eagerly anticipated British-based pro team that will debut in the pro ranks in 2010. When the man behind that project, the British Cycling performance director Dave Brailsford, unveiled the first concrete details of his plan in February 2009, the press at home and abroad was quick to assume that I'd be the fulcrum and figurehead of the team. The *Sun* newspaper even dedicated almost a full page to a picture of me winning Stage 5 of the Tour, alongside an article speculating that I could be bought out of a contract worth "about £1.2m" a year with Columbia. They were wrong on two counts—once, spectacularly, on the value of my current deal, then again on the likelihood of me wriggling out of that deal before its expiration date.

So what are those reasons? Well, one is that, although Sky looks set to be one of the richest teams, if not *the* richest, in the peloton—and logic certainly dictates that it'd be willing to fork out more for Britain's most high-profile Tour rider than any Spanish, Italian, or, for that matter, American-based outfit—the wealth that motivates me is not the kind that appears on my bank statement. If they could guarantee me wins in

Tour stages or Classics like Paris-Roubaix and Milan–San Remo, that would be another matter, but that's the other issue: I solemnly swear that I couldn't guarantee the results I've had this year with different teammates. And what if I really couldn't? What then? Well, just flick back a few chapters and reread what I said about the implications of burning bridges with other riders. The very same applies to auctioning off your services to the highest bidder; for one, two, or maybe three years, you cash the checks and watch the zeroes multiply, but what happens the next time you come to negotiate, when your price has plummeted because you haven't won any races, and you haven't won any races because although your new teammates are good, your old ones were the best? Is it just me, or is it not more sensible to invest first in your potential as a bike rider, then skim off the material benefits as and when they arrive as a consequence of success?

I'd chatted once or twice with Lance Armstrong about this over the past few months. Lance texted George after my first win at the 2008 Tour, inviting George to pass on his congratulations, "unless he's a dickhead." George apparently replied that, nah, I wasn't all that bad, really, and that I actually reminded him a fair bit of a young Lance, perhaps alluding as much to my fearless approach to racing as my fiery temperament.

Lance and I finally met at the Interbike trade show in Las Vegas in September 2008, and then again on our bikes, in the second race of his comeback, the Tour of California. It was there that he gave me a piece of advice as simple as its source is authoritative: "Don't waste your money." I told him he needn't worry; my directeur sportif Valerio Piva may tut and shake his head at my designer jeans, and I may have developed an expensive habit of buying glitzy watches for myself and my teammates, but I know the value of money. There's hardly a top Italian pro these days who doesn't own a Ferrari or, at the very least, a Porsche. They can keep them; if and when I next buy a car to replace our Lexus 4×4, it'll probably be secondhand, and it certainly won't have a prancing horse on the bonnet.

As for the other attractions of joining Team Sky, and the idea that I'd rather be in a team where the majority or at least a significant proportion of the riders will be British, I'd respond that I love my current teammates and my current directeurs sportifs and struggle to imagine an environment where I could feel more comfortable. I get on well with Brad Wiggins, Geraint Thomas, and Dave Millar—all of whom would be expected to ride for Sky at some point, whether it be next year or further down the line—but I won't be offending any of those guys when I say that I'm equally close to Bernhard Eisel, George Hincapie, Adam Hansen, and a number of other teammates. Again, I don't want to prejudge Team Sky or indeed any other team in the peloton; I do, though, believe that my team has an X-factor—a unique mix of ability, camaraderie, and unity—that would be nigh on impossible to re-create elsewhere. Among the twenty-nine of us, we won seventy-seven races in 2008—more than any other team—yet the atmosphere remained that of a bunch of mates meeting up for a joke and a laugh. George, Bernie, and another one of my most experienced teammates, Michael Rogers, all say the same—they've never had this much fun in any of their previous teams.

Much as I would like to vacuum-pack and deep-freeze what we had in 2008 and more specifically at the Tour, of course I'm not naive enough to think our team won't evolve and change. To an extent, at the end of 2008, that had already happened, as the German pair, Gerald Ciolek and Linus Gerdemann, both left for the Milram team. As I've already intimated more than once, while I may not have welcomed Gerald's departure, it certainly made sense, and not solely on financial grounds. He's too good to be straitjacketed to the role of lead-out man—and won't have to be at his new team. Incidentally, there's plenty more about another rider who didn't renew his Columbia contract, Brad Wiggins, in the next chapter.

The crucial thing, of course, is that the team carries on winning, whoever the personnel, whatever the color of the jersey—which, to my slight regret, changed from the blue neon that illuminated the Tour to a yellow-and-white design for 2009. Tweaking our kit design wasn't (but perhaps could have been) one way of disguising me and disguising the fact that after my four stage wins at the Tour, suddenly me winning a sprint was treated by fans and the media as a formality, and losing as a major story. Fortunately, in the second half of 2008 and the first few weeks of 2009, the ratio remained clearly in my favor, thanks to my winning three out of three bunch sprints at the Tour of Ireland in August 2008, three out of five at the Tour of Missouri a month later, two out of two in the Tour of Qatar in February 2009, and two out of three at the Tour of California later the same month. Most reassuringly, on every occasion bar one or two that the final 200 meters of a race were a test of pure sprinting ability, and my lead-out train was on time and unencumbered—which was usually the case—the press was left to write about the formality of victory rather than the calamity of defeat.

One of my main sprint rivals, Tom Boonen, knows all about this predicament—the pressure of having amassed enough trophies and accolades in your early 20s for a lifetime's achievement, and the expectations that come with such precocity. Boonen has freely admitted over the past couple of years that, after winning the World Championship road race in Madrid at 24, he began to lack motivation. Depending on what you read, and whose version of his positive test for cocaine in 2008 and multiple driving offenses over the past couple of years you believe, either Boonen has slightly lost his way and the odd sprint or, for a brief period, he lost the plot entirely.

In theory, I could be vulnerable to the same malaise. I've also won a lot at a young age. In common with Tom, I'll never win the Tour de France or the Giro d'Italia. Sometimes, I'll confess, in those rare moments in the winter of 2008 when I could reflect on the previous, heady summer, I even wondered how on earth I'd done it all—and more importantly, how I could possibly do it all again.

Does this mean I'm doubting myself? No, more a case of acknowledging that a rider winning four stages in a single Tour is a twice-a-decade occurrence—and that no one has accomplished the feat twice in the same decade since Eddy Merckx in the 1970s. If fans in Britain and abroad expected me to reel off another four or more in 2009, I could only very much hope that I wouldn't disappoint—but I'd also like them to appreciate that any such deed wouldn't be a case of normal service resuming. It would, in fact, be like climbing to the pinnacle as high as anything in the Alps or Pyrenees—pretty much the peak of what a sprinter can achieve—for the second time in twelve months.

I'm glad to say that, for me at least, motivation shouldn't be a problem. Besides stage wins at the Tour, I hope one day to wear and take home the green jersey that rewards the winner of the points competition—a race within a race running parallel to the Tour's general classification and offering a sliding scale of points for the first three riders over intermediate finish lines, dotted along the route of every stage, and for finishing positions on each stage. The fact that the green jersey is also occasionally referred to as the sprinters' jersey tells you what kind of rider usually contends. Unfortunately, there are also points available on mountain stages, plus of course there is the obligation to finish the Tour to qualify—which means that the sprinter sporting green in Paris is often not the fastest but the most consistent and the most resilient in the mountains.

Prize jerseys in the Tour and indeed other stage races are one goal that should help to keep me occupied and focused for a few years yet, not to mention a good incentive to work on my climbing. When I say "work," I should really say "continue working," or even "let nature take its course," given that the more I race, the more mountains I climb, the more I improve. By my own admission, I'm currently one of the worst climbers in the pro peloton, although the perception of what that status entails sometimes frustrates me. No, contrary to what a lot of the "aficionados" on Internet forums think and write, I don't get dropped "every time a race goes over a railway bridge"; take the time to examine the route details of one stage that I won in the Giro in particular last year, and you'll discover that it wasn't flat, wasn't merely "hilly," but did in fact require me to climb a mountain higher than Ben Nevis.

What every cycling fan knows as the Classics is another source of intrigue and stimulation. I mentioned in a previous chapter that the first races to inspire and excite me when I was a teenager were also the most brutal events on the calendar—the Tour of Flanders and Paris-Roubaix, with their cobbles and crosswinds and iron-willed, iron-jawed Belgian and Dutch stars. The Grote Scheldeprijs may not rival either of these monuments in terms of prestige, but my wins there in 2007 and 2008 certainly deepened my fascination with the hotbed of racing that straddles the Benelux countries and northern France. At our training camp in Majorca in January 2008, Brian Holm had introduced me to a brilliant documentary about the 1976 Paris-Roubaix called *A Sunday in Hell*; I watch that film now and think that's the era when I wish I was riding. The guy who won was a Belgian by the name of Marc Derneyer. You watch that film and can only marvel at how hard someone like Derneyer was—or the Italian Francesco Moser, who finished the race with his undervest flapping over his mud-splattered shorts. That's cycling—279 kilometers, over cobbles that rattle your bones like 10,000 volts of electricity, in the wind and cold, with mud flying up into your face, into your eyes and mouth, with some big Belgian bastard on the front who wants to rip your legs off. That's cycling. Some of the blokes who race these days spend too much time worrying about their tan lines.

The Tour's green jersey, Paris-Roubaix, a World Championship road race that's due to take place on a sprinter-friendly course in Melbourne in 2010 or in Copenhagen in 2011, the Olympic road race in London in 2012, and the Tour of Flanders when I'm a touch older and stronger—there's plenty still to aim at. My interest is in leaving a lasting imprint on this sport, and I know you don't do that by enjoying one or two good seasons, winning a few Tour stages, then burying your head in a bowl of powder. Thankfully, those two years at Barclays also taught me to value what I have and that I should think very long and very hard before doing anything that might compromise a career and a wonderful life. It would be both disrespectful and wrong to suggest that there were any cautionary tales among the six lads with whom I shared some fantastic adventures at the Academy in 2004 and 2005, but it's worth reminding myself every now and again that given the odd piece of misfortune here, the odd lapse in focus there, the odd injury, the dream can soon disappear. In their own ways, Christian Varley, Bruce Edgar, and Tom White were all more talented than me, yet all stopped racing years ago; Matt Brammeier, again at least as gifted as me, now races for a small, Belgian-based team run by the former rider Sean Kelly; Geraint Thomas rode the 2007 Tour de France with Barloworld but has yet to win a pro road race; Ed Clancy, like Geraint, is now an MBE after his gold-medal-winning ride in the team pursuit in the Beijing Olympics but on the road competes mainly in Britain for the Halfords Bikehut team.

What has set me apart so far is my passion—and the logical conclusion would be that I'll cease to flourish and maybe even cease to survive as a pro as soon as that runs dry. The logical conclusion might also be the correct one; fortunately, at the moment, I can't conceive of how a feeling so raw and so real could possibly evaporate, at least for the foreseeable future. When it does, there'll be only one, sad but necessary, course of action: Hang up my bike and retire—very probably to a slightly more slow-moving life on the Isle of Man with Melissa and, who knows, maybe a couple of little boy or girl racers.

What I do know for certain is that I'll carry on splitting opinion, carry on wearing my soppy big heart on my sleeve, carry on smiling when I win and scowling, swearing, and spitting the dummy when I lose. A bit like the 2008 Tour de France, it's been one hell of a journey to this point and, at 24 years of age, I think it's fair to say and hope that it's only just begun.

STAGE 14: NÎMES–DIGNE LES BAINS, 194.5 KM

1. Oscar Freire Gomez (Spa), Rabobank, 4:13:08 (46.102 kph)
108. Mark Cavendish (GBr), Team Columbia, 3:27

GENERAL CLASSIFICATION

1. Cadel Evans (Aus), Silence-Lotto, 59:01:55
140. Mark Cavendish (GBr), Team Columbia, 1:55:31

MILAN–SAN REMO

2009

Go, Brad! They're gonna blow. They're gonna blow . . . !"
As Bradley's hand dropped into mine—a bullet into a gun barrel—my arm drew back, then the trigger released, and a huge roar of excitement and anticipation filled the track, as if everyone in the velodrome had read my lips. Maybe that had been the problem for the last forty-five minutes—if the crowd didn't know what we were saying, they definitely seemed to know what we were plotting. Thus, every time Brad started cranking up those massive levers or my shorter, stumpier little pistons started pumping—and one of us moved a few meters off the front—the noise from the stands alerted our opponents to the danger. All through the race, we'd been attacking—powerfully, relentlessly—yet every time, it seemed, as much as the crowd's support was inspiring us, it was also creating a wave of sound on which every team was hitching a ride.

This time, I sensed it was different straightaway. The Madison is considered an endurance event—and in terms of track cycling, 200 laps of the velodrome and 50 kilometers are a long way, even if you do ride in teams of two and share the distance. In road cycling, of course, 50 kilometers is nothing—a quarter, a fifth, or even a sixth the distance of the most prestigious one-day races. That was why I was telling Brad the others would blow; with 30 laps to go and over 40 kilometers already ridden, this was where Brad and I, both of us full-time road pros who dabbled in track racing, would come into our own.

We needed a lap. Just one lap would do it. There are two ways to score in the Madison: finishing in the first four positions in sprints worth 5, 3, 2, and 1 points at predetermined times in the race or lapping the rest of the field. The winning pair is the one that has gained the most laps at the end of the race; in practice, at the end of a Madison, there are often multiple teams tied on the same number of laps, and that's when the number of points gained in sprints becomes the decisive factor. If you like, sprint points are the "goal difference" of the Madison.

One lap. Easier said than done, especially as several teams had already opened their account. That meant two things—one, that it was no good dragging them with us for them to gain a second lap while we notched our first, and two, they would spit blood, teeth, and guts to stop us getting away. In other words, we'd have to do it on our own—one team against seventeen other pairs, logic, science, and the bounds of belief. Watching Brad streak away now, don't ask me why, but I liked our chances. . . .

An hour later, we were standing on the top step of the podium with gold medals draped around our necks, smiles on our faces, lumps in our throats, a Union Jack above our heads, and "God Save the Queen" ringing in our ears. As the final bell had rung out, Brad and I now miraculously level on laps with six other teams, I'd glanced at the scoreboard for a final check on what we needed in the final sprint to ensure victory. The board had displayed only positions five to eight, meaning I'd just have to sprint and hope for the best. As the same scoreboard now finally indicated, my 3rd place had been more than enough:

1. Great Britain 19 pts Mark Cavendish Bradley Wiggins
2. Germany 13 pts Roger Kluge Olaf Pollack
3. Denmark one lap and 11 pts Michael Morkov Alex Rasmussen

It was Manchester, March, and we were World Champions. Now we just had to do it all again in five months' time in Beijing.

My two World Madison titles both relied on a lot of luck—not because I didn't deserve them but because, in theory, I shouldn't have been riding on either occasion, in Los Angeles in 2005 or in Manchester in 2008.

In the winter before LA, I was only penciled in to partner Rob Hayles when Geraint Thomas ruptured his spleen in a crash as we were riding to the Sydney velodrome during a training camp in Australia. Privately, I'd felt pretty miffed when Gee had been selected ahead of me in the first place, then quite vindicated when, having been told that I'd replace him, I finished second in the Sydney World Cup Madison with Tom White, another one of the Academy lads. Tom, smug and southern, and me, northern and narky, had never been great mates, not that there was any real malice intended when, a few days after our Madison in Sydney, I took a brand-new pair of shorts out of his suitcase and put them back in the wardrobe as he was packing for Bendigo, the next stop on our trip. Someone grassed; Tom was furious, and so was Rod—so furious that he told me I'd just lost my place in the team for LA Worlds. Tom then, ironically, probably saved me by announcing in the briefing at a circuit race in Bendigo a few days later that he refused to ride for me. Four years on, Rod says now that he should have put his foot down and given Tom a choice—follow orders, lead me out, or not race at all. As it turned out, we all rode, Ed and Matt Brammeier did a fantastic job, and I won ahead of . . . Tom White. Not only had Tom's irritation backfired on him, it ended up returning me to the moral high ground and, after more discussions between Rod and Dave Brailsford, to my place for the Worlds.

Three years later, before Manchester, I'd at least been one of the first-choice pairing, though not before the British Federation had told me I'd have to prove myself first by interrupting my winter break after my first full road season with T-Mobile to ride the Madison with Bradley at the World Cups in Sydney and Beijing. Again, I was pissed off; I'd been riding World Cup and World Championship Madisons for years, never finishing outside the top four; I'd been a world champion at 19 in LA; I'd proven myself in Six Days like Ghent and Dortmund, where the Madisons were notoriously tough. Yet here they were telling me I *still* had to go to the other side of the world to prove myself if I wanted to ride the Worlds and, later, the Olympics. One logic was that we still had to rack up World Cup points to even *qualify* for Beijing, but it was Great Britain as a nation that still needed to qualify—it didn't need to be Bradley and me. To me, it would have made much more sense to send one of the glut of good young Madison riders on the Federation's books to Beijing and Sydney for points and experience. Meanwhile, I could have spent the winter getting the rest that, who knows, might have translated into freshness and speed and medals months later in Manchester and then again in China. But no—Brad and I went to Sydney and Beijing, did the necessary, then returned to Europe to face what would be a long, tough road season punctuated by the two most prestigious Madison races on the calendar.

When I said I shouldn't have ridden in Manchester, I wasn't referring to the convoluted, contentious process of securing my place in the team. What I meant, and what very few people know, is that the day before the Madison, after a crap ride in the points race, when I felt strong but strangely one-paced, I climbed off my bike and felt a splitting pain in my groin. I played it down that night, mainly because I hate it when other people make excuses for poor performances, but after two hours of physio, it was still hurting. Same the next morning. To the coaches' question of whether I'd be fit to race, I said I honestly couldn't give a confident answer, whereupon they decided that Geraint would take my place and partner Bradley. Half an hour later, I could sense an improvement and let them know. "Look, I'm not going to bullshit you and say I'm okay when I'm not. I'm the last person who wants to go out and look like an idiot. . . ." They took a lot of convincing but eventually relented, and the rest, our win and gold medal included, is history.

The volume and the intensity of the support in the Manchester velodrome that day will remain one of my best memories in cycling. The same, purely in terms of gratification, applies to the text message that Bradley, a multiple world and Olympic champion on the track, sent me that night saying it had been the best of all his major wins on the track. One reason, said Brad, was that it was his major first title in a nontimed event—in other words, where he'd been racing other riders rather than the clock. The other was that it had come in an event where his dad had once been one of the world's top riders. His dad, a few weeks earlier, had been murdered in Australia.

The Parisian post-Tour party that nearly never was, at least for Melissa and me, also marked the end of my post-Tour rest. Actually, that's not strictly true, not only because in the week since I'd abandoned it, the Tour had carried on—it just carried on without me—but also because I'd been out on my bike every day. Every cyclist or fan worth their salt will tell you that while tiredness is an inevitability two or three weeks into the Tour, fantastic form for another two, three, or maybe four weeks after the race ends is one of its major boons. My problem in that week on the Isle of Man was resisting the temptation to milk that magic feeling when every ride is pure, unadulterated enjoyment. In a month's time, I'd be riding the Olympic Madison, and the only way to be at my best in Beijing was to ease off now, then build up again over the next three weeks. The solution? Stopping for coffee twice on every ride.

From the Isle of Man, I'd flown to Paris, and from Paris headed to Belgium for the week of post-Tour criteriums that I mentioned in the previous chapter. As I also mentioned in the previous chapter, these races brought an opportunity not only to swell my fan base but also, crucially, to develop a good training base from which to start my final preparations for Beijing. Rod agreed that these races, which typically lasted a couple of hard, frenetic hours, were the ideal appetizer for the track work I was about to start with him in Manchester.

Rod wasn't in charge of the Madison, so to speak. Nobody was. Nobody ever had been. The man at the top of the British Cycling pyramid, Dave Brailsford, had rejigged the coaching staff and reevaluated their approach after parting with Simon Jones in 2007, but as far as I could see, one thing that hadn't changed was the coaches' obsession with the timed events and particularly the team pursuit. At least now they were winning World Championships and beating world records, which hadn't been the case under Jonesy. But that still didn't help me. Bradley didn't mind, of course, because not only was he entered for both the individual and team pursuits, and not only were they easier to predict and control, they also came before the Madison on the track program in Beijing. From my point of view, at every major track championship I'd attended, the coaches had shown zero interest in the Madison until twenty-four hours before the race, when the team pursuit was over. Now, partly because the Madison was the last of Brad's three events and partly because no one at the Federation was putting any pressure on him to give it any thought, it would have been naive of me to expect him to start focusing on the race more than a few hours before we lined up together in the Laoshan velodrome on 19 August.

When I started a nine-day block of training with Rod before flying to China, the rest of the GB track team, Brad included, was training at the *other* British Cycling velodrome, in Newport, South Wales. Why wasn't I with them? Simple—for the reasons I've just explained and above all the fact that if I'd gone to Newport, it would have been no different from the Worlds in LA in 2005 or in Bordeaux the following year, or at the training camp with Jonesy in Perth at the end of 2006. I didn't want to spend hours twiddling my thumbs in the middle of the track, waiting for the team pursuiters to take their breaks and leave me to train uninterrupted. There was no one there to coach me, in any case, whereas in Manchester I would have Rod and his undivided attention.

The training was hard. I'd just ridden the ultimate endurance event, the Tour, where the explosive efforts, the five- or ten-second leg-wreckers, came hours apart, but now you could make that minutes or sometimes seconds. It was hard, but there were no excuses—I wasn't still tired from the Tour, mentally or physically. On the contrary; one day, after the riders who'd been in Newport had left for Beijing, Melissa and I sat in the hotel that was our Manchester base camp and watched the opening ceremony, goggle-eyed. While road cycling was my first love and my bread and butter, and the Tour the axis of my season and my universe, the Olympics was still the Olympics.

I may have been critical of the British Cycling Federation's attitude toward the Madison, but there was no denying that other aspects of its Olympic planning were spot-on. One good example was a system whereby, in the first three years of every Olympic cycle, we traveled to and from events on inexpensive flights, with the money saved going into a fund to buy business-class outward flights in Olympics year. This was particularly useful for me, as my legs have always reacted badly to long-haul flights. Apparently, it's the same for anyone with big leg muscles—after a long flight, fluid collects in your thighs and calves, and for days afterward your legs can feel swollen and lifeless. A comfy pillow and extra legroom may not solve everything, but it certainly can't do any harm.

I arrived in China a week before the start of the four-day track program and ten days before the Madison. I don't know quite what I expected when I was met at the airport by a British Olympic Committee chaperone and driven to the Olympic village, but I wasn't blown away. The blurb said 9,000 rooms in 42 buildings spread over a 66-hectare site and capable of housing 17,000 guests; the canteen alone could seat 5,000. The village also had a McDonald's. If that wasn't enough of a temptation (and not one to which I succumbed, in case you're wondering), there were plenty of other potential distractions, from games arcades to an Internet café, from a supermarket to almost mowing down the 14-year-old diver Tom Daley on my bike, which I nearly did on the way to collect my accreditation.

My apartment slept four—me and Bradley, both in single rooms, and Ed Clancy and Geraint, both of whom were riding the team pursuit. It was good to see the lads—Gee, Ed, Chris Hoy, Jason Kenny, Jamie Staff, and especially Bradley—but it was also tense. Everyone was tense. The track lot always are. The atmosphere's so different in road teams, especially *my* road team. By comparison, we're free spirits, whereas the track boys seem to thrive in a controlled environment, whether it's on or off the bike.

In Beijing, often you could walk around the apartment block and think you'd stumbled into a church. Everyone seemed to be in their rooms, in their beds, in the compression tights supposed to flush the toxins from your legs after a hard training session. Meanwhile, conscious of the need to maintain my endurance for the rest of the season, I headed out on my road bike with Shane Sutton. I needed Shane and his tales from the other side of the pro cycling tracks to alleviate the boredom of grinding up and down the highway, which was pretty much the only training route available. When Shane had finally run out of jokes, it was left to whoever was sending the weather. One day, it didn't so much rain as monsoon, and we rode back not so much through puddles as through a vast lake.

Soon there was another activity besides training to keep me occupied: counting the British cycling medals. By the time the Madison came around at five thirty p.m. on 19 August, we'd won golds in the team sprint (Hoy, Staff, and Kenny), gold and bronze in the individual pursuit (Bradley and Steven Burke, respectively), gold and silver in the keirin (Hoy and Ross Edgar), bronze in the points race (Chris Newton), gold and silver in the women's individual pursuit (Rebecca Romero and Wendy Houvenaghel), and gold in the team pursuit (Bradley, Ed, Geraint, and Paul Manning). Another way of putting it was that every rider in the GB track team who'd competed had won a medal.

No pressure, Cav.

Five gold medals in, I suppose Dave Brailsford could be forgiven for start-ing to believe his own hype. Dave's a down-to-earth bloke, an averagely talented former rider who had the good sense to abandon his aims of riding the Tour and get himself an MBA degree. A mazy career path took him to a middle-management role at the British Cycling Federation in the late 1990s, after which he impressed enough to be appointed performance director in 2002. Since then, and especially now in Beijing, the track team's success had made Dave a bit of a media darling and minor celebrity—or so, we thought, he'd have liked to think.

The perfect opportunity to test our theory presented itself on the day of the Madison in the restaurant at the Olympic village. Shane and I were homing in on three free seats while Dave went searching for cutlery when I saw the British Olympic team's chef de mission, Simon Clegg, beckoning me over. "Mark, Mark, this is Bernie Ecclestone," he said, pointing to the wizened, bespectacled gentleman sitting opposite. "Bernie, this is Mark. He won four stages of the Tour de France. . . ." And there I was, face-to-face with the grand exalted majordomo of Formula 1 motor racing.

No more than a minute or two later, Shane and I were tucking in to our lunch when Dave finally arrived. Shane winked at me, but I could have spotted the mischief in his eyes from double the distance.

"Ah, Dave. There you are, mate. We were just chatting to Bernie Ecclestone over there," Shane squawked, gesturing toward the wealthiest man in the room. "He wanted to meet Cav. Then he asked where you were. . . ."

A look of confusion, then pleasant surprise, spread across Dave's face. "Oh, all right," he said. "I'll go over and say hello. . . ."

As we watched and giggled a few meters away, the next thing to spread across Dave's face, then across his hairless dome, was a crimson-colored curtain of embarrassment. We later found out what he'd said on seeing Ecclestone's blank expression: "Er, hello, Bernie, I'm a friend of Mark's. . . ."

There weren't many more opportunities to laugh over the next few hours. There was, though, bizarrely enough, a last, failed attempt by me to change Bradley's mind about leaving Columbia for Garmin at the end of the season. Hardly the ideal mental preparation for the Olympic

Madison, you might say—but then neither were Ed and Geraint clattering back into the flat and waking me up after a night of boozy celebration. They'd gotten their gold medals; they could afford to relax.

But there were no mitigating circumstances: Until the starter's gun sounded—I'll be honest—we were in good spirits and confident. There'd been a bit of debate before the race about whether Brad might be exhausted after his individual pursuit heat, then final, and the same again for the team pursuit, the final having taken place only the previous day. But the schedule at the Worlds in Manchester in March had been almost as arduous (at the Olympics, there were three rounds per event, as compared with two at the Worlds), and we'd not just pulled but stormed through. I had reservations as well about Brad's lack of specific preparation for the Madison, but as I completed my half-hour warm-up in the middle of the track, I felt strong and optimistic. No, forget the optimism—it was as close as you could come to a cast-iron certainty that we were about to win without teetering into complacency.

Melissa, my mum, Prime Minister Tony Blair, and of course Bernie Ecclestone were all there in the stands, waiting for the next installment of the British Gold Rush. Neither I nor Dave Brailsford was going to need any introduction after this one. . . .

"Fuck!"

Yet again, as it had in Manchester five months earlier, one stifled shout on a changeover told the story of our race. I say "changeover," but what I actually mean is "failed changeover," since Brad missed me as I swung down the track, left arm out, ready for him to grab it—hence the obscenity. It also said a lot about our day that all of this took place right under the nose of Tony Blair—and easily within his hearing range.

The missed change was annoying, symptomatic, but no more than a minor inconvenience; basically it meant Brad had to do an extra lap before handing over to me. In a Madison of 200 laps, like this one, it's up to each pairing exactly when and how often they change, according to strategy and tiredness. An extra lap for either one of you isn't the end of the world, but, as I said, it *was* symptomatic of what was fast turning into a nightmare.

In Manchester, Brad had been a Trojan. Here, I didn't know what was going on. On the changes when we weren't grasping at air, in those few milliseconds when we locked hands, I quizzed him—"Brad, you okay?" "You good?" "Something wrong?" But nothing. No reply. Just a grunt or a nod, then off he or I went.

He couldn't seem to move up. Every time, when he'd throw me into the track, I'd try to pull us up to the front, to a position where we could at least contemplate an attack, or winning the next sprint; then I'd sling Bradley back in, and he'd drift back. I said I didn't know what was going on, but it was actually pretty classic behavior for someone who was struggling, or "swinging," as we call it. The back of a bunch is one of the hardest places to be in any bike race; in the Madison, it's doubly difficult because, in the chaos and congestion of changeovers, the rider at the back finds himself weaving in and out of the riders from opposition teams peeling to the side of the track as they finish their turns. It's double the effort to slot into the pack and almost double the distance, what with all the detours around the riders choking the track. Even once you'd negotiated that traffic, it cost as much energy to move from the back to the front third of the group as it did to gain half a lap. With fifty laps, I knew it was all over. We both did. You could see it in our body language. I'd tried to attack, tried to gain a lap, but the marking was skintight, and Brad seemed absent. Even if we had broken free and gained a lap, it was going to be in vain, as there were other teams who had already scored and who were well ahead of us on sprint points. The tactic before the race had been to consistently pick up sprints along the way and use our strength to gain a lap, as we had at the Worlds; from the arse-end of the race, however strong I was feeling, that simply wasn't going to happen. For those last fifty laps, we went through the motions.

As the Argentines celebrated their gold medal, we slowed, then pulled to the middle of the track without even glancing in each other's direction, let alone beginning a postmortem. Brad was soon slumped on a chair, talking to British Cycling psychiatrist Steve Peters, while I picked up my road bike and headed straight for the ramp leading out of the arena and into the changing area. A few minutes later, I was back to collect my rucksack. Again, I wasn't in the mood for hanging around—although I did take time to congratulate Vicky Pendleton when she came off the track after her gold-medal-winning ride in the women's individual sprint. Vicky's was the penultimate track cycling event of the Games; the men's sprint that gave Chris Hoy his third gold medal at seven thirty the same night was the last. It was now official: I was the only British track rider who would go home without a medal.

I watched Chris and Vicky receive their medals from the stands while Melissa tried to console me. I then called Rod, who was back in England. As ever, while I ranted, he listened.

"I gave 100 percent, but I didn't get it in return," I told him over and over again.

I was talking about Bradley but also about the Federation. For the past three years, ever since my World Championship win in LA, they'd wanted me to keep proving myself, keep eating into my road commitments, yet they hadn't reciprocated with anything like the same resources they'd devoted to other events. Every other member of the team was going home a hero, with medals around their necks and the coaches basking in the golden reflection. I wasn't just going to be the forgotten man now; I'd been the forgotten man all along.

As the age-old parental admonishment goes, I wasn't angry with Bradley, just disappointed. I didn't feel that three events were too much to ride—I felt that in my event, our event, he'd given up too easily and too early. In the past, and especially at the World Cup events the previous winter, Brad had carried me, but, at the same time, I'd had to dig in as hard as at any point during my career to allow myself to be saved. Now, in Beijing, I felt that I hadn't been able to carry him because, realizing he wasn't at his best, he hadn't given me 100 percent. There was also another, key issue, albeit one that I'd been aware of all along—the fact that Bradley had spent weeks training to do 4-kilometer efforts for the team pursuit and now found himself totally unprepared for the completely different nature of a 50-kilometer Madison.

In our separate ways, Brad and I had both found ourselves in an unfamiliar position that day. I hadn't known how to deal with being the strongest rider on the track—which is what I felt I was—and Bradley hadn't known how to cope with *not* being the strongest rider. It came down to how we'd grown up as cyclists. I'd come up as the underdog, the physiological mongrel, if you like, who'd learned to scrap and scratch because it was the only way for me to survive. Brad, on the other hand, was a thoroughbred who, in my opinion, was so used to relying on his natural talent that he perhaps hadn't learned how he could still win when that innate ability wasn't functioning. It was a classic role reversal: I didn't know how to take control when I was on the front foot, and Brad didn't know how to react with his back to the wall. In short, like a lot of supremely gifted athletes, Brad perhaps hadn't learned to *suffer* like I had. It's just my view, but perhaps that was also why his achievements on the road didn't match the success he'd had on the track.

Some of these points I made to Rod on the phone, some I made to Dave Brailsford when I went back to the village that night. After dropping Mum at her hotel, Melissa and I had gone for a short and none-too-celebratory drink, after which we'd taken taxis home—she to the hotel and I to the village. On my way into the apartment block, I'd walked past a large contingent of the track team, all dappered up and ready to go out. I'd kept my eyes on the pavement, walked past, and said nothing.

Dave Brailsford came to find me in my room. My tune hadn't changed: I'd given more than I'd gotten back; I'd had to prove myself over and over again, yet in the end it had been me who'd been let down; Brad hadn't given me 100 percent.

"We're disappointed, too," said Dave.

"Well, it's too late now," I replied.

Next to tackle the beast was Jamie Staff. I'd always liked Jamie, just as I liked Chris Hoy and Jason Kenny, his fellow gold medalists in the team sprint, and now Jamie proved what a lovely guy he was by sticking around to commiserate with me when, really, he should have been out on the piss with everyone else. As I sobbed on the bed, he told me the story of his disastrous Games in Athens in 2004 and how he'd felt similar then. My nightmare day ended when Jamie left the room, the light went off, and I fell fast asleep.

The next morning, I was back on my road bike, back on that mind-numbing highway—but really I'd rather have been anywhere in the world other than Beijing. My flight back to the UK was booked in four days' time, but now I wanted out as quickly as possible. The flight could be switched to the next day without any problem—the only glitch was that, whether I left the next day or four days later, as the only track cyclist who was going home without a medal, I'd also be the only one going home in economy class.

Luckily, I was booked on the same flight back as Jason Kenny. I say "luckily" because not only did Jason have two medals—one his gold from the team sprint, one his silver from the individual sprint—but he also had the bright idea of lending me his silver at the check-in desk. It was an ingenious plan but one that appeared doomed when the lady at the check-in desk told us the flight was full and the medals-for-upgrades arrangement British Airways had laid on wouldn't apply.

Economy class it was, then. Or at least so we thought until, an hour or so later, we were in the departure lounge, waiting to board, when we saw an air hostess walking promisingly in our direction.

"Are either of you two medal winners? We've got two seats in first class. . . ."

"Yeah, both of us. . . ." I smiled innocently, producing Jason's silver while Jason waved his gold.

As she frowned, her eyes settled suspiciously on my medal. "That's not your medal, is it?"

"Er, how do you know that?"

"I know exactly who you are . . ." she paused . . . "but you're lucky because my dad and my husband are both cyclists, and I know you won four stages of the Tour de France. On you go, here are your first-class tickets."

Her dad and her husband will have been grateful that she bent rules; a few weeks later, for her troubles, they had a signed jersey that I'd worn in the Tour.

Not since the winter of 2005–2006, when Ed and I returned from our first season with Sparkasse in Germany, had I felt as unmotivated as in August and September 2008. It perhaps didn't show at the Tour of Ireland, where I won three stages, or at what turned out to be my final race of the season, the Tour of Missouri, where I fired off another three, but I'd traveled from Beijing back to the Isle of Man with no desire to train, no desire to do anything. Anything, that is, except eat junk—just as I had in that 2005 winter of discontent. By the time I turned up in Ireland, a week after leaving Beijing, I'd already started to put on weight.

What got me down most were the well-meaning but infuriating comments I kept hearing on the Isle of Man. Every time I left my front door, it seemed, someone would mince up, ready to tell me, "Hard luck on the Olympics"—and almost never mentioning the Tour. I carried on riding and training throughout, but instead of enjoying the afterglow of my record-breaking Tour performances, I was almost starting to ask myself whether it had all been worth the bother.

Of course I shouldn't have taken it personally, and I didn't—it wasn't my fault that the British public hadn't grown up with road cycling so didn't appreciate it in the same way as the Belgians, Italians, or French—but by the same token, it was pointless moaning when I'd known all along that this was the status quo. If I'd wanted my picture in *Hello!* or a guest appearance on *Richard & Judy*, I would have focused on the track long ago. I didn't, and so I hadn't.

At the end of October, at around about the same time that I began work on this book, the *Observer Sport Monthly* magazine named me one of their athletes of the year and published an interview in which I was critical of the British Federation and its role in the Madison fiasco. I phoned up Dave Brailsford shortly afterward to clarify that I hadn't been misquoted and that I stood by what I said. In his own defense, Dave made the same justifiable point he'd made back in Beijing, namely, that it was his job to win gold medals, and it was much easier to do that in events where more variables could be controlled, like the team and individual pursuits. "But it'll be different now. We're changing things," he said, referring to a restructuring that had seen my coach, Rod, handed responsibility for all "bunch" races on the track, i.e., the Madison, the points race, and the scratch race. Dave also argued that he wasn't to blame for Bradley having a bad day in the Madison.

"Dave," I told him, "I know what you're saying, but if you're getting credit and awards for the team's success in Beijing, you've also got to take the flak for whatever goes wrong. . . ."

One of Dave's awards—the most prestigious—would be the Coach of the Year at the BBC Sports Personality of the Year ceremony in December. The shortlist of ten for the title of actual Sports Personality had been unveiled on 1 December, when I was with my Columbia teammates at our first training camp in Majorca. Knowing what fervor had been whipped up around the Olympics, and the comparatively low profile of the Tour in Britain, I wasn't hopeful for a nomination. And sure enough, when the list appeared on the BBC web site, my name wasn't among the ten. I had—it's true—received six votes in the top-tens submitted by twenty-eight newspaper and magazine editors as part of the initial selection process, but five other cyclists—all Olympic medal winners—had received more honorable mentions, and four had made the final ten.

"Blimey, look at that—four cyclists nominated for Sports Personality of the Year," I told my roommate in Majorca, Bernie Eisel, as I surveyed the list open on my laptop.

"Oh, yeah?" Bernie said. "You reckon you've got a chance?"

When I'd finished pointing out to him that, no, I didn't have a chance because I wasn't on the list, I ran through the lucky quartet of riders who had made it. He knew of all four except Rebecca Romero. I explained that she'd won the women's individual pursuit in Beijing. By this stage, four months on from Beijing, I was quite calm about the whole thing—or at least resigned. The same, evidently, could not be said about Bernie. . . .

"Yeah, but you won four stages, *four* stages of the Tour de France!" he bellowed. "I can't, I can't understand it, I don't believe . . . it's fucking ridiculous. It must be a British government conspiracy to kill road cycling!"

Two weeks later, on the night of the program itself, I was watching with Melissa in our upstairs lounge at home on the Isle of Man. The Olympic cycling team, of which I, strictly speaking, was a member— albeit an insignificant, non-medal-winning one—won the Team of the Year prize. As I've already mentioned, Dave Brailsford was the Coach of the Year, and Chris Hoy a deserved Sports Personality of the Year. I was thrilled for Chris—a lovely bloke and a great ambassador for his sport.

It would be wrong to say that I received no coverage; I was given precisely four seconds—as long as it took Sue Barker to say the words ". . . and Mark Cavendish won a record-breaking four stages of the Tour de France." Or as many seconds as I won stages.

The nomination, or lack of one, hadn't fazed me. Those four seconds, however, were like four daggers through my heart.

By the time March arrived, just two months into the 2009 season, I'd already won two stages at the Tour of Qatar and another two at the Tour of California, which, in its third year, was now regarded (or at least hyped) as possibly the third most prestigious stage race in cycling, behind the Tour de France and the Giro d'Italia. I was also now deep into my preparation for arguably cycling's single most illustrious one-day race, barring the World Championships: Milan–San Remo, or "La Classicissima," as the Italian fans, or *tifosi*, referred to it. I said "barring" the World Championships; what I ought to point out is that for Italian riders, Milan–San Remo *is* the World Championships.

The 2009 edition of La Classicissima was to mark the race's centenary, and a universal truth of cycling almost as old stated that a 23-year-old would lack the stamina to win a race that, at 298 km, was the longest single-day event in the sport. In addition to that cliché about endurance being a quality you acquired with age and experience in cycling, there were three more substantial hurdles to overcome, and they were called Le Mànie, Cipressa, and Poggio. To experts, these three sacred places of cycle racing will require no introduction; for the benefit of nonaficionados, they are the three principal climbs on the San Remo course and also the three main obstacles to a sprinter triumphing in San Remo at the end of La Classicissima. In the race's 100-year history, these three climbs had been added to the traditional route along the Ligurian Riviera in three phases, every time the sprinters had threatened to develop a stranglehold. The most recent and most troublesome adjunct had been Le Mànie in 2008; at 4.6 kilometers and with an average gradient of just under 7 percent, it was no Alpine or Pyrenean mountain pass, but even 94 kilometers from the finish, it was difficult enough for me to know that this sprinter, at least, would be out of contention by the time the peloton swung onto the San Remo seafront around seven and a half hours after leaving Milan on 21 March.

I had, it's true, noticed a discernible improvement in my climbing at the Tour of California in February. A knee injury I'd sustained playing—embarrassingly—a snowboard simulator on the Nintendo Wii at the end of October meant a month's delay to the start of my preparation for 2009, a month in which I wasn't possessed by the ravenous hunger that often took hold when I was back on the Island training, the weather was cold, and the racing season was still a prospect as distant as the Cumbrian fells I could see across the Irish Sea on a clear day. I'd eaten sensibly and scrupulously, and as a result, without any great effort or purges, I was now three kilograms lighter than at the same point in 2008, without having lost any of the speed and power that were the dual pillars of my sprinting prowess.

The first week of March was spent in Manchester with Melissa, attending to various forms of marriage-related bureaucracy to do with our October ceremony in Cheshire. That week, I'd also hooked up with my old friend and Madison partner Rob Hayles, who lived in the nearby Peak District. The rides with Rob that week were literal trips down or rather up not one but several memory lanes—climbs that had been regular fixtures in our training sessions with the Academy and where I had once been subjected to the same pride-shattering ordeal on every ascent. I knew I'd improved in the space of five years, but it was only now, as I coasted up hills that had once supplied the contoured backdrop for my nightmares, that I could measure just how much I'd progressed.

If I'd surprised myself with the way I was climbing then, at the end of that week, I'd gone to Italy for the Eroica one-day race and surpassed even my own, newly revised expectations. The Eroica has been described as the Italian equivalent of Paris-Roubaix, largely by virtue of the fact that, while a succession of long and brutal cobbled stretches have earned the former the nickname "Hell of the North," almost 60 kilometers of unpaved *strade bianche*, or white roads, fulfill the same purpose of decimating the field in the latter. That, at least, is the popular misconception; in reality, it's the Tuscan hills that those *strade bianche* wind up and down that make the race a war of attrition and that prompted me to write off my chances of winning even before I arrived on the start line in Gaiole in Chianti. Five hours later, while thrilled with my teammate Thomas Lövkvist's victory, I was left ruing the fact that I'd not shown more faith in myself; had I done so, I'd have been attacking the corners at the front of the peloton and been much better placed to stick with the leaders at least until the steep rise to the finish in Siena. As it was, I had to be content with a nonetheless encouraging 24th place and yet another, startling vote of confidence for my climbing that had come from weaving through riders on those climbs like Ryan Giggs on a mazy dribble.

Luckily, my impressive form in the Eroica passed almost unnoticed in the media. Why luckily? Well, a week earlier, I'd been informed that one bookmaker had me down as a short-odds favorite for San Remo, a revelation that didn't cause me too much concern but did create undue pressure—undue because the notion that a 23-year-old sprinter who the previous year had been possibly the worst climber in the Tour de France could get over Le Mànie, *and* the Cipressa, *and* the Poggio, *and* win the concluding bunch gallop, in his very first appearance in the race, ought to have been nothing short of preposterous.

Ought to have been preposterous. *Ought* to. That was just it—those training sessions with Rob Hayles in the Pennines and now L'Eroica had started to give me ideas. I hadn't shouted about it, mainly because, once having seemed "preposterous," that notion that the bookies had down as a ten-to-one shot now appeared merely far-fetched. In the off-season, Bob Stapleton had recruited recently retired sprint legend and five-time San Remo winner Erik Zabel as a technical consultant, and now, from L'Eroica in Tuscany, I traveled north with Erik, our Italian directeur sportif Valerio Piva, Tommy Lövkvist, Bernie Eisel, and two other teammates, Edvald Boasson Hagen and Michael Albasini, for a two-day scouting mission on that last stretch of Ligurian coastline that, every spring, plays host to the most nervous, nail-biting racing on the calendar. Over the next forty-eight hours, I'd already decided, I'd find out whether I really could win Milan–San Remo or not.

Not that it mattered, in light of the eventual response, but the answer to my question had to wait until the second day of our San Remo field trip. It finally arrived when, having *only* ridden the last 85 kilometers of the race route, and *only* climbed the Cipressa and the Poggio, we turned right in the village of Noli, a small road sign announced the start of Le Mànie, and the road suddenly tapered through a narrow archway and shot upward. Five minutes later, my heart thumping like techno music and my body and backside rocking to a much slower beat, I turned to the lads, shook my head grimly, and summoned all the breath left in my lungs to utter a single sentence: "There's no fucking way I'm getting over this. . . ."

Was I being my usual melodramatic self? Without a doubt—but I was also being my usual, realistic self. The previous day, I'd tried to simulate race pace on the Cipressa, and I'd felt lactic acid gushing through my legs as I clambered toward the top. Now, twenty-four hours later, Tommy, Bernie, and the other guys set the same infernal rhythm to test me on the same climb, and not only did I hold on, I attacked them as the road twisted around the olive groves that hugged the hillside and toward the summit. On the Poggio, too, the last and easiest but also what could be the most crucial of the three ascents, I'd felt comfortable enough to coast alongside Valerio in the team car and assure him, "This isn't going to be a problem."

No, the problem was that the actual problem came around 85 kilometers back up the coast, back toward Milan, where the road narrowed and pointed toward Le Mànie.

The last and most important stepping-stone in my preparation for San Remo started forty-eight hours after that final reconnaissance, back around the Riviera in Tuscany. A sought-after stage race in itself, the Tirreno-Adriatico is also widely regarded as the best litmus test of pre–San Remo form, particularly among the top sprinters, who always turn out in force. This year, if a sprinter really was going to survive the Mànie-Cipressa-Poggio triple whammy and triumph in San Remo, it would almost certainly be the one who emerged with bragging rights from what was to be a battle royal between the world's fastest finishers over the next seven stages. Everyone was here: proven Classics winners like Tom Boonen and Thor Hushovd, sprinters who'd come close at San Remo several times before like Robbie McEwen, sprinters who could climb like Alessandro Petacchi and Daniele Bennati, dark horses like my old team-mate Gerald Ciolek, then a favorite who felt like an outsider, i.e., me.

Little did I know it when I took to the start line that Wednesday morning, but the first stage of Tirreno was to turn my and the media's impressions of my chances in San Remo on their head. That evening, on examining the Tirreno results sheet and seeing Daniele Bennati, Alessandro Petacchi, and Tom Boonen's names occupying positions three to five, just twelve seconds behind the rogue breakaway winner, the Frenchman Julien El Farès, then scrolling all the way down to my name, the 182nd on the list, over seven minutes adrift of El Farès, the pundits were all thinking the same thing. That night, in the press room at Capannori, judging by reports the next day, more than one conversation between journalists no doubt went like this:

"Ah, so Cavendish came a cropper on that last climb, then. . . ."

"What, that one 17 kilometers from the finish? The one a bit like the Poggio?"

"Yep, you got it."

"Ah, I knew it. I guess we can forget about him for San Remo, then. . . ."

Had they known the reality, or rather, if they'd seen me skimming serenely up that very same final hill after a mechanical problem had dumped me out of the main peloton on the approach to the climb, they'd at least have reserved judgment. That was what I had done after our sighting rides of the San Remo, but now, forget "reserved"; I'd seen and felt enough on that last incline to *reverse* whatever premature conclusions I'd been tempted to draw. That night, I turned to my teammates, much as I had four days earlier: "Guys," I said simply, "I think I can get over Le Mànie."

That little announcement raised a few eyebrows. My next one, to my directeurs sportifs, would be even more unexpected. While one reason for me to be perturbed by my favorite's billing was the burden of expectation, another, more relevant consideration was that the more the other sprinters feared me, the more likely they were to focus on eliminating me before the Poggio, and certainly before the finishing straight in San Remo. They'd know, as I knew, that there'd be one surefire way of achieving this goal, and that was marshaling their teammates to set a punishing pace on Le Mànie.

They had their tactic, but I also had mine. Now, clearly to the consternation of my directeurs sportifs, I unveiled my master plan: "Over the next few stages, I'm not going to bust a gut on the climbs. I want to keep a low profile, keep the rest of them thinking I'll never get over the climbs at San Remo. . . . Guys, I'm going to bluff them."

"It's fucking worked. It's only fucking worked. . . ."

I hope you'll grant me two final lapses into profanity for the sake of describing my reaction to what I saw on the pink pages of *La Gazzetta dello Sport* on the morning of 21 March, the morning of Milan–San Remo. Before every major race, *La Gazzetta* assessed the likely favorites with a sliding star rating, with maybe the dozen top contenders awarded one to five stars, according to the strength of their credentials per the newspaper. Now I looked at what *La Gazzetta* had come up with for La Classicissima, a race that the newspaper's parent company owned: Alessandro Petacchi, five stars; Daniele Bennati, five stars . . . and so on and so on until, finally, I saw my name.

Mark Cavendish . . . one star.

I was absolutely buzzing.

Tirreno had ended the previous Tuesday—and it had ended with my first stage win of the race; I'm afraid my bluffing didn't extend to losing sprints, especially as that was exactly what I'd done four days earlier, finishing 2nd to the American Tyler Farrar. Where I could maintain the charade was in my press conference in San Benedetto del Tronto on that last evening. Asked how I rated my own chances in Milan–San Remo at the weekend, I smiled meekly. "San Remo is one of the most difficult races on the calendar. I am only 23 years old and don't expect too much. . . ." I said.

Over the next three days, after we'd journeyed north to our hotel on the outskirts of Milan, I was extremely nervous. Which was a good sign because it meant that, contrary to what I'd been saying all year and even in the last week about "just going for the experience," now I was really starting to believe that I might have the slimmest of chances of emulating Tom Simpson, the only previous British winner of La Classicissima. Had I not believed it myself, my roommate, Bernie, had enough faith for both of us: "You know, Cav, you can do it. You really can," he kept saying.

On the Friday night before the race, as was the case before every race, we were handed our race numbers. Mine was 213. I looked hard at those three figures. "Hey, Bernie," I said, "look at that: 213. What does that say to you?" He looked puzzled. "*Two, one, three*, Bernie," I insisted. "The twenty-first of the third, Bernie—the twenty-first of March. Tomorrow's date."

I couldn't quite put my finger on it, but something felt special—and that special something was making me even more nervous.

The race began under luminous blue skies. I was still apprehensive, but at least I was riding protected by the most formidable human shield in professional cycling: my seven Columbia-Highroad teammates, George Hincapie, Bernie Eisel, Tommy Lövkvist, the Canadian Michael Barry, whose presence I'd specifically requested after he'd babysat me through the entire Tour of California, the Norwegian Edvald Boasson Hagen, and two of our new signings, the Belgian Maxime Monfort and the Aussie Mark Renshaw.

Almost immediately, the attacks started and the peloton unraveled into one raking, 300-meter line, as it always does when the pace nudges 50 or even 60 kph. I waited for the first signs of tightness in my legs or my lungs—except they never came. I was floating on that magic carpet again, in spite of the wind that was gusting across the featureless landscape, which persisted all the way to the bottom of the first major climb of the race, and also the highest—the Passo del Turchino. At one point, after the road had been dragging slowly toward the treeline for what seemed like just a couple of kilometers, I asked George Hincapie, "George, when does the hard part start?" He didn't have time to answer before Tommy chipped in, "What do you mean? We're almost at the summit."

The descent off the Turchino fed onto the coast road, the Via Aurelia, which would take us all the way to San Remo via three brief detours inland to Le Mànie, the Cipressa, and the Poggio. Michael Barry and I made one last toilet stop as we hit the Aurelia. "Right, now I'm racing," I told Michael as we sped off.

Edvald and Michael had been given the task of bringing me to the foot of Le Mànie in the first ten or twelve positions in what, 200 kilometers into the race, was still a 170-strong main bunch. Three kilometers from that ominous right-hand turn in the village of Noli, Edvald was bludgeoning his way to the front of the pack with me on his wheel; for the next 2 kilometers, it was Michael; then, just as Michael began to flag, Edvald reappeared like the proverbial phoenix, revived, to sprint into that keyhole of a slip road that led into the climb and drop me off in fifth position.

I waited again, this time for the other sprinters' teams to converge on the front of the bunch, ready to crank up the pace and send me spiraling back down this 4.7-kilometer staircase to hell. I kept waiting. Nothing. Not even the teams whose only chance was eliminating *all* of the sprinters, and not only me, seemed to be riding that fast. Or maybe it *was* just me and my magic legs; as we neared the summit, close to the point where, two weeks earlier, I'd officially declared my San Remo challenge over, Maxime, a climber, looked across at me, dumbfounded. "Wow, you're climbing well!"

I later discovered that once we reached the summit, swooped down the other side, and rejoined the Aurelia, Maxime dropped back to speak to Valerio in the team car. "Get over in the main bunch? He was climbing better than me . . . !" Maxime said.

I'd cracked it. Made it over Le Mànie unscathed. Or had I? The leg muscles that had felt light and elastic in those first 200 kilometers of racing were now tighter, less springy. I could only hope that everyone else's were the same. . . .

Eighty-five kilometers. An hour and three-quarters, maybe two. Cipressa and Poggio—that was all. Well, apart from the Capi—three ripples of headland that served the same purpose as speed bumps as the race rattled toward the Cipressa but that today, to me, on this form, with Bernie Eisel's wheels in front and the wind gusting behind, seemed like precisely that—speed bumps.

Forty-five, 40, 30 kilometers to go. Cipressa and Poggio.

On the radio: "Cav, how are you feeling?"

"Really, really good." It was like a shopping rush before Christmas—the peloton vortexing, people jumping lines, shouldering each other out of the way, all at 55 kph—but I meant what I said: I felt really, really good.

As it had at Noli, toward Le Mànie, in San Lorenzo al Mare, the road kicked right and diagonally toward the hilltop in the distance known locally as La Cipressa. In 2008, on these same first half-dozen hairpin bends of the climb, Tommy Lövkvist had attacked, but now he was sacrificing his own chances to bubble-wrap me safely in the first twenty positions of the peloton. I was surprised again by how comfortable it all felt; yes, I was slowly drifting backward, but on that two-day reconnaissance mission with Erik Zabel, on both evenings we'd studied videos of the 2007 and 2008 races and seen how you could survive both the Cipressa and the Poggio by maintaining a good, steady rhythm, while others who'd invariably get lured into the stampede up the first two-thirds of the 5.6-kilometer climb would be vulnerable on the steeper ramps toward the top. Now, sure enough, to my delight and amazement, riders who'd charged past a few minutes earlier were boomeranging back toward me as I gained momentum. Riders like Tom Boonen—the same Tom Boonen who'd said in his pre-race interviews that I'd be long gone by the time the race reached the Cipressa.

Another foreign rider from what was in theory a rival team, Juan Antonio Flecha of Rabobank, drew alongside as I neared the summit, tucked in behind Petacchi and two of his teammates. After passing Boonen, I'd been tempted to surge again and make up the ten seconds that separated me from the leading group of twenty or thirty riders, but

I'd decided to sit tight and save energy in Petacchi's slipstream. Flecha now glanced at me in much the same way as Monfort had on Le Mànie. "You can win this," he said.

Eighteen kilometers.

In my earpiece, I heard Valerio: "Cav, you've got George. He's going to be there for you all the way. Stay with him on the Poggio. . . ."

"Okay, I can see him."

Fifteen kilometers, 14, 13, 12 . . . 6 to the base of the Poggio, and then 9 to the top.

Come on, Cav, keep it there. Keep it there.

That was easier said than done: On those final 5 kilometers of coast road there may have been only fifty riders left in the hunt, but the group was now less a peloton than a rolling riot. "Shit fight" is actually the technical term.

Nine point nine kilometers. The Poggio. Another right turn, like the ones to Le Mànie and La Cipressa, only this one just a gentle flick inland, hardly gaining altitude. Unfortunately, the pace wasn't gentle—but at least I had George. He'd ushered me into the first ten or twelve positions in the group, and now I just had to hold the wheels. That, too, was easier said than done.

Come on, Cav, keep it there. Keep it there.

"The Poggio's not going to be a problem," I'd told Valerio a fortnight earlier. And it wouldn't be, or rather it wasn't, except for a short stretch of false flat a few hundred meters from the top where, everyone knew, the riders who'd have no hope in a bunch sprint always made their move. Now who should accelerate off the front but Filippo Pozzato—Flash Filippo, the show pony. As he attacked, I also pushed harder on the pedals, taking myself from around thirtieth to twentieth position in a fast-fractioning bunch. Pozzato and his handful of breakaway companions turned left as they entered the village of Poggio di San Remo and began their descent seven seconds before I swung past the same spot. Seven seconds that were never going to be enough.

Come on, Cav. Three point three kilometers downhill. The easy bit. Bernie, Flecha, they were right—you can win this, you can fucking win this. Come on, Cav.

At the bottom of the descent, the road widened. I picked my way in between the twenty or thirty riders in front of me, including Pozzato—and that was when I also saw George. There was no one in the world whom I'd rather have seen at that moment than George Hincapie—second-nicest man in the world, after his brother, and as far as I was concerned, second-best pilot in New York, behind the fella who landed the plane on the Hudson River. George slowed and nodded to his rear wheel. With less than 2 kilometers to go, I was in his jetstream.

Into San Remo. Onto the seafront.

Twelve hundred meters. One thousand. Eight hundred.

Cav, you can fucking win this.

Well, yeah, I could, but I could also lose it. George was now committed. It was too early to commit, but then, 298 kilometers in, timing and tactics became irrelevant; it was about eking out whatever energy was left.

At 500 meters to go, George's bottomless tank finally ran dry.

Four hundred fifty. Four hundred twenty-five; here it comes, Cav. Brace yourself.

And suddenly I was swamped, stifled, suffocated by the Garmin rider Julian Dean, who was trying to sprint through the meter-wide channel between me and the barriers on the left-hand side of the road but who was running out of puff and was now boxing me in. I couldn't move, couldn't sprint, couldn't do anything except watch in horror as, to the left of Dean, a black jersey suddenly flashed past and into clear daylight. It was the German Heinrich Haussler.

Haussler's getting away, Cav. He's getting away, and no one's moving. He's going and going, and there's no gap, but you've got to go, Cav. You've got to go now—it's not a gap, but you've gotta go, Cav. You've gotta gamble.

So I veered left, pushed all of my chips into the middle of the table.

He's too far, Cav, too far. But I was getting closer, and it was 125, and then 100, and all my weight was going through the pedals, and my nose was almost grazing my front wheel, just like when I was a junior, and it was 75, and Haussler was starting to tire, zigzagging all over the road. . . .

Seventy, 60, 55, 35, Cav, you can fucking win this. You can fucking win this.

At 20 meters to go, my front wheel was level with Haussler's back one; at 15 it was level with his thigh; at 10 it was his shin; at 5 it was his front wheel; at 1 meter it was still his front wheel.

We both lunged over the line, and I had no idea who'd won. But then silence ended, broken not by the screaming *tifosi* but by Haussler's cry. An anguished cry. Not the cry of a man who'd just won Milan–San Remo.

The best ten seconds of my life. The last ten.

EPILOGUE

From one hallowed ground and prize of Italian cycling, Milan–San Remo, my unstoppable momentum swept straight to another, the Giro d'Italia and its pink jersey. The 20.5-km team time trial around the Venice Lido that kicked off the centenary edition of the Corsa Rosa on the second Saturday of May had ended with me raining expletives on my teammate Marco Pinotti and being pinned down in our team bus by Mark Renshaw and Michael Rogers as I continued my rant about how "we could have gone fucking faster." It turned out that they were right, and we hadn't needed to; we'd won not only the phony war that I'd sparked a day earlier with some disparaging comments about Garmin but also the race, by six seconds, from . . . Garmin. By virtue of having crossed the line first, as agreed in our pre-race meeting, I now donned my first leader's jersey in a major tour. I also became the first-ever Briton to pull on the *maglia rosa*, the pink jersey of the Giro leader.

I'd end up staying on the Giro until the end of week two—long enough to learn the lessons of my surprise defeat to Alessandro Petacchi on Stage 1 and win three bunch sprints, the last of which came, aptly, in Florence, just up the road from my adopted home in Quarrata. The race would continue without me to its spectacular conclusion under Rome's Colosseum a week later; I bowed out safe in the knowledge that my aura and fitness were peaking nicely ahead of the Tour de France.

The day after the Giro ended with the Russian Denis Menchov's overall victory, I was to be found in London's Soho at a press conference arranged to coincide with the launch of this book's hardback edition. Months earlier, I'd been asked whether I wanted the book to carry a dedication and had no hesitation in choosing my fiancée, Melissa. Now, as I sat at one end of the launch venue, the swanky Bar Italia, holding up my handiwork and grinning into the flashbulbs, Melissa sat at the other end of the room, sobbing, trying to come to terms with the bombshell I'd dropped on my return from Italy a few hours earlier: There would be no wedding and, in all likelihood, no further chapter in our eight-year romance.

I'm sure I don't need to tell anyone who has experienced a breakup that both parties could write their own epic, soul-baring tomes on the topic. Not only is there neither space nor time to do that here, but Melissa and her dignity, if not mine, deserve better than to have her private life exposed in print. The truth is that she was blameless. Whether that means I lived up to the self-portrait put forward elsewhere in this book—"selfish," "an arsehole"—is for others to judge, but I acknowledge that if I was guilty of anything, having reached the age of 24 and a matter of months away from a lifetime commitment to my girlfriend of eight years, it was of the self-indulgence that has been largely absent from other areas of my life and my career. I'd had my fears and doubts for several months. With hindsight, I can see that they were bound to erupt. Better, probably, for Melissa's sake and mine that the breakup happened when it did.

Emotionally, it made those few weeks leading up to the Tour a constant torment. Physically, I'm almost ashamed to say that it was a help more than a hindrance, as the stress kicked in and the weight dropped off my already honed, toned muscles. For five or six weeks before Milan–San Remo, I'd made calories my enemy and brought new meaning to the clichéd notion in cycling of living like a monk. Now I went even further, for longer, and my appetite for once cooperated. I had also been careful to coax and nurture the form I'd built in the Giro, as I proved in my last big warm-up race, the Tour of Switzerland in mid-June. Out of seven stages there, I won two and my team six, adding up to a domination that, in professional cycling, was always likely to arouse more suspicion than admiration. It shouldn't have; our secret was as simple as picking the team member best suited for the day's stage and pooling all of our energy and resources behind that rider. In the mountainous stages, this meant me giving everything I had for Tony Martin or Kim Kirchen, both of whom won stages. One day, I overheard Filippo Pozzato mocking another rider for being "in the same group as Cavendish in the mountains." But even preening Pippo knew that was now no disgrace.

My strong display in Switzerland only served to whip yet more hype about what I might achieve at the Tour. In choosing Monaco for the start, the Tour organizers had opted for a Grand Départ in keeping not only with the glitz and glamour surrounding Lance Armstrong's come-back but also what, I could sense, was increasingly my public profile. Our pre-race press conference in the Grimaldi Forum in Monte Carlo was, predictably, a cluster-fuck. Bob Stapleton had secured a major new sponsorship deal with the mobile phone company HTC a week or two earlier, and now that agreement and our slightly redesigned jersey were presented along with me and my eight teammates. I'd never seen so many journalists as I would over the next forty-eight hours—or hear the same, single question repeated more times: "Mark, Mark, how many stages do you think you can win?" My answers were deadpan: "I don't know. I'll try to win what I can."

Bob now dictated the names of the eight riders who, for the next three weeks, would be my teammates, soulmates, and partners in adventure: Bert Grabsch, Bernhard Eisel, Maxime Monfort, Kim Kirchen, Michael Rogers, Tony Martin, George Hincapie, and Mark Renshaw.

The curtain call mirrored the crescendo we'd soon be reenacting on the road. But whereas now, after a dramatic pause, Bob called me onto the stage and I stepped into a cacophony of clicking cameras, out there I'd wait for my lead-out man, Renshaw, to peel away and help me find that special silence.

It had been a year since the last time. I didn't intend to wait much longer.

Officially, the 2010 Tour de France started with a 15-km time trial around the Monte Carlo port, the Swiss sprinter Fabian Cancellara's widely predicted stage win, and race favorite Alberto Contador's ominous 2nd place. I stress "officially" because although I crossed the line like the 198 other riders in the field that afternoon, I'd already come to the realization, after three Tours de France, that the Tour begins and often feels as though it's about to end somewhere else. Cycling parlance has the good humor to call that "somewhere" the "neutralized zone." In Stage 1 of the Tour, as I've already established elsewhere in this book, "war zone" would be a better description.

As usual, it was chaos. Mayhem. Carnage. If you've ever been to Monaco, you'll know that steep mountains surround the principality on all sides. One of those mountains, the 491-meter La Turbie, was the first major climb on the 2010 Tour route, its summit just 8.5 km into Stage 1. I can remember gliding along in the middle of the bunch, feeling fantastic yet treating every unfamiliar wheel like a land mine. One rider who's known to everyone in the bunch as a crash magnet, the Colombian Mauricio Soler, had already sent me sprawling and had possibly cost me a stage win at the Giro. But with legs like the ones I had at the start of the race, I could already tell that nothing was going to stop me today. Just before the summit, George Hincapie appeared on my shoulder and looked down at my legs whirring like Catherine wheels. "Wow, Cav! You're fucking flying!" he said. George's voice was followed by Brian Holm's in my radio. Brian's rundown of the riders already dropped was music to my ears.

Fuck, it was hot, though. I wasn't keeping count, but I must have gone through thirty bottles, each half a liter. All day, my teammates were ferrying back and forth to the car. I'd get one bottle and down it within 5 kilometers, and then someone else would be there with a replacement.

The order to hit the front came with 50 kilometers to go. For me, this meant finding Mark Renshaw, locking on to his back wheel, and tunneling my vision for the next 49.8 kilometers. When Gerald Ciolek had left for Milram the previous winter, Mark had been just one of several riders whom Rolf and Bob had mooted as his replacement—and not necessarily my preferred candidate. But after one botched lead-out right at the start of the season at the Tour of California, I'd quickly realized that Mark's bike handling, positional sense, coolness under pressure, and pace judgment—not to mention his speed—made him to setting up sprints what I was to finishing them: the best. A horse-drawn Volvo couldn't have given me a surer, more comfortable, more stylish ride to the finish line. It bordered on embarrassing, how easy Mark made winning sprints.

But of course, that was in other races. This was the Tour. Everything here was different, amplified, magnified, overblown—including, clearly, the Milram team's confidence in its ability to booby-trap our train. World time trial champ Bert Grabsch drew level with the Milram riders, opened up the throttle, and blazed away like a Lamborghini from a Lada. Seven or eight wheels back, on Renshaw's wheel, I didn't flinch.

Rogers, Monfort, Hincapie, and Martin all buried themselves. Not sure if Kirchen did anything in that stage (or some of the later stages, come to think of it). We didn't need him. Inside the last 500, like in San Remo, I felt Julian Dean of Garmin surge on the right and, tucked in behind him, his teammate Tyler Farrar do what he always does—flap. Tyler's a good sprinter and a good bloke, but sometimes I can't figure him out. Why not just sit on my wheel? Why waste energy trying to fight with me? Why flap around in my face? If you fight with me, you can come in front of me, but I'll get past anyway. George went, and I kicked once. Then Mark went, and I kicked again, past Farrar, around Mark with 250 to go, and into the heat, the noise, the silence, the emptiness. I kicked hard—as hard as I could, harder than I needed to. I saw the line, looked down at my legs, then back at the line, flung my arms in the air, and let the feeling electrify me. One-, two-, three-tenths of a second—one, two, three bike-lengths—and Farrar finally crossed the line. Not since Milan–San Remo had I given 100 percent in a sprint, and not until the Champs-Élysées in nearly three weeks' time would I do it again. The result, and message, in all three cases was emphatic and the same.

I'd dreamt about pulling on the green points jersey—often also called the sprinter's jersey, though that's not quite accurate, as points toward it accumulate elsewhere along the course, not solely in the sprints—since the age of 14. In that era, the man who was now my mentor, Erik Zabel, rarely rode without it at the Tour. Erik took the jersey to Paris no fewer than six times—consecutively, no less. Now on the podium in Brignoles, it was mine, temporarily, for the first time.

There was elation at having won the first sprint of a major tour for the first time—a goal that had been foremost in my planning with Rod before the Tour—but no great sense of relief or release. The day before the Tour started, in Monaco, I'd had a long, tearful phone conversation with Melissa, and no doubt the breakup was still preying on my mind, as it would throughout the Tour. Really, though, I was just too preoccupied. Too focused. Too hungry.

The next stage started in Marseille and hugged the coast heading west, cutting through the vast, marshy plains that comprise the Camargue region, famous for its wild horses, flamingos, and wind. The wind we could definitely vouch for. My sprint the previous afternoon had been perfect except for one thing: I'd won too easily. We now paid the price as we looked around for other teams to contribute to the pace-making and might as well have been recruiting volunteers for a mass striptease. The general gist of their expressions was "You must be fucking joking."

With 40 kilometers to go, the wind was still howling into Bernie Eisel's and Bert Grabsch's faces at the front of the line. A few wheels back, George rode level with me and said we should drop into the belly of the bunch, where we wouldn't be so exposed to occasional gusts that somehow found their way through or around the rider in front. I nodded, and back we went.

It can't have been more than a minute or two later before I next heard George's voice. "Fuck!" I looked up and saw a 90-degree right turn about 200 meters ahead of us. Instinctively, we both stood on the pedals and sprinted up the gutter—past Contador, past Armstrong, and, finally, into the top thirty positions as we reached the bend. A bunny-hop over a traffic island won me another half-dozen places. Then, of course, as we shifted direction, the wind hit us from the left, and the same thought entered all our minds. For perhaps thirty seconds, no one dared say it until, finally, Michael Rogers reached for the microphone under his jersey and gave the order: "Guys, let's do it."

As Mick veered to the right-hand side of the road, you could sense the waves of panic spreading through the peloton behind us. Within seconds, they were actual, physical ripples, or "echelons." In layman's terms, these occur when the wind gusts across the road from one side and the man, or men, at the front peels to the opposite side of the road to leave the riders behind either exposed or flailing around in the gutter, trying desperately to keep a body and bike between them and the direction of the wind. Eventually, maybe ten wheels back, maybe twenty, maybe thirty, someone runs out of space, strength, or shelter, and the line snaps.

Now twenty-eight men made the front group, driven like sled dogs by my entire team. Lance Armstrong was there. According to the press the next day, the first of the worst—the man who left the first gap and provoked the split—was Armstrong's Astana teammate, the Tour favorite Alberto Contador.

The last 32 kilometers were exhilarating. At first, I took turns on the front like everyone else. The time gap quickly rose to nearly a minute, after which I settled back into the middle of the group as Armstrong called two of his teammates to the front to help with the pace-making. That night, the press implied that Lance had somehow conspired with his old mate George to bring about the split and scupper Contador, but that was bollocks. The breakaway happened maybe fifty seconds after George and I saw the road pivot to the right—barely enough time to sprint through the peloton, let alone hatch some elaborate plan with Lance. Lance hit the nail on the head in his interviews that night: Every bike racer knows, or at least should know, that in windy conditions, and especially crosswinds, you ride as close to the front as possible. George, Lance, and twenty-six others, including me, got it right; Contador got it wrong.

For me, the time we were gaining on general classification was immaterial. What mattered was that I'd be sprinting for my second stage win against 27 riders instead of 179. The man who wanted my green jersey, Thor Hushovd, was in that number, but he was the only sprinter of any real pedigree. A kilometer from the line, under the red flag, a lone rider shot off the front of the bunch. Rather than accelerate after him, Mark Renshaw called on his track experience, maintained his cool, and kept the pace steady. Two hundred meters from the line, Mark let himself drift to the left, and I barreled past, with Thor a safe distance behind.

Maybe 50 meters from the line, I started thinking about my celebration. Before the Grand Départ in Monaco, I'd tried to talk Jason Gordon from our new sponsor, HTC, into giving me one of the Hero handsets HTC was about to release, only to be told that there were one or two technical issues that had to be resolved before the company launched the phone. The night before, in Marseille, I'd texted him: "Jason, I've got a surprise for you tomorrow, and, when you see what it is, I reckon you'll give me a Hero." The surprise was me crossing the line with my right hand cocked around my ear like a telephone and left index finger pointing to the HTC logo on my jersey.

As I'd hoped and expected, the people at HTC were beside themselves. Soon the image graced their advertising campaigns all over the world.

Less happily for their employees, a 100-foot-high, ego-sized reproduction also graced the facade of their company headquarters.

In theory, I could have equaled my quartet of stage wins from the previous Tour even before we reached the Pyrenees. After a mildly disappointing 5th in the 38-kilometer team time trial around Monaco on Stage 4, we all thought we were homing in on win number three when, 30 kilometers from the finish line in Perpignan on Stage 5, a six-man breakaway group had a forty-second lead. Twenty kilometers later, it was an even less daunting thirty seconds, yet, for some inexplicable reason, we couldn't get any closer. I say "inexplicable," but as the Tour wore on, I was noticing a recurring theme: TV and press motorbikes getting a little too close to the action and sucking riders into their slipstream. The end result was a solo stage win for Thomas Voeckler and the only other remnant of that five-man break, the Russian Mikhail Ignatiev, robbing me of four vital green jersey points by pipping me on the line for 2nd place.

The next day's stage from Gerona in Spain to Barcelona was another ball-ache. The rain in Spain falls mainly on the plain, they say . . . well, everywhere I looked there were hills, and it was still pissing down. Luckily, I was climbing like a Sherpa and was in the front group over all five of the category 3 and 4 climbs on the profile, while others got washed away. The finish line was also at the top of a hill—the 1.7-km rise to the Olympic stadium in the Parc de Montjuïc. The roadbook gave the impression that it was harder than was actually the case—more up Kirchen's street than mine—and we committed too early. To add insult to injury, while Kim and I trailed in 16th with legs to spare, Hushovd won the charge to the line to take the stage and draw within a point of my green jersey.

The Pyrenees now loomed, as did nightmares of the previous year's ordeal. Secretly, though, I knew I'd be okay this time. My mantle as the Tour's worst climber had been inherited by Kenny Van Hummel—a curly-mopped Dutch sprinter from the Skil-Shimano team with a Houdiniesque knack of escaping time limits. In Holland, he'd become a cult hero by the end of the Tour. In the peloton, his tall tales of survival were greeted with a smile and a raised eyebrow. It was hard to begrudge him his fifteen minutes of fame because, although he wasn't a great sprinter, he was undeniably a decent bloke.

On Stage 7 to Andorra, while Kenny was chugging along at the back, and up front Contador rode everyone off his wheel, I was coasting along in the middle of the gruppetto. That was the big difference between 2008 and 2009. Whereas then I was grinding myself into the tarmac to hold on to the gruppetto and sometimes just to sneak inside the time limit—not helped by the Riccò pantomime up the road—now I had the option of either economizing in the gruppetto or straining to stick with the second-to-last group. It was an easy choice. At the Tour, any effort that's not strictly necessary is an effort you simply shouldn't be making. In 2008, my exertions at Hautacam had still been hurting me days later, and eventually caused me to quit the race. Similarly, anything you eat or drink on the Tour has an impact not only on the next 20 kilometers but, potentially, on the next week or fortnight. The same now applied to every extra watt, every extra heartbeat, every extra kilometer per hour that it would have taken to cross the line twenty-eight minutes after the stage winner instead of thirty.

In Tarbes at the end of Stage 9, having survived the Tourmalet and hence the last of the Pyrenees, I crossed the line in a forty-six-man gruppetto, grunted a sentence or two about "surviving the mountains" for the TV cameras, then scuttled off in search of our team bus. From there, after a quick shower, we'd head to the airport, where two planes were waiting to fly us north to Limoges, base camp for the Tour's first rest day. The Pyrenean stages had been stiflingly hot, and the airport was almost as clammy. Everyone just wanted to get to Limoges quickly—except, apparently, a gentleman with a French accent dithering at the front of the queue. "Fucking Frenchie," I cursed under my breath.

Why do I remember saying this? Well, I don't. I mean, it's quite possible that I did say it, but I have no precise recollection. According to L'Équipe newspaper two days later, though, one rider did. He didn't want to give his name—neither did the journalist to whom we were all indebted for this vital nugget of public information—but he remembered, all right. He also had clear memories of me "ranting and raving at my teammates in the gruppetto."

My alleged "racism" would be the next day's talking point. First we had a stage from Limoges to Issoudun, through some pretty featureless flatlands in central France, as well as the Tour organizers' first stab at a ban on intercom radios. At least, that was the plan. Their hope was that a day of aggressive, unpredictable racing would be the best possible advertisement for a lasting radio embargo—the perfect antidote to the formulaic tactics that team managers dictate to riders through their earpieces.

Oh, how very wrong they would be.

Here's the thing: Unlike my team managers, I'm in favor of banning radios. I've already written in this book about the senseless, scattergun attacks you see in the first hour of races, particularly from French riders, and to my mind the reason for a lot of that madness is the use and abuse of radios. Directeurs hear over the *other* radio, central race radio, that a rider has attacked, or a break has gone without one of their guys in it, and their instinct tells them to scream into the intercom: "Attack, attack, attack!" And their riders don't want to attack—don't need to attack because often they can see that the split is insignificant—but they end up following instructions. As a result, the first 100 kilometers of every Tour stage are crazy, ballistic. Whereas without radios, the guys who really want to be in breaks would hover around the front of the bunch and wait until the right moment, and then the ship would sail and everyone else could just settle into a nice, even tempo.

The funny thing was that exactly that did happen—but the four guys in the break were clearly so bereft without their radios that they didn't know what to do next. Fairly soon, they seemed to realize that, actually, they weren't so keen on staying on the front after all, and they started to slow. The main bunch, in turn, also eased off, keen not to pounce too early and therefore encourage further, more troublesome attacks closer to the finish line. Meanwhile, the journalists in the pressroom either scratched their heads or speculated that this was the organized go-slow that had been rumored in the morning. It was no such thing.

Radio or no radio, from 20 kilometers out (when the gap was down to thirty-eight seconds), and then when we gobbled up the last of the breakaway quartet 2 kilometers from home, it was business as usual. Armstrong knew the script—"Bastille Day. A Brit will win tho," he'd tweeted that morning—as did Mark Renshaw, who executed yet another perfect lead-out. From there, it was just a question of which sponsor I was going to salute this time. I chose my sunglasses supplier Oakley, whipping off my green Radar frames and pretending to clean the lenses as I came over the line well clear of Hushovd and Farrar.

In an interview with a British magazine after the Tour, the Bouygues Télécom directeur sportif Didier Rous called my victory celebrations "disrespectful." I'd face much more offensive charges in the following morning's *L'Équipe*. Apparently, at least one French rider—the eager-eared sleuth who'd evidently been scribbling down my every word in the Tarbes airport two days earlier—thought I was also "racist" and "anti-French." "He'd better watch what he says," said the peloton's anonymous Head of International Relations. "We're not going to just keep letting it pass."

I was furious—up to a point. The very suggestion that I was racist was so downright ridiculous that it was easy to dismiss. If saying "Fucking Frenchie" meant I was anti-French, then I must also have been anti-British when we went on training camps in Majorca and I clocked a "fucking Brit" getting tanked up on Bacardi Breezers, then lobstering himself on the beach. Or when, on a training ride with the team, a few of us would stop for a piss and the "fucking Germans" wouldn't wait. If that all made me xenophobic, then I owe you all an apology: The book you're reading ought to be called *Boy Racist*, not *Boy Racer*.

As for the identity of my accuser, I had my suspicions when I read the subsequent press coverage, and in particular comments from a selection of French riders. Most saw it for what it was—the petty jealousy of a small, insignificant rider. Conversations after the Tour confirmed to me that I was dead right about who he was. I won't ruin the suspense here. I just invite you to watch out for a breakaway specialist who, from now on, won't get into too many breakaways if my team or I can help it. That'll be your man.

Ten stages in, some pundits were already complaining that the real drama was taking too long to warm up, with the unfancied Italian Rinaldo Nocentini still in the yellow jersey and the big Alpine stages still a week away. Three stage wins to the good, I wasn't whining. According to the roadbook, Stage 11 to Saint Fargeau could serve up another chance, although word also got back to us from Erik Zabel that the uphill finish was a good bit stiffer than it looked on paper. As he did every day, Erik had driven ahead to the finish line and relayed info back to our directeurs in the team cars, who then passed it on to us via our radios. Having toyed with the idea of swapping Renshaw with Hincapie to catapult me up the slope, we eventually decided to stick with the winning formula, only delaying and shortening everyone's final turn on the front to account for the 500-meter rise to the line.

Many predicted that the uphill finish would rule me out. Who? That was what I wanted to know when the suggestion was put to me by Ned Boulting of ITV minutes after I'd held off Hushovd and Farrar to win Stage 4. "Internet forum people?" I asked, my face a thesis on indignation. Even in the afterglow of victory, even after years of hearing the same old crap, certain misconceptions about my ability as a bike rider still grated. Everyone had heard me poke fun at my own climbing and drawn the conclusion that I was a liability on any surface more undulating than a supermodel's chest. They wrote that I'd never win Ghent-Wevelgem because I couldn't make it over the infamous Kemmelberg—perhaps not realizing an uphill stretch of about a kilometer doesn't even qualify as a climb, or not having seen me attack there with Tom Boonen in the Three Days of De Panne in April 2009. When I talked about climbs, I meant Alps, Pyrenees, Dolomites. A 2-kilometer climb is a sprint anyway.

All that needed to change was where my train reached its destination, Renshaw dropping me off 100 meters from the line instead of 200.

Of course, none of this really mattered. My Tour could have ended in Saint Fargeau and been viewed as an unqualified success. I, though, now wanted to take the green jersey all the way to Paris. To that end, I went for and won the first intermediate sprint of Stage 12 from Tonnerre to Vatan to add six points to my total. A seven-man break then went clear and had built up a lead of nearly five minutes with 100 kilometers to go. The sun throbbed. Rivers of sweat cascaded down foreheads. With the break still motoring, our team directeur Valerio Piva came over the radio and urged us to start the chase. I looked into the tired, straining eyes of my teammates, their sinking shoulders, and squeezed the mic under my jersey. "Not today, Valerio," I said. "The guys need a rest." While the Dane Nicki Sørensen seized his opportunity to attack from the breakaway group and take the stage, I consoled myself by leading the peloton over the line to increase my lead over Hushovd to ten points in the points competition.

The slate skies and icy rain that provided the backdrop for Stage 13 through Alsace and Vosges mountains were, I now know, a faithful reflection of how my green-jersey campaign was about to take a definite turn for the worse. With Hushovd's teammate Heinrich Haussler en route to an epic solo win and the general classification contenders too busy trying to avoid hypothermia to throw off the material and metaphorical gloves, Thor hung on over the climbs to finish 6th and snaffle fifteen vital points. Seventeen minutes later, in the third big group on the road, I crossed the line in 118th position for zero points and a day in normal Columbia-HTC colors.

Stage 14, the last before the Alps, was now crucial. It was also eventful from the start, with attacks going off like fireworks on Guy Fawkes night. The lumpy route profile suggested that a sprint was a possibility but not a formality, especially with the other teams less willing than ever to help us reel in breakaways and my guys becoming increasingly tired as a result. Given that a group was sure to go early on, the least I could do was go with that break and win the first one or two intermediate sprints before dropping back to the peloton. Why even drop back, you say? As if I'd have a choice; given that they didn't even want to sprint against me in a peloton of 180, the chances of them working with me in a group of 5 or 10 were nonexistent.

It was all going perfectly when the Russian Sergey Ivanov accelerated and I was one of thirteen riders to jump with him. George was also on board. The gap rose to twenty, thirty seconds. We were away with the mixer.

I was moving up the line, head down, legs singing, when I suddenly became aware of a lime-green jersey entering my field of vision. *"Oo! Cavendish, che cazzo fai?"* It was the Liquigas rider Daniele Bennati, kicking off about something, telling me to go back to the peloton. A few seconds later, another Liquigas rider, the Belgian Frederik Willems, joined in: "Hey, you've got to go back. If you stay here, you'll screw it up for everyone. Cervélo's chasing behind. . . ."

Even if Bennati was being a dick, what they were saying sort of made sense. Only sort of. There was a Cervélo rider with us in the break—Hayden Roulston. They also didn't have the kind of team that could lead a high-speed chase on the flat. I radioed back to the car to check but couldn't get any signal. As I tried to talk into the mic, I could still hear Bennati squawking away in my ear. Against my better judgment, confused and resigned, I decided to shut him up and go back, no more than 10 tantalizing kilometers before that first intermediate sprint of the day.

No sooner had I been absorbed back into the field than I heard more voices. I glanced across and saw Rabobank's Juan Antonio Flecha.

"What the fuck are you doing? Why did you come back?" he said.

"I thought Cervélo were chasing," I stammered. "The Liquigas guys said . . ."

Flecha shook his head in disapproval. Next to him, Fabian Cancellara did the same. Cervélo chasing? My teammates didn't know whether to laugh or cry.

At least, in the break, George was now homing in on the yellow jersey. Though certain that he would lose the jersey the next day on the big climb to Verbier, George needed to finish no less than five minutes, forty-one seconds in front of Nocentini to take the golden fleece today. Nocentini's AG2R team had made it clear it wasn't going to commit to the chase, so responsibility fell to the lineup that probably *would* inherit the yellow jersey in twenty four hours' time—Astana. We spoke to Armstrong, who said his team would aim to keep the gap at around six or seven minutes. That didn't leave George with much room to maneuver, but we couldn't tell Astana how to race. Instead we nodded and crossed our fingers.

With 10 kilometers to go, it was still looking good. Then something incredible, inexplicable, despicable happened: Garmin riders began to flood the front of the peloton. Dave Zabriskie, George's friend; Ryder Hesjedal, the guy who'd gotten his first pro contract on George's recommendation; Julian Dean; Dave Millar. All full gas. What the fuck was going on? Brad Wiggins shrugged and said the order had come from their directeur sportif Matt White. Apparently an American rider from a rival American team getting the jersey wasn't part of the Garmin game plan. Yet again, they seemed more preoccupied with fucking up other teams than with achieving something themselves.

Whatever the motivation, I now had a problem: I had to sprint for 13th place and the accompanying 13 points, but I had to do it as slowly as possible, for George's sake. We rounded the last bend, a gentle right-hander, with 150 meters to go. A Cofidis rider jumped on my left. I now had to go. I kicked past Renshaw, holding my line against the right-hand barriers, looked to my left and saw no one coming, then eased off to save George what could potentially have been a vital few fractions of a second. Alas, they weren't; we'd crossed the line five seconds too early, and Nocentini had retained the yellow jersey by that margin.

Perhaps 20 meters beyond the line, as I squeezed the brakes, someone shouted behind me. A second or two later, Hushovd was by my side, in my face. "Do you think that was fair?" he barked, as angry as I've ever seen him.

I didn't know what he was talking about. "Calm down, Thor," I said, a touch patronizingly, then rode off toward our team bus.

When I got there, George's head was buried in his hands. His whole family was in France to see him, and in what was his fourteenth and possibly last Tour de France, only Garmin's shameful tactics had denied him a yellow jersey that would have been the crowning glory of a brilliant career.

After a somber journey to the team hotel, Mark Renshaw and I went up to our room and, as we often did, turned the TV on to catch the end of the highlights and post-race analysis. The stage results flashed onto the screen. I did a double take; my name wasn't there. I'd been disqualified. I phoned Valerio. He said not to worry; they wouldn't let this lie. A few minutes later, I was facedown on the massage bed, being bashed and kneaded by my Latvian masseur, Aldis, when our team manager, Rolf Aldag, appeared in the doorway. He looked glum.

"Sorry, Cav," Rolf said. "You've lost the points."

I burst into tears. The TV replays merely confirmed what I knew at the time: I'd done nothing wrong. Commentating on Eurosport, the Irish Classics legend Sean Kelly said exactly the same thing. I could have shifted left to let Thor through, but I was under no obligation to do so. I've never thought about other riders when I've been sprinting. Thor said I was trying to outmaneuver him; I say that was the voice of desperation. Why would I have to outmaneuver Thor when I'd proved in every head-to-head sprint in the race so far that I was simply far quicker?

My dismay turned to disgust the following day when Brian Holm and Rolf Aldag went in search of the UCI race commissaire who had apparently made the decision to disqualify me, a Dutchman by the name of Martin Bruyn. Brian asked Bruyn whether, on reflection, he felt he'd made the right call. Bruyn's reply? That he'd spoken with his countrymen from the Skil-Shimano team, who'd wholeheartedly backed his ruling.

So at least that was settled, eh? We could all sleep easy in the knowledge that the destiny of the Tour de France's green jersey hinged on the secondhand account of a rival team. Fucking fantastic.

No, fucking disgraceful. Bruyn had already cost Erik Zabel one green jersey with a similar gaffe years ago. Now he had done the same to me.

Months later, when the damage was done, we'd consider submitting a formal protest to the Court of Arbitration for Sport, only to withdraw for fear of setting a dangerous precedent. The injustice would therefore remain. Together with my anger.

The next day, a tough 207-km stage from Pontarlier on the edge of the Jura Mountains to Verbier in the Swiss Alps, was the last thing I needed in my already fragile emotional state. In all, I'd end up weeping into my Oakleys three times that day—twice over a toboggan ride of a first 100 kilometers featuring four category 3 climbs and once on the final ascent to Verbier. The constant, emotional peaks and troughs of the previous two weeks had stretched my tired nerves like strands of fraying elastic. As the road wound toward Verbier and, several hairpins above our heads, Contador was effectively winning the Tour, Hushovd appeared at my side in the green jersey that should still have been mine.

"Can we talk?" he asked.

No, we couldn't. "Fuck off, Thor," I hissed, and rode off.

If that was rash, my comments to radio FiveLive the following day, a rest day in Verbier, would be no less emotive. I told them Thor's green jersey now "had a stain on it." The web site Cyclingnews.com, which all of the riders read, then posted the offending quotations, whipping up yet another storm with Mark Cavendish at its epicenter.

Plenty of people assumed that Hushovd's long, solo raid over three Alpine passes on Stage 17—particularly the moment when he tugged demonstratively at his green jersey while grinning into the TV camera—was a direct response to my "stain" remarks. They also said the breakaway and two intermediate sprints he'd picked up on the way exemplified why Thor was going to beat me to the green jersey: He was a better climber and better at accumulating points in the intermediate sprints. The green jersey isn't exactly a sprinter's jersey, anyway, they said. All I could say to this was "Bullshit." Why? Because first place in an intermediate sprint, of which there were typically two or three per stage, was worth six points, whereas my stage wins were each worth thirty-five. In other words, you'd have to win six intermediate sprints to score one more point than comes with crossing the line first at the end of a stage once.

I won't deny that Stage 17 was a massively frustrating one. After an injury-plagued spring and disappointing Tour to that point, Kim Kirchen had announced in the briefing that morning that he wanted to redeem his Tour and needed as much help as we could give him. This meant me and the rest of the team forgetting about the green jersey for a day—and in particular Maxime Monfort, George Hincapie, and Tony Martin, who'd have key roles in launching Kim toward a stage win. For the rest of us, the priority would be survival as usual in the Alps, beyond whatever little assistance we could offer Kim in the early part of the stage.

Hushovd attacked on the descent off the first climb of the day, the Cormet de Roseland. On the second ascent, I noticed Kim climbing behind me; we tried to move him up, but he said no. Not "Guys, I haven't got the legs—forget working for me," just "No." We went over another mountain; the gruppetto formed; then we came to the hardest climb of the day, the Col de Romme. As we hit the lower slopes, who should I see but Kim, surrounded by the whole team, then climbing *behind* the whole team a few hundred meters later. I noticed his fed-up, disinterested expression. His heart wasn't in it. I'd sacrificed the chance to send someone away with Hushovd and potentially deny him those points for the sake of a bloke who seemed like he couldn't be bothered. When I ask for the team's support, I may not always win, I may not always have good legs, but I always see it as my duty to give everything. Kim apparently didn't have the same sense of gratitude or responsibility.

The green jersey was now slipping further and further away. Paris, fortunately, was getting closer. Only four more days. The first was a time trial around Lake Annecy—what ought to have been as good as a rest day had I not panicked on hearing the earlier time splits and needlessly ridden the second half full gas. For a moment, I'd feared I was going to miss the time limit. I'd also wasted several seconds on the single uphill section to stop pedaling completely and glare at a British fan whose idea of cheering on a countryman was telling me, "Cavendish, get up off your fat arse!"

My thoughts were now fixed on what was likely to be my last remaining chance of a stage win—every sprinter's theater of dreams, the Champs-Élysées in Paris. That night in Annecy, though, the manager of the Saxo Bank team, Bjarne Riis, strolled across the hotel dining room bearing an expected gift: Leaning over the table where Brian Holm and I were sitting, he told me the 787-meter Col d'Escrinet, 16 kilometers from the end of the following day's nineteenth stage to Aubenas, needn't stop me winning that one either. "It's steep at the bottom, but after that you can settle into a rhythm," Riis told me with a wink.

A Eurosport documentary later showed Johan Bruyneel in the Astana team bus the following morning telling his men, "Cavendish will get dropped on the climb." Meanwhile, in our bus, I'd been promising my teammates that I could make it with their help, just like I'd made it over the Cipressa and Poggio at Milan–San Remo. That was exactly what ended up happening. The whole stage, up to the bottom of the climb, was blistering, with guys even getting dropped on the flat. But the Escrinet itself was exactly how Riis had described it—steep for 3 or 4 kilometers, then more gradual for 10. Shielded by my teammates, I thought back to San Remo and how, on the Cipressa, the TV cameras had lingered next to me, filming close-ups of my face. As they did the same now, I was careful to show none of the signs of strain that might excite rival directeurs sportifs watching monitors in their cars. As long as I looked comfortable, they'd know there was no point in upping the pace.

The reigning world champion, Alessandro Ballan, crossed the summit with the Frenchman Pierrick Fédrigo. A few seconds later, at the front of the main bunch, I started the descent. The kilometers ticked by, and we still didn't seem to be getting any closer. Finally, as the road kicked up toward the finish with 1 kilometer to go, George vacuumed them up. Now I only had Tony Martin, who was going to have to pull off the lead-out of the century, from a kilometer out, all uphill. It was going to take something special—and Tony is a special young rider. From 200 meters to go, when his bionic legs finally started chopping, all I had to do was the easy bit and outsprint Gerald Ciolek to take what was maybe my unlikeliest Tour stage win to date, given the nature of the route.

Five wins. And counting. The Belgian Freddy Maertens was the last man to win six, in 1981. I now had forty-eight hours to wait for my chance to join him. On top of a Mont Ventoux that must have lost 50 meters in altitude that day, such was the weight of the crowd on the slopes, I warmed up by playfully beating Thor in a sprint for 104th place. Mathematically, I could still win the green jersey, but only if Thor had some kind of problem or an accident on the Champs-Élysées. Our sprint on the Ventoux was part peace offering, part crowd-pleaser, part private joke at the expense of the media. "Let's sprint just to confuse them. They think we hate each other," I'd whispered to Thor in sight of the summit.

The start of the twenty-first and final stage in Montereau Fault–Yonne wasn't so amusing. In fact, it was shit, literally: I stood in some dog dirt on the way to the team bus. But I was too zoned in for that or anything else to bother me. I'd told our team press officer, Kristy, not to make me do any interviews. I was also dressed head-to-toe in brand-new kit. While, as per tradition, the other 155 riders left in the field joked and sipped from champagne glasses until we reached the first of eight laps of the Champs-Élysées, I thought only of the last of those laps—the one I intended to complete with my arms aloft.

Nothing about the Champs failed to exceed my expectations. The noise, the color, the view—the goosebumps when it all hit me. Incredible. As we knew they would, the second we hit the Champs, the attacks started, but we were in total control, from the first lap to the last. As we rounded the bend in front of the Arc de Triomphe for the final time, whole teams were strung out parallel to our train, trying to swamp us. "Stay together! Stay together!" I screamed—and we did. All except Michael Rogers, who'd punctured on the penultimate lap, leaving us one man short.

Oh, the irony—it'd be Garmin that did Mick's work for him and for us, taking it on around the last, sweeping, left-hand bend. In every sprint until then, we'd all kept something in reserve, except me on Stage 2, but now we didn't need to hold anything back. Dave Millar took us under the kilometer-to-go flag, then George smashed past and onto the front. Boom—from the overhead cameras, it looked as though a bomb had dropped into the middle of the peloton.

Eight hundred meters to go. Seven hundred. George pulls off. Renshaw takes over. Into the Place de la Concorde. Into the last right-hand bend, too fast, way too fast, only I'm on Mark Renshaw's wheel, and if there's one man skillful enough to get around that bend, at that speed, it's Mark Renshaw. Still, I wince. Wait for the impact with the barriers. Nothing. Relief.

Into the straight. Five hunded meters. Mark kicks. Four hundred, 300. I could go, but Mark's still accelerating. I wait until 250, maybe 200, and he launches me. A laser-guided missile. Giving it everything. And we leave everyone behind—so much so that, had I known, I'd have sat up and let Mark come through for the win.

Instead I screamed as I crossed the line and threw up my arms. Behind me, Mark did the same. Contador may have won the Tour, Hushovd may have beaten me to the green jersey by ten points and by default, but the performance the whole of Paris would remember had come from my team.

The moment was unforgettable. The moment was ours.

They say the pinnacle of every sprinter's career in cycling is victory on the Champs-Élysées. At age 24, I, for one, was hopeful and confident that plenty more highs lay beyond the horizon of the 2009 Tour.

The truth was that the months that followed would be the toughest of my career and maybe my life, albeit not for the lurid reasons that the naysayers had predicted, having seen me change car, girlfriend, and, they mistakenly thought, attitude. On the road, August had been low-key yet successful thanks to wins in a couple of the traditional post-Tour criteriums, in the Sparkasse Giro Bochum in Germany, and then in a stage of the Tour of Ireland. From Ireland, via a couple of weeks' training in Italy, I was due to head to the Tour of Missouri.

A few hours before I was to leave for America, I got back from training and noticed a missed call on my phone from my younger brother, Andy. I'm not proud to say it, but Andy and I aren't close, and I may not even have returned the call had he not then sent me a text message asking if I had a suit he could borrow back home on the Isle of Man. He said he needed it for a job interview. Bemused but pleased for him about the interview, I said I had one Paul Smith suit in my wardrobe. He was welcome to use it.

It was sometime the following day, when I was stuck in Frankfurt, waiting eight hours for my connection to States, that my phone rang and I saw Melissa's name on the display. It was Andy, she said. He'd been arrested. Something to do with drugs. Cannabis and cocaine. That was all she knew. It's also about as much detail as I want to go into here.

What I will say is that, naturally, I wasn't in great emotional shape when I finally got on the plane, then arrived on U.S. soil eight hours later. Physically, I didn't feel much better; despite my roommate Bernie Eisel's best efforts to cheer me up, I could sense that I was coming down with something. I managed to muddle through and win the first stage the following day, but that was a dubious blessing, as I now had a race leader's yellow jersey to defend. I then won the second stage and felt compelled to stay another day, as what was now clearly a nasty lung infection deteriorated. After I practically collapsed over the line to finish 5th on Stage 3, we decided I could go no farther. I spent the rest of the week in bed, in Kansas City, potentially contemplating the end of my season but much more worried about what was happening to my brother thousands of miles away.

My health improved quickly back in Italy. The World Championships were taking place in Mendrisio, Switzerland, in the last week of the month. I could still just about get fit in time. The Friday before the Worlds, I went out training with my mate from the Isle of Man, Jonny Bellis, and in the evening we headed into Quarrata for a meal. Jonny had done pretty well in his first pro season, but he was riding for Saxo Bank, one of the top teams in the world, and had found his opportunities limited. For that reason, Rod had provisionally left him off the roster of the British road race team for Mendrisio.

After the meal, we stopped for an ice cream, then headed back to Quarrata—me in my Audi R8, as you'd expect, rather faster than Jonny on his Vespa. Jonny said he was going to stop at our usual haunt in Quarrata, Bar Grazia, for a coffee. I told him I was tired and was going straight to bed. "See you tomorrow," I said.

The next morning, I was awakened by my phone ringing twice in quick succession. I glanced at the clock: six thirty. I rubbed my eyes, rolled over, and tried to get back to sleep. A few seconds later, more ringing. This time, I answered. It was Max. He sounded funny, shocked. "Cav," he said, "it's Jonny. He's had an accident on his scooter. I'm at hospital with him in Florence. . . . I don't think he's going to make it."

I didn't think. In those moments, you don't. Instead I scrambled out of bed, threw on some clothes, and drove straight to the hospital. When I got there, Max was talking simultaneously on two different phones. Then he told me the story: Jonny had been found in the middle of the night, having crashed his Vespa. He'd been taken to Pistoia hospital, where they'd said Max should call his parents because he wasn't going to make it. Max had asked whether they were sure they couldn't do anything, and they'd said no, they were sure. Max then called the Italian national coach, his mate Franco Ballerini, whose son had recently survived a brain tumor. Ballerini had told him to get Jonny transferred to Florence, which was twenty minutes away and had the best brain department in Italy. When they'd got there, Jonny had been rushed straight into the operating room, which was where he was now.

One hour passed. Two. Three. Four. Midday, and still no news. I left Max to get a coffee. A few minutes later, as I came back up the stairs, I was greeted by a vision so horrific that it'll be forever imprinted on my memory: Jonny, or at least what was left of him.

Max and I were crying in each other's arms. It was all too awful, too distressing. I'd seen Jonny five hours after he'd first been admitted; Max had been there when they'd said he was dead. Nobody can understand what that's like. You hear about cyclists having that kind of injury—like the Rabobank rider Kai Reus in 2007—but unless you see it with your own eyes, you can't imagine how close to death they are.

Now, apparently, there was a tiny chance, but only tiny. Jonny's parents arrived in the evening, having had to catch a flight from the Isle of Man to London, then one from there to Italy. I couldn't begin to imagine how they felt.

He made it through one day, then two, unconscious but alive. We kept bracing ourselves for the worst possible news, which we all knew could come at any moment. We were allowed in the hospital ward twice a day, but even that was sometimes for no more than five minutes at a time, what with all his operations and treatments. He survived another day, then another, until it was a week that had felt like a year. The second week was full of complications, but again, he pulled through. After three weeks, the doctors took him out of what was by then a medically induced coma.

Jonny and I hadn't always been best mates, but it didn't take a lifetime of shared experiences for all this to have a profound effect on me. While I'd found and fallen in love with cycling in my early teens, Jonny, who was three years younger, had done all kinds of sports before finally settling on cycling when I was about to turn pro. Over the past year, our time living and training together in Quarrata—and our chippy Manx sense of humor—had brought us close. Now I watched his parents suffering and thought about my relationship with my mum and dad. I thought about the phone calls I sometimes ignored, the distance that had somehow grown between us, and what had just happened with Andy. The pause for reflection wasn't nice, but it was necessary. From now on, I decided, I needed to make more effort.

About five weeks after the crash, Jonny almost died again from peritonitis when the tube pumping food into his stomach came loose and sprayed all over his organs, but it turned out to be just a short-lived, if horrendous, scare. As they had throughout his recovery to that point, his mental and physical strength saw him through. The doctors marveled at how far he'd come and how quickly. By this time, my illness in Missouri, compounded by the stress of the past few weeks, had forced me to skip Paris-Tours in October and end my season. Brian Holm, Bob Stapleton, and others worried about me holding it together over the winter after a traumatic few weeks since September. They were part of a support system that now included my new girlfriend, Fiorella; my old one, Melissa, who had remained my close friend; Max Sciandri; Rod; and my teammates, particularly George, who unfortunately left Columbia-HTC for the BMC team at the end of 2009.

In the end, come the end of 2009, Jonny B and I were fighting for the same thing. His battle may have been a lot more arduous than mine—he'd been moved to a rehab unit in London, where he'd spend another three months, making phenomenal progress, to the point where a comeback in late 2010 seemed possible—but what kept us both battling was our love of life. A life that, for both of us, was in cycling. It might have been easier and more fun for me to drink myself into oblivion to forget about my problems, but instead I remembered all the positives that had come out of my years in cycling and reminded myself that I could carry on doing all that in the future, for as long as I wanted. I was going to be racing again in February; I wanted to be racing and enjoying it, not suffering because I hadn't put in the hard work.

As far as the 2010 Tour was concerned, it would be hard if not impossible to keep outdoing myself, to win *more* sprints, but by leaving Paris in 2009 without the green jersey, I may actually have done myself a huge favor. Now I knew exactly what I'd be aiming at in July 2010. And what I hoped I'd be wearing.

ACKNOWLEDGMENTS

The opportunity to write this book arose mainly thanks to my four stage wins in the 2008 Tour de France. That opportunity therefore owes as much to the countless individuals who have supported my career as did those four, life-altering achievements.

Mum, Dad, brother Andy, uncles, aunts, cousins, grandparents, Melissa and her family—all have witnessed, encouraged, and celebrated my transformation from cheeky, chubby teenager to Tour de France stage winner. All deserve my heartfelt appreciation. The same applies to my many mates on the Isle of Man and elsewhere, inside and outside cycling, too numerous to list here, but who know who they are, and who will always be my anchor in reality, whatever riches, success, disappointment, and failure I go on to enjoy or endure.

In different periods, British Cycling and my current team, HTC-Columbia, have been my two "families" in cycling. Rod Ellingworth has been the bridge between those phases in my life—a coach and a constant source of advice, sympathy, friendship, and necessary bollockings. At Columbia, Bob Stapleton, Brian Holm, Rolf Aldag, and Allan Peiper, in particular, all showed faith in me when there were other, more obvious candidates for their confidence. The extraordinary, selfless performances of my teammates—some mentioned here, some not—have been a mere continuation of that trust. Lads, I love every second we spend racing together.

I thank my manager, Fran Millar, my literary agent, David Luxton, and everyone at Ebury Press for their great help in taking this book off the drawing board and into publication. I would also like to show my gratitude to Daniel Friebe for the same reason, and for his commitment at every stage of the project.